The Double Binds of Neoliberalism

EXPERIMENTS/ON THE POLITICAL

Series Editors

Iain Mackenzie, University of Kent
Amanda Giorgio, UMass Amherst

This series reflects on how interdisciplinary and/or practice-led thought can create the conditions for experimental thinking about politics and the political. What if the domain of the political is not what we usually think it is? Are there ways of thinking about the nature of politics and the political that can take us beyond frameworks of conflict and cooperation? These questions derive from a commitment to the idea that political thought has not yet exhausted its creative potential with regard to what constitutes the political domain. It is also motivated by the desire for political theory to become a genuinely creative discipline, open to collaborative interdisciplinary efforts in innovation. Moreover, if our understanding of the political world is to keep pace with political events then it is important that political theorists do not simply presume that they express one or other of these dominant models of the political; rather they should remain open to the possibility that experiments in politics may be happening 'on the street' in ways that require theorists to think differently about what is meant by 'the political'.

Titles in the Series

The Political Space of Art: The Dardenne Brothers, Ai Weiwei, Burial and Arundhati Roy
  Benoît Dillet and Tara Puri
Comedy and Critical Thought: Laughter as Resistance
  Edited by Iain MacKenzie, Fred Francis and Krista Bonello Rutter Giappone
Meanderings Through the Politics of Everyday Life
  Robert Porter
The Aesthetics of Necropolitics
  Natasha Lushetich
The Double Binds of Neoliberalism: Theory and Culture After 1968
  Edited by Guillaume Collett, Krista Bonello Rutter Giappone, and Iain MacKenzie

The Double Binds of Neoliberalism

Theory and Culture After 1968

Edited by
Guillaume Collett
Krista Bonello Rutter Giappone
Iain MacKenzie

ROWMAN & LITTLEFIELD
Lanham • Boulder • New York • London

Published by Rowman & Littlefield
An imprint of The Rowman & Littlefield Publishing Group, Inc.
4501 Forbes Boulevard, Suite 200, Lanham, Maryland 20706
www.rowman.com

86-90 Paul Street, London EC2A 4NE

Copyright © 2022 by The Rowman & Littlefield Publishing Group, Inc.

All rights reserved. No part of this book may be reproduced in any form or by any electronic or mechanical means, including information storage and retrieval systems, without written permission from the publisher, except by a reviewer who may quote passages in a review.

British Library Cataloguing in Publication Information Available

Library of Congress Cataloging-in-Publication Data Available

ISBN 978-1-5381-5452-6 (cloth : alk. paper)
ISBN 978-1-5381-5454-0 (electronic)

♾️ The paper used in this publication meets the minimum requirements of American National Standard for Information Sciences—Permanence of Paper for Printed Library Materials, ANSI/NISO Z39.48-1992.

Contents

List of Figures ... vii

Acknowledgements ... ix

1 Introduction: Revolution Today ... 1
  Guillaume Collett

PART I: 1968 AND MARXISM

2 Communism as the Riddle Posed to History ... 39
  Jose Rosales

3 Workers and Capitalists: Two Different Worlds? Immanence and Antagonism in Marx's *Capital* ... 67
  Daniel Fraser

4 The Unfulfilled Promises of the Italian 1968 Protest Movement ... 89
  Franco Manni

PART II: FREEDOM AND RIGHTS

5 On Ludic Servitude ... 103
  Natasha Lushetich

6 Contrasting Legacies of '68: Deleuze and Human Rights ... 123
  Christos Marneros

7 '68 and Sexuality: Disentangling the Double Bind ... 139
  Blanche Plaquevent

PART III: COLLECTIVE PRACTICES AND INSTITUTIONS

8	Two Kinds of Critical Pragmatism *Iain MacKenzie*	161
9	May '68: An Institutional Event *Gabriela Hernández De La Fuente*	183
10	Communist Guilt, Public Happiness and the Feelings of Collective Attachment *aylon cohen*	201
11	Community, Theatre and Political Labour: Unworking the Socialist Legacy of 1968 *Ben Dunn*	225

Index 247

About the Contributors 251

List of Figures

Figure 3.1.	*From the Depths.* Print illustration by William Balfour Kerr.	68
Figure 11.1.	*ALBERT DRIVE performance.* Photograph by Alan Dimmick.	231
Figure 11.2.	*Everybody's House.* Photograph by Abigail Howkins; House designed by Andrew McAvoy.	239

Acknowledgements

We would like to thank everyone involved in this project, from its inception at the conference that launched this conversation and exchange on the fiftieth anniversary of '68 ('Double Binds of '68,' University of Kent, 2018)—an event that was more than a retrospective, intensely rooted as it was in present concerns—right up to publication (a journey in fraught times, also reflected in the volume's continued engagement with recent events). We would like to thank the University of Kent, in particular the Centre for Critical Thought and the School of Politics and International Relations, for supporting and hosting the event. Special thanks go out to all of our contributors, who make this volume what it is. We would also like to thank Rebecca Anastasi, Mark Kerr, Ivy Roberts and their team at Rowman & Littlefield, for all their help with the preparation and finalising of the manuscript.

Early versions of Jose Rosales's and Christos Marneros's chapters were published as articles in *La Deleuziana*, no. 8 (2018). We thank the journal's editors for their permission to re-publish parts of those articles. Jose Rosales, '1968–2018: plus ça change, plus c'est la même chose (?),' 28–38; Christos Marneros, 'Deleuze and Human Rights: The Optimism and Pessimism of '68,' 39–52.

Chapter One

Introduction

Revolution Today

Guillaume Collett[1]

1.

This volume is concerned with helping to elucidate how, over the past fifty-plus years, the after-effects of the global 1968 uprisings have given rise to an array of double binds, of irreconcilable tensions without obvious solutions, across society, culture and critical thought. These double binds define the fate of resistance to capitalism today, helping account for the maze of impasses in which the left finds itself. We refer to this situation as the 'double binds of neoliberalism,' so as to foreground the disjunction between 1968's revolutionary intentions and potentials, and its effects of co-optation by capitalism which has shown itself to be particularly effective at exploiting these tensions.

Today, neoliberalism's ongoing crisis of legitimacy and hegemony, particularly as intensified by the 2007–2008 global financial crisis and its economic and political after-effects, calls for a return to '68 so as to better understand the contours of the never-ending *interregnum* of the present, and potentially a way out.[2] For although '68 gave rise to a series of double binds, we believe these to be perhaps more the double binds of neoliberalism than those of '68 itself, as they only later became sedimented as binds, even if they may already have existed as tensions. Thinking-acting beyond today's double binds, which continue to define the conditions of possibility of the left's thought and practice, also means, therefore, returning to '68.

The chapters in this volume centre on these double binds that paralyse our present but also attempt to reveal their limits and to indicate the possibility of an outside. Before providing an outline of the book and its chapters in the concluding sections, I will first sketch out some of the contrasting ways in which neoliberalism's and '68's double binds have been understood by contemporary critical thought and try to synthesise aspects of these arguments in order to provide an initial overview of the fate of revolution today.

2.

For numerous commentators, the double binds of neoliberalism are best understood as the result of the exploitation of a disjunctive synthesis—unstably experimented with during '68—of two distinct conceptions of freedom which can helpfully be termed 'negative' and 'positive.' In the context of '68, negative freedom is the freedom both from the state's encroachment on the individual (including the social-democratic institution of organised work) and from capitalist forms of alienation, upholding both the individual's right to choose and to experience an authentic self, free from commodification and standardisation as well as from normalisation and oppression. On the other hand, positive freedom anchors resistance to substantive social objectives understood rationally and experimented with both theoretically and practically. The aims and objectives of the different forms of resistance associated with these two conceptions of freedom are not necessarily compatible with one another and in some cases diametrically opposed.

For David Harvey:

> Pursuit of social justice presupposes social solidarities and a willingness to submerge individual wants, needs, and desires in the cause of some more general struggle for, say, social equality or environmental justice. . . . Neoliberal rhetoric, with its foundational emphasis upon individual freedoms, has the power to split off libertarianism, identity politics, multiculturalism, and eventually narcissistic consumerism from the social forces ranged in pursuit of social justice through the conquest of state power. It has long proved extremely difficult within the US left, for example, to forge the collective discipline required for political action to achieve social justice without offending the desire of political actors for individual freedom and for full recognition and expression of particular identities. Neoliberalism did not create these distinctions, but it could easily exploit, if not foment, them.[3]

Harvey notes that 'The objectives of social justice and individual freedom were uneasily fused in the movement of '68.'[4] He emphasises the hostility that emerged in the French '68 between students and workers, as representatives of the two different types of freedom being sought. For him, today, neoliberalism's exploitation of the left's disorganisation speaks for itself: for instance, while productivity in the United States steadily increased over the second half of last century, average salaries in 2000 were the same as at the start of the 1980s, wages having reached their peak in the early 1970s. Instead, increases in productivity have accrued to the highest 1 percent, and particularly the highest 0.1 percent.[5] Data from the United Kingdom and other societies that have pursued neoliberal policies the most brazenly show a similar picture. If '68 rejected the very notion of class as the driving factor in revolutionary movements, neoliberalism, for Harvey, has exploited this over the last fifty years in order to effect an immense re-entrenchment of class power—while superficially appeasing non-class-based demands.

Harvey is not alone in drawing attention to '68's double binds. Many on the left consider the, in many respects laudable, flowering of identity politics and new social movements in the late 1960s and 1970s to have an ambivalent legacy. Writing about second-wave feminism, Nancy Fraser considers it to have pointed to 'two different possible futures' when it first erupted on the scene.[6] As Fraser contends:

> in a first scenario, it prefigured a world in which emancipation went hand in hand with participatory democracy and expanded social solidarity; in a second, by contrast, women's liberation promised a new form of liberalism . . . individual autonomy, increased choice, meritocratic advancement, and the career open to talents. . . . Compatible with either of two different visions of society, it was susceptible to two different historical elaborations.[7]

She argues that it unwittingly formed a 'dangerous liaison' with neoliberalism—though, for her, today's crises offer new hope for a return to the first of its possible futures.[8]

Robert Pfaller concisely sums up the broadly socialist reading of the dynamic tension between these two freedoms as follows: 'The general ideological task of postmodernism is to present all existing injustice as an effect of discrimination. . . . [P]rogressive neoliberalism massively increases social inequality, while distributing all minority groups in an "equal" way over the unequal places.'[9]

3.

During the years of postwar reconstruction ending with the oil shocks of the early 1970s—the so-called *Trente Glorieuses*—whose audacious penultimate chapter was the *soixante-huitards*' rejection of work itself as the route to freedom,[10] the state had been a privileged rallying point for the left. On the basis of the Bretton Woods Agreement of 1944, the state sedimented itself as a buffer against the excesses of monopoly capitalism, through systems of monetary regulation designed to make finance serve industry rather than itself—even if critics of postwar 'state monopoly capitalism' understood this more fundamentally as serving as a bulwark against the twin threats of communism and fascism, ultimately shoring up capital accumulation in the medium term, and as being spearheaded by an American militarism (the military-industrial complex) designed to absorb surpluses rather than redistribute them.[11] Be that as it may, during this time the working class made historic gains in terms of workers' rights, social protections, the rise of meritocracy through qualifications, and especially remuneration, the proportion of capital apportioned to labour costs rising to what, in some advanced economies, has been a historic highpoint.[12]

Yet, at the same time, the rights of white, male workers were safeguarded on the basis of a system that oppressed all other minorities not principally structured by class, that enforced strict work discipline and that established high levels of standardisation, both in production and consumption, as well as in subjectivity. As Nick Srnicek and Alex Williams put it:

> There can be no return to Fordism. The capitalist 'golden era' was premised on the production paradigm of the orderly factory environment, where (male) workers received security and a basic standard of living in return for a lifetime of stultifying boredom and social repression. Such a system relied upon an international hierarchy of colonies, empires, and an underdeveloped periphery; a national hierarchy of racism and sexism; and a rigid family hierarchy of female subjugation.[13]

This is part of what makes '68 such an ambiguous revolution comprised of internal tensions: the very system that enshrined the rights of workers was rejected on the basis of a newly emerging set of demands.

Despite having appeared to 'soften' its approach and to incorporate various of '68's criticisms into its development, the proposition to 'return' to the state today is far from being the silver bullet that would spell the end of neoliberalism's reassertion of finance over industry and capital over labour. Recently, calls for a 'mission-oriented capitalism'[14] centring on a Green New Deal appear to be gaining mainstream traction, as a desirable alternative to the excessive economic and political instability occasioned by the putative neo(il)liberal 'deconstruction of the administrative state.'[15] However, early indications suggest that the different variants of a Green New Deal currently being implemented are designed primarily as a life support system for capital and for business, or as another iteration of the kind of 'Keynesianism for the rich' witnessed after 2008. This also seems true of the post-COVID-19 era, during which time the state, finance and big business have continued merging in the Global North to a point where they are almost indistinguishable.[16]

4.

Anchoring the left's hopes to a nostalgic image of state capitalism raises additional questions about the nature of exploitation today. Irreversible shifts in the nature of work—especially since the late 1970s, although already in evidence from after the Second Word War, if not earlier—have displaced the site of class struggle from the spatio-temporally bounded institution of productive labour (the factory), to society at large. This has blurred the distinction between work and leisure, and dissolved the traditional conceptions of class identity and solidarity rooted in industrial labour, on which basis demands addressed to the state had been formulated in the postwar era.

The feminist Marxist left's critique of the exploitation of domestic work has been instrumental in shifting focus from struggles over productive labour to struggles over reproductive work.[17] From this vantage point, the capitalist exploitation of women's domestic or reproductive work—defined by capitalism as non-work and thus unremunerated—has always been internal to the exploitation of (initially, primarily male) productive activity.

The mature Marx understood the production of surplus-value through the exploitation of work through a model of 'socially necessary labour.'[18] Marx distinguishes between 'necessary labour-time,' which is the quantity of remunerated labour worked during the day that is needed to clothe, feed and house the worker, so that they can turn up to work the next day ('reproduction'), and 'surplus labour-time,' which is the quantity of unremunerated labour worked during the same day that, being unremunerated, provides a surplus for the capitalist (surplus labour-time congealed as 'surplus-value').[19] 'Socially' necessary labour is the productivity of a given quantity of labour-time averaged out within a particular sphere of work, which also implicates reproduction at a social and not simply an individual level.[20] During what Marx calls the 'real subsumption of labour under capital,' which he considers the properly capitalist mode of production, production becomes subsumed under, or reorganised by, capital which it now serves—the individual worker increasingly becoming not the most important factor in production, which is now rather the overall system designed to maximise surplus-value.[21]

For autonomist Marxism, this system extends to reproduction, or the social, due to its key role within the (re)production of surplus-value. As Mario Tronti writes in 'Factory and Society,' during real subsumption:

> the social relation is never separated from the relation of production; the relation of production is identified ever more with the social relation of the factory. . . . When the factory seizes the whole of society—all of social production is turned into industrial production. . . . When the whole of society is reduced to the factory, the factory—as such—appears to disappear.[22]

The exploitation of the social interaction not factored into the worker's salary becomes particularly significant under de-industrialised, knowledge-based production which, being inherently collaborative and diffuse, cannot be pinpointed and quantified in terms of the productive labour-time of the individual. As Paolo Virno puts it, 'In post-Fordism "production time" includes non-labor time, during which social cooperation takes its root. . . . Hence I define "production time" as that indissoluble unity of remunerated life and non-remunerated life, labor and non-labor, emerged social cooperation and submerged social cooperation.'[23]

5.

It has been argued that '68 was itself a response to an intensified encroachment of capital upon the social and upon subjectivity, long before the use of smart phones to check work emails outside working hours and the design of open plan offices intended to spark informal exchanges of ideas. As Félix Guattari and Antonio Negri put it:

> The great conflagration of 1968 demonstrated that the new economic techniques now implicated the domain of social reproduction. . . . The events of 1968 posed themselves as an antagonistic recognition of this transformation of the social quality of production and work procedures. . . . 1968 represents the subjective side of production.[24]

Postwar capitalism saw not only the beginning of a third industrial revolution that imported scientific advances into production techniques but, consequently, also the rise of education and of the use of information within production which, for Guattari and Negri, necessarily implicate the social due to the inherently collective and impersonal nature of knowledge.[25] The dividing lines between production and reproduction, work and the maintenance of life, and even consciousness and the unconscious,[26] lines that were already dotted rather than hard, continued to break down during this period, just as the welfare state was in the process of being built. Consequently, for Guattari and Negri, and other writers informed by the experience of '68, the welfare state is seen as a part of production itself, rather than acting as a social defence against capitalist exploitation.[27]

Hence, for Guattari, 'the problem of the university is . . . the problem of society as a whole.'[28] The students rejected the postwar model of organised labour not only because they opposed standardisation at work, hierarchical unions and institutional discipline, but also because they already sensed the creeping exploitation to come (even if they also played a role in accelerating this very process), and which they would be the ones to bear the brunt of due to their generation's higher education levels and thus greater absorption into the social factory.[29] From this vantage point, it made no sense to defend the institution of work and the welfare state as a buffer against capital. These were being incorporated into the postwar evolution of production which, becoming dislocated from factories and relocated to society at large, could no longer be opposed simply through strike action and from within factories.

Writing in a more specifically political register, Kristin Ross speaks of May '68 as entailing a movement of deterritorialisation and a 'dislocation' of politics itself: a '*de*classification' of social and economic groups, as students, workers and farmers went to meet each other through a 'physical dislocation,' in which they strayed outside their normal spaces but also, in so doing, reimagined the city, the social and the self (recalling the 'psychogeography' of the Situationists). Ross understands this as a 'political opening to otherness,' through which students and factory workers could break with their social identities and with their self-interests, in order to 'acced[e] to something larger': a rupture with their very conception of the system, a conception on which 'the state based its authority to govern.'[30] Ross notes that the policing of these transgressive mixtures by the state during the uprisings, and the vehemence with which the police and other state actors tried to prevent it,[31] reflect the stakes involved.[32]

From the perspective of the social factory, these 'transgressive mixtures' physically embodied, in a way, the transversal relinkages actively produced as/by the social factory itself, as well as the tension that exists between the emerging social factory (transversal relinkage) and older state institutions (rigid segmentation) within the postwar capitalist state, while seeking to break with both. This intermingling of groups was less than a strategic revolutionary act with tangible objectives, yet '68 thought would argue that it was more than merely a symbolic performance or an imaginary reverie, being closer to an experiment in the real rupturing of subjectivity.[33] In France, the uprisings did not stop once the de Gaulle government made concessions to the historic strikes that erupted across France. Revolution's aims could no longer be modelled on the surpassing of the dialectic of work and capital that, within a decade, would seemingly be consigned to history as an outdated conception of social dynamics.[34]

6.

While, on the left, questions of identity politics and social justice would later become more disarticulated, the poles of positive and negative freedom that they each tend towards appear to find a common ground in the notion of social factory, which transversally bypasses the distinctions micro- / macropolitics, subjective / objective, public / private. '68 thought theorises this blurring in terms of something like a real experience of intersectional resistance, drawing on the 'dislocated' politics of May '68.[35] This theory's level of analysis does not seek to transcend identitarian differences in favour of a disembodied model of social justice that would ignore these groups' distinct histories of oppression and embodied specificities. Nor does it wish to remain at the level of siloed identities, which do not reflect the real functioning of capital, power and oppression across their differences.[36]

Having a multiplicity of social objectives—where one marginalised group is not prioritised over, or even completely distinguished from, another but, rather, the common, if complex, intersections of their oppression are seen as foundational—would appear to lack the unitary focus of a Leninist revolutionary strategy guided from above by the Marxist scientist or theoretician. Yet, '68 thought considers this a major anti-Marxist-Leninist lesson of '68. While the negative freedoms expressed during '68 have been criticised by the socialist tradition and more widely for their subjectivism and anticipation of selfish individualism, '68 thought has understood this as something like an experimental—certainly incomplete, though potentially illuminating—use of the experience of negative freedom to revitalise conceptions of positive freedom. Marxism-Leninism is seen by this tradition to guide revolutionary strategy through a preestablished and transcendent conception of the social (modelled on the dialectic of labour and capital and its historical overcoming within/as communism), which is given priority over the multiplicity of desires embodied by the social actors present therein.[37]

'68 thought seeks instead to articulate a more immanent conception of revolutionary praxis, where the concepts guiding social justice are constructed on the basis of a multiplicity of concrete affects within a given socioeconomic field—and, moreover, on the basis of these affects' inherent if still-underdefined directionality, a notion which pierces the myth of the double bind of either stultifying form or the chaos of the unformed.[38] This is what Gilles Deleuze terms an affective subjectless 'becoming,' understood as a horizontal synthetic process that neither privileges any one point or term (subjectified affect) in a set of relations over another (preventing one term from being raised above the others as their principle of unity), nor leaves these differences dispersed in a bottomless chaos of indistinct forces.[39] Rather, becoming sticks to the level of affects' relationality—which is prioritised over the terms being related and without cancelling their differences—as well as to these relations' emergent directionality, understood as their common, if shifting and open-ended, effect. Hence, after '68, Deleuze will speak of a 'becoming-revolutionary,'[40] which can be understood as a kind of intersectionality rooted in a shared if composite affectivity, as a transversal alternative to the double bind of either the Marxist-Leninist prioritisation of the collective over the individual or its liberal reversal.

Rather than attributing this becoming to a spontaneism of forces, as if they alone contained the principle of their auto-synthesis—according to a naive naturalism or vitalism that would see nature as inherently resistant to hierarchies and thus innately revolutionary—Deleuze and Guattari are keen to emphasise the need for an additional component lying outside, if strictly built alongside, the domain of forces themselves, which they term an 'abstract machine.'[41] This is a unifying element built in conversation with, and ultimately giving internal consistency to, the inherent proto-convergences of a set of affective vectors that seek to escape the territory within which they are currently trapped. This unifying element is historically conditioned by the concrete territories trapping a set of affects in a given time and place, whose proto-convergence these territories oppositionally determine. Yet, insofar as it is a ruptural 'event' that abstracts itself from actual history, the abstract machine cannot be reduced to these historical conditions, as necessary as they are.[42] The abstract machine emerges instead from affective potentiality in its resistance to history—a potentiality that, nonetheless, can only be synthetically expressed by the historical sequence in and through which this event is aborted. In a way, the abstract machine can be understood as the cutting edge of history.

The abstract machine, or event, thus auto-synthesises itself both in and against history, as a new basis for revolutionary praxis that rejects the teleology of earlier variants of historical materialism, as well as the Jacobin notion of a general will based in reflexive subjectivity. Instead, becoming-revolutionary spontaneously emerges as an experience rooted in emergent, counter-historical affectivity.[43]

7.

Éric Alliez and Maurizio Lazzarato have helped clarify the workings of the abstract machine of 1968.[44] Building on Federici, they show how, during the Cold War, Western capitalism instituted a system of 'containment': a rigid and totalising integration of categorisations and hierarchies, which incorporated the division of the sexes (housework versus production), the 'endo-colonisation' of racial and ethnic differences (as national internalisations of its histories of colonisation), and the geopolitical polarisation of Western capitalists versus Eastern communists, into the worker/capitalist dialectic itself—which was itself given its socioeconomic impetus by this system of differences, while also acting as a centralising container of any opposition to this system.[45] Using Alliez and Lazzarato's work, we can describe the postwar system as being unstably positioned between the social factory and its transversal relinkages, on the one hand and, on the other, the containment of those linkages within a system of rigidly interlocking differences organised around their overdetermination of the relation of labour/capital.[46]

The global '68 uprisings took advantage of this instability, being the 'crack up' of this integrated system of differences, while also being internally assembled by it.[47] '68 derived its internal coherence from a shared rejection of containment, meaning that women's rights, anti-racism, and all types of subjective resistance to normalising oppression, combined with anti-capitalism and anti-state sentiment—converging on their shared rejection of a system designed to integrate and control all these differences. '68 functioned in this respect as an abstract machine, insofar as it synthesised the totality of what, prior to '68, had been discrete sites of built-up pressure and partial leakage (affects' tendency to escape oppression) that had not yet been connected with one another (such as the civil rights movement of the mid-1950s to late 1960s, or the antiwar movement of the late 1960s). Not being connected (or only subterraneanly), these sites of blockage/leakage had not yet fully ruptured or caused a subjective break with the system that contained them. They needed linking up in order, symmetrically, to construct an adequate image of the face of their opponent, and to oppose that self-same image by synthesising what was already partially leaking from a number of sites, to a point where they could 'become' an experience of all-out rupture. Having synthetically apperceived and thus diagnosed the ultimate source of their oppression, these sites of leakage could thus synthesise themselves on the other side—or in the mirror image—of their opponent's synthesised visage—that is, as a total rupture with it.

8.

If May '68 in particular correctly diagnosed the new nature of exploitation and oppression, and seemed to offer a theory and practice of revolution that acknowledged these new conditions, why is it that it failed to bring about meaningful progressive change in the years that followed? As intense as it was, the spectre of civil war in May '68 soon evaporated as Charles de Gaulle was re-elected with an increased majority in June. The 1970s saw a continued liberalisation of French society, already begun in the 1960s, opening France further up to global capital. The 1970s gave way to the election of a socialist president who, in 1984, began a series of austerity measures designed to make France more competitive internationally. Furthermore, if May '68 was a response to the conditions of the social factory, why is it that more revolutions on the same scale and in the same transversal mold haven't appeared as forthcoming, given the expansion of the social factory in the intervening years?

The second question can be answered more readily, if we consider that May '68's success depended on its rejection of a system of integrated oppression that manifested itself, at one level, in state institutions. Those institutions provided a manifest expression of this system of exploitation, a visible target and unifier of resistance to its totalising form of oppression. This system of postwar disciplinary normalisation having been fundamentally displaced and reformatted after '68, post-'68 revolutions lack the abstract machine or revolutionary unifier that postwar institutions had oppositionally conditioned. At the same time, as we know the social factory has only continued expanding and intensifying its transversal networks, which can be much less easily identified and opposed, particularly when disarticulated from visible and/or more disciplinary institutions, as became the case in the years following 1968.[48]

The first question prompts a turn to the question of institutions and their relation to affects and concepts. To do this, we need to look at the two-sidedness of revolution, as understood by '68 thought: revolution as event and revolution proper, which I shall approach in this order.

9.

'Becoming-revolutionary's' strength as pure event (emerging in history against history) lies precisely in its momentary suspension of any institutional mediation or retranslation, as well as any teleological progression, and not only in its affective rupture with the status quo. While Guattari considers 1917 to have also functioned as an abstract machine or event, insofar as it effected a mass subjective break with the exploitative organisation of affects within prerevolutionary Russia, this rupture was effectively already compromised by its institutional expression through the theory-practice of soviets, which would soon be secondary to centralised state power, the Party, and the Army—leading to these affects' repression under Stalinism. For Deleuze and Guattari, this history was encoded in the concept (or 'order-word') of the revolutionary institution of the soviet ('All power to the soviets!'), because this concept *preexisted* the social body to which it was retrospectively applied and which became magnetised (or binarised) by it, effecting a conversion simultaneously 'from the masses to a guiding proletariat'[49] and 'from the proletariat to a directing vanguard.'[50]

Writing a month before May '68, Guattari criticised Leninism's 'mistrust of the spontaneity of the masses.'[51] Shortly after '68, Guattari remarked:

> The activity of the militant group [as an 'analytical activity actually among the masses' not in a 'vanguard standing apart from them'] is not aiming to provide ready-made rational answers to the questions they think people should be asking, but on the contrary, to deepen the problematic, and to bring out the singularity of each step of the historical process. ... The group's analytical activity was not directed to adjusting individuals to the group, but to ensuring that the group ... would not become a substitute for the mass movement [and its critique of institutional closure].[52]

Thanks to this new praxis, May '68 as pure event remained a kind of virtuality or potentiality in suspended animation, a reopening of the field of possibles (and in a way that wasn't already compromised by the form of this reopening), even if this only lasted a few weeks.[53]

One line of argument considers May '68 as necessarily stopping here, its strength lying precisely in its being an 'impossible revolution'—a revolution in the very idea of revolution as something having tangible historical effects—given that it is only on the basis of such a negation of its historical retranslation by means of institutional mediation (which always reintroduces a dimension of power) that it can reflect and bring to light the totality of the forces of oppression at work in a society.[54] For Guattari, a defensive strategy ('We are building barricades, but that is all') was needed as an initial first step—a collective phantasy framing and beckoning the other—understood as a 'method of revelation' functioning as a 'self-training to recognise instances of oppression in all their forms.'[55]

While such an experience of affective rupture can powerfully inform the theory and practice of emancipation, the risk is that remaining at the level of negative freedom will fail to bring about a socioeconomic alternative. Thus becoming-revolutionary arguably needs to ultimately serve a theory-practice of positive freedom at the level of actual revolution. This, in a sense, is the Leninist lesson ('obviously, if [the barricades] are attacked, we will have to defend them').[56]

10.

Writing in 1973, Guattari thought that, while May '68 had 'profound consequences' that are 'still being felt at all sorts of levels,' its effects were micro-political or 'molecular,' being 'no longer visible on a national scale,' and failing to effect a subjective break on the scale of 1917. He chalks this up 'undoubtedly' to the absence in '68 of a 'large scale machine for revolutionary war.'[57] Deleuze and Guattari developed the concept of a revolutionary 'war machine' as the necessary complement to their theory of becoming-revolutionary.[58] They understand it as a strategic theory-practice of revolution capable of immanently synthesising the affective proto-convergences of the abstract machine of becoming-revolutionary, in a way that will give them sufficient consistency to construct an alternative to, and thus fully break with, the socioeconomic organisation of affects being opposed. If May '68 as pure event entailed a momentary affective rupture, the lack of a war machine to synthesise these affects meant that the becoming-revolutionary itself did not lead to a subjective break in the longer term (or if it did, in part, this would be through other channels).

Their concept of a revolutionary war machine acts as a third, mediating (or, even, schematising) term between the pure event of becoming-revolutionary and its institutionalisation within actual history—that is, within institutions as concrete machines, or assemblages of parts, that are 'selected' by the war machine as capable of effectuating affects' potentialities (or proto-convergences) in a way that does not in turn repress them. That is to say, in a way that does not fully 'recode' these 'decoded' desires, but allows them a margin of indeterminacy reflective of their immanent existence as open-ended relations rooted in embodied social actors with multiple aims and objectives.[59] This completes Deleuze and Guattari's theory of the abstract 'machine,' as not only poised between history and becoming but also able to actively ('machinically') intervene in and between both dimensions.

The point is to channel becoming-revolutionary towards concrete social objectives, and even institutions capable of solidifying the experience of liberation in the longer term, but without this entailing that they also turn their backs on it. To avoid the over-sedimentation and repression of desire, there needs to be a constant and ongoing communication between the revolutionary war machine and its institutionalisation, a perpetual revolutionisation of institutions—even if also by means of institutions, which are therefore also a necessary complement to the theory of becoming-revolutionary and its war machine.

Thus a 'micro-politics' of desire needs to be undertaken strictly in correspondence with a macro-politics of institutions. As Deleuze and Guattari put it:

> It is wrongly said . . . that a society is defined by its contradictions. That is true only on the larger scale of things. From the viewpoint of micropolitics, a society is defined by its lines of flight, which are molecular [as opposed to 'molar'] . . . May 1968 in France was molecular. . . . The reverse, however, is also true: *molecular escapes and movements would be nothing if they did not return to*

the molar organisations to reshuffle their segments, their binary distributions of sexes, classes, and parties.⁶⁰

This theory, I have suggested above, is the result of '68 thought's attempt to immanentise the transcendent use of concepts in Marxism-Leninism, so that concepts are constructed on the basis of the affects that these concepts (partially and reversibly) concretise within institutions.

11.

Writing in 1984—the year that the Mitterrand government began to implement austerity measures in France, after the capitulation of the government's communist faction—Deleuze and Guattari reasserted this failure to establish either the war machine or institutions needed to bring the virtual or pure 'event' of May '68 down to earth, as it were, and give it historical existence.⁶¹ As they write in their (perhaps premature) eulogy 'May '68 Did Not Take Place': 'When a social mutation appears. . . . [s]ociety must be capable of forming collective agencies of enunciation that match the new subjectivity [the "becoming-revolutionary"], in such a way that it desires the mutation. That's what it is, a veritable redeployment [of subjectivity].'⁶² Again, subjective ruptures (redeployments) are only possible through collective institutions capable of historically embodying the becoming-revolutionary, and in a way that allows the liberated desires to continue desiring in and through the institution that expresses them. As Lazzarato reminds us, what the left still lacks today is such a revolutionary war machine.⁶³

Nevertheless, if today the left is lacking both the strategies and institutions that would have been needed to concretely effectuate '68's revolutionary break, and thus draw out various of its potentials as real historical consequences, it cannot be said that 1968 was not itself revolutionary in a substantive sense, that its revolutionary break wasn't concretely implemented through new strategies and institutions. As we know, after '68, the old postwar normalising and disciplinary institutions were irrevocably changed: neoliberalism turned '68 against both itself and the postwar system that '68 had rejected, putting '68's liberated energies to work within institutions that ultimately turned against these energies. In a certain way, we can therefore suggest that, in the years immediately following Deleuze and Guattari's titular article (till perhaps roughly the turn of the century), *May '68 did take place*—only not as the left would have wished or imagined.

If neoliberalism can aptly be termed a counterrevolution rather than simply a restoration, it is because it intercepted the revolutionary baton fumbled by the left, expressing '68 in and as a historically effectuated counterrevolution of its own making. As Alliez and Lazzarato argue, this perpetual counterrevolution is of a piece with the construction of a global capitalist war machine, whose 'creative destruction' and ongoing revolution of all the old ways of life (and even recently established ones) for the purposes of capital accumulation gives us the dominant contemporary form of revolutionary strategy, albeit in the name of the right. Capital's 'far from equilibrium' global markets, as the outcome of the dismantling of central planning, require a strategy able to flexibly adapt to its constant changes, so that the war machine takes precedence over its local and temporary institutionalisations.[64] Nonetheless, this capitalist war machine is itself 'virtual,' a piloting strategy (materialised within global financial, media, and informational systems, and in the decisions of policy makers) that needs to be further embodied in, and expressed by, localised institutions.

12.

We can understand the firm as a privileged neoliberal institution. Through a system of individualised salaries and competitive bonuses, as well as flexibilised contracts, the neoliberal firm restructures work independently of labour law and the collective agreements instituted by postwar social democracy, giving rise to a more intensive and destabilising exploitation driven by an unleashed spirit of competitive individualism, self-affirmation and entrepreneurship, while treating individual differences and identity politics with the utmost respect (or at least giving that impression).[65] At the same time, the autonomisation of the firm away from central planning and state management opens it up to global horizontal (and even pseudo-'rhizomatic')[66] networks stabilised through short-term 'projects' (taking place either inside or outside the firm), in which the entrepreneurial individual seeks to extract value from the novel connections they have established, as well as to increase their human capital, allowing for a greater degree of excitement, 'connection,' 'flexibility' of working conditions, autonomy and creativity than under the old system.[67] The firm can therefore be understood to broadly function, at its own localised level, as what Foucault called a *dispositif*, that is, an apparatus capable of redressing an 'event's' reversal of power relations by reincorporating the event into the development of a new governmental apparatus that effectuates a distinctly new model of subjectivation.[68]

13.

Conversely, Michael Hardt and Antonio Negri forward the view that, post-'68, governmentality has migrated to global de-centred networks which treat workers, neither as factory labourers involved in collective bargaining nor as competitive individuals seeking bonuses, but as ultimately impersonal intellectual labourers in the global social factory of re/production ('Empire').[69] For Hardt and Negri, this makes the contemporary world of work the site both of exploitation (since remuneration does not account for the fundamentally social, reproductive activities informing it) and of potential self-subversion. This is because the impersonal social energies exploited by intellectual production are at the same time constructed or assembled by it (as an impersonal 'multitude' or open collection of singular affects)—potentially, for them, enabling May '68's non-workerist notion of an emerging collectivity (becoming-revolutionary) to be realised in, through and against the development of neoliberal capitalism. For Hardt and Negri, capitalism is pregnant with an 'altermodernity,' pointing neither backwards to Fordism and postwar discipline nor forwards to the kind of modernity envisioned by capitalism, but to a self-developing communism-within-capitalism.[70]

For Hardt and Negri, revolution must come from the abolition of identities, given these are themselves built upon the liberal notion of property.[71] Yet, just as autonomism sought to do away not with workers per se but the identity of worker (as defined in relation to capital), so too must identities (sex, gender, race, etc.) move away from their hierarchical relations and differences from one another towards what they have in *common*: communal flows of affects or impersonal singularities constructed by the development of the social factory.[72] Be that as it may, strategically, it is still necessary to start with these identities (even if only to ultimately turn against them), since it is on these identities that governmentality acts. Their vision of an altermodernity is not simply opposed to identity politics but seeks to identify their common 'intersections,' symmetrically in terms both of their exploitation and resistance to it. For them, negative freedom (as the liberation from identity itself) is the means to achieving positive freedom (communism-within-capitalism), as a joint project involving strategic alliances across all identities.[73] This 'revolutionary parallelism' of identities requires contingent events to select and bring two or more of them together, and institutions to stabilise their convergence—on the condition that these institutions be constituted through conflict, and be 'continually transformed by the singularities that compose them.'[74]

14.

Published a year before Hardt and Negri's *Empire*, Luc Boltanski and Ève Chiapello's *The New Spirit of Capitalism* also analyses the dynamic relation between capital and anti-capitalism. However, they see this relation as actually driving the development of capitalism (if not necessarily strengthening it), rather than leading to the auto-production of a communism-within-capitalism. Although it has its own limitations, which I will come to, this text is key to understanding an important aspect of today's double binds, which show less sign of buckling than Hardt and Negri's analysis would suggest— as already indicated by Alliez and Lazzarato's critique. Moreover, Boltanski and Chiapello's work throws into particularly sharp relief the insight that it is extremely difficult to disentangle the left's failures from capital's successes, the two being so closely tied.

Boltanski and Chiapello centre their analysis on the notion of critique, and the dialectical manner in which capitalism develops as a function of its varying ability to incorporate its critiques into itself, which in turn morph as this incorporation develops and becomes undone. Moreover, critique for them is itself split in two, producing a secondary tension within the initial tension between capitalism and critique. Capitalism throws up a range of indignations which 'it is virtually impossible to combine . . . into a coherent framework.'[75] From these indignations, two types of critique have accompanied the development of capitalism: an 'artistic critique' and a 'social critique.' The artistic critique, typified by Baudelaire, is rooted in the nineteenth-century bohemian search for authentic self-expression in a world of capitalist standardisation and commodification. The social critique is derived from socialism and Marxism.[76]

In the French '68, we can see that these two critiques of capitalism merged with anti-state sentiment, being coarticulated in terms of what was broadly introduced earlier as two kinds of freedom. For Boltanski and Chiapello, what was specific to '68 was the manner in which the critiques were combined, the artistic taking on a proportionally bigger role than in the nineteenth century.[77] This is significant, since it was particularly the artistic critique that the 'neo-capitalism' emerging in the second half of the 1980s and 1990s sought to appease, in its construction of a new justificatory framework designed to re-establish consent. Moreover, we can see that the artistic critique being merged with anti-state sentiment during '68 allowed neo-capitalism's distorting valorisation of the artistic critique to cover over anti-capitalist sentiment with anti-state sentiment, to provide justificatory support for its own objectives of deregulation. This enabled the new spirit of capitalism that would emerge to repackage negative freedom as libertarian individualism, suppressing the artistic critique of capitalist alienation.[78]

'68's demands for greater autonomy at work, greater flexibility, more self-management, creativity and excitement, along with less standardised processes and products, were in large part answered by neo-capitalism. Yet, this meant that neo-capitalism's dismantling of Taylorism and its creation of new forms of work distracted from its jettisoning of the attendant social protections and stability Fordism had provided, as well as from its re-intensification of commodification. The creative entrepreneur of the self was its effect, the artistic critique's demands for authentic self-expression outside the state and outside capital being folded into a 'new spirit of capitalism,' that merged the public and the private by putting negative freedom to work within capital accumulation, as a commodification of anti-capitalism.

While this history is well known, Boltanski and Chiapello do not seek to blame '68's participants, but to explain the mechanics of the neo-capitalist co-optation. They hypothesise that capitalism 'has a tendency to take back on one level what it offers on the other,'[79] producing an effect of disorientation as one critique becomes occluded for a time by the other and indeed, as we have seen, this tension becomes redoubled within the artistic critique itself. Co-optation always inevitably reinforces both forms of alienation due to their interconnectedness,[80] individual self-expression needing solid social foundations to prosper, even as it tends to jeopardise those same foundations under neo-capitalism and indeed to become further alienated by this at its own level. This disorientation explains why, for them, it was not until the late 1990s that the social critique began to fully reemerge, the effects of neo-capitalism's appeasement of the artistic critique taking some time to register.[81] That is, to have both its economic effects of rising social inequality (as a function of the suppression of the artistic critique) and its subjective effects of intensified alienation, which in turn also retriggered the artistic critique.[82]

15.

While for Boltanski and Chiapello, neo-capitalism is an inherently unstable formation due to the weak solutions it offers long-term to both the artistic critique and the social critique, they themselves do not provide answers as to why another (properly leftist) '68 didn't take off at the end of the 1990s.[83] Lazzarato, on the other hand, suggests that the co-optation of the artistic critique is an insufficient framework for understanding developments in capitalism, particularly after 1999 when the *New Spirit of Capitalism* was published.[84] For Lazzarato, the dot.com crash of 2000–2001, and then the financial crisis of 2007–2008, spelled the end of the neoliberal entrepreneur of the self, creatively exploring networks for personal gain—the primary model of co-opted artistic critique in Boltanski and Chiapello's work.[85] In its stead came a more cynical, purely extractive model of financialised capital accumulation, less in need of artistically inflected justificatory frameworks to cleanse the consciences of '68's participants enlisted into neo-capitalism's management class.

Since 2008, finance, driving capital accumulation more generally ever since the end of the 1970s, has increasingly detached itself from all productive activity, be it industrial or in services and IT. Instead, it has embedded itself ever more deeply in rent-seeking and extractive practices—financialised assets such as privately owned housing, liabilities such as private debt and services such as real estate, the credit industry and the monetisation of the digital commons—rather than value-generating ones rooted in the exploitation of work. Indeed, it has been argued that global stock markets became finally detached from the real economy on 12 August 2020, after the COVID-19-induced stock market crash prompted another round of financial Keynesianism that finally swung finance out of orbit—markets having been kept afloat since 2008 only through the printing of money by central banks. Speculators and investors have finally cottoned on to the fictitious nature of finance capital, its disconnect from production, labour and the real economy, and the state's willing complicity in this.[86]

The implications of this for the left need reckoning with: if capitalism has now become detached from human labour (as value-generating exploitation), what does this mean for strategies of resistance? And at this point, can we even speak of capitalism, rather than of a return to a kind of 'digital feudalism,' in which competitive markets previously generating value and profits through exploitation have now been replaced by monopolistic platforms that extract value independently of the market and labour?[87]

As early as 1999, Boltanski and Chiapello had argued that global networks of self-entrepreneurs generating value by establishing novel connections had replaced markets, capitalism for them being a mode of production that relies on markets only when no other option is available, given the tendency for market competition to drive down prices and thus profits.[88] Yet, what we are seeing now is the emergence of networks that no longer require even intellectual labour and which function primarily by means of algorithmic 'work,' which amounts to the extraction and purification of the raw material of human social interaction as algorithmic 'fuel.'[89]

16.

If we go back to shifts that have occurred since the turn of the century, another aspect of neoliberalism's history, which is becoming ever more prevalent, is its increasing hybridisation with neoconservativism and neo-fascism. This provides further explanations as to why another '68 did not take off either in the late 1990s or in the years following 2008.

When the co-optation of demands for authentic self-expression (issuing from the artistic critique) fails to gain ground, due to the reemergence of the social critique (for instance after an economic crisis, as in the early and late 2000s), neo-capitalism is capable of driving consent through more authoritarian means, from enslavement by debt[90] to the engineering of anxiety,[91] by appealing to nationalistic and jingoistic sentiments,[92] and by sowing division and hate.[93] In the case of more recent populist neo-fascisms, the neoliberal co-optation of the artistic critique (itself designed to save capitalism after the 1960s) appears to be directly targeted. However, this is less in order to give a faltering post-2008 capitalism a new, if inevitably brief, lease on life—given the shift towards extractive capitalism which depends less upon the liberal subjectivation of capitalism's critics, and even workers as such—and more to manage the generalised crises in governmentality resulting from ever-widening social inequality.[94] Neo-fascism hinges on a rejection of neoliberalism's incorporation of the artistic critique at the expense of the social critique—and especially the identity politics and new social movements that later became at least partially disarticulated from it—though without doing anything to reassert the latter against the former. It does not have the necessary concepts, having traded them for affects.

We must consider this as being at least partially connected to the sedimenting of a disconnect between economy and politics, capitalism and work. Today, (post-)capitalism's aim is no longer primarily to motivate productive activity as complicit in its processes of accumulation and exploitation, but to extract value independently of workers' involvement. This means that its governmentality has a tendency to increasingly bear on a political rather than an economic form of subjectivation and, therefore, may be tending towards more authoritarian methods given, historically, the alliance between the capitalist exploitation of work and more 'liberal' forms of power (following Foucault, power *stricto sensu* involves a tacit form of willing complicity or self-subjection, key to maximising workers' effectiveness[95]—therefore what we see today is sometimes closer to war[96]). According to this line of argument, (post-)capitalism—at least in terms of its tendency towards automating work—needs primarily to manipulate and deflect the resistance of its populations, and less and less to also motivate workers through power relations (governmentality), and/or inspirational visions and models of justice.[97]

17.

Boltanski and Chiapello emphasise within capitalist dynamics the necessary imbrication of justificatory frameworks capable of effectively responding to critique, given that capital's *raison d'être* is endless accumulation for its own sake (i.e. tending towards worldly abstraction), which is both fundamentally meaningless in itself and liable to generate a variety of indignations.[98] However, they overlook how capital can use meaningless affects just as readily as it uses justificatory concepts, when embedding itself within a given cultural milieu—especially when contemporary critique is itself at risk of being overtaken by affects. While '68 thought shows how collective affects of indignation (becomings) can be used to drive the construction of new concepts (institutions), today these becomings or events are already blocked the moment they appear.

As neo-capitalism continues to both extend and reorganise its networks—while haemorrhaging legitimacy, triggering new connections and affects—we are not seeing the emergence of a leftist multitude, but something much more variegated. Negri notes how, whereas May '68 'established itself on the foundations of a continuum of workers' struggles'—between industry on the one hand and an emerging social factory on the other—France's recent *Gilets Jaunes* protests are 'internally divided,' unified only by a shared rejection of the government.[99] Today, affects of indignation too often lack a sufficiently shared and consistent socioeconomic basis (in either industrial labour or intellectual work) to form the continuums and becomings on whose basis social critique could construct concepts adequate to the expression of a world capable of responding to these affects.[100]

Pronounced variations in earnings and working conditions—made more complex by intergenerational and regional differences, as well as by the automation of industry, services and intellectual labour—are actively amplified by the politics of division and hate, which pits sexes, generations, regions and ethnicities against one another. To this, we must also add finance's progressive devaluation of work as central to the economy and the rise of a digital feudalism. In this landscape, affective continuums rooted in manual or intellectual work (as analysed by Hardt and Negri in *Empire*) are fragmented, blocking the becomings-revolutionary that might otherwise emerge from these sites.

Conversely, there is a functional disconnect between experiences of indignation and the concepts the left at present has at its disposal (such as left accelerationism), which are arguably too general to be capable of being affectively rooted in the kinds of local struggle that would provide them with the transversal functionality needed to be politically effective.[101] On the other hand, if neo-fascist or right-wing populisms are so effective at electoral mobilisation, leaving to one side their additional use of algorithmic manipulation of affects, it is because their impoverished concepts are designed to succeed at superficially unifying these fragmented affects of indignation, that is, on non-socioeconomic grounds.

18.

All the authors in this volume engage in some manner with the problem of critique in a time of crisis—including the crisis of critique—and in an attempt to (dis-)articulate neoliberalism's double binds post-'68. The chapters are organised into three parts corresponding to: (I) '1968 and Marxism' (chapters 2–4), (II) 'Freedom and Rights' (chapters 5–7) and (III) 'Collective Practices and Institutions' (chapters 8–11). There are, of course, areas of overlap between all the chapters.

The first three chapters develop re-readings of the histories of postwar Marxist thought and practice, and their articulations with 1968, shining a light on the sobering scale of the impasses confronting our contemporary moment.

For Jose Rosales, as they put it in their title, after the French '68 in particular, we must consider that communism is the riddle posed to history rather than, as Marx had claimed, 'the riddle of history solved.' May '68's rejection of the Marxist conception of revolution—be it Leninist or Maoist—and of a collective subject of history, repositions communism as a virtual horizon rather than a foreseeable actuality. For this reason, it subsists in the present as a problem, orienting our revolutionary horizon through its absence. Hence, for Rosales, we are caught in a double bind with respect to '68, as the fleeting manifestation of a virtual communism. On the one hand, if we seek to recuperate '68 from the past so as to realise it in the present, as if it had contingently 'failed' and can be completed today, we fail to recognise its truth as the rejection of any preexisting conception of revolution, its necessary failure being what leftist praxis should learn from. On the other, if we seek to go backwards in time in order to anchor our present strategy to '68, in order to extend and draw out its contemporary applicability, we fail to acknowledge the extent to which today's conditions have changed with respect to the late 1960s. Our contemporary conditions of 'access' to this 'impossible revolution' preemptively bar us from effectively returning to what is in any case already an impossible site. Unless these points are understood, for Rosales, the left will be doomed to repeating May '68's failure as failure, either through melancholic reflection or farcical repetition.

Daniel Fraser's chapter, 'Workers and Capitalists: Two Different Worlds? Immanence and Antagonism in Marx's *Capital*,' develops a contemporary analysis of the Marxist understanding of the possibility of resistance and communist actuality. Fraser focuses on a fundamental irresolvable tension that exists within Marxism's theoretical corpus, particularly the work of the mature Marx and its reception by post-'68 heterodox Marxism. This is the double bind of antagonism and immanence, which figures as a rejection *avant la lettre* of both Marxist-Leninist revolution and social democratic compromise, the latter being namely the belief that there exists a capital-labour dialectic functioning between two derived, interlocking terms, which can ultimately be overcome, either through synthesis or overturning. For Fraser, there is no functioning dialectic, only a double bind of (capitalist) immanence and (workerist) antagonism: neither an immanent unity internal to the logical movement of capital itself, foreclosing any outside, nor a position for labour under capitalism of radical, antagonistic autonomy. Fraser uses this double bind to reassess, on the one hand, the interpretation of Marx found in the New Reading (*Neue Marx-Lektüre*) and the value-critique (*Wertkritik*) school, which emerged in Europe in the 1960s and anticipated '68's break with Marxist orthodoxy. And on the other, to interrogate Italian post-workerism (*autonomia*), whose theories concerning workers' potential autonomy from capital were fundamentally inflected by the events of 1968.

Franco Manni's chapter, 'The Unfulfilled Promises of the Italian 1968 Protest Movement,' also examines the history of postwar Marxism, this time from the perspective of the Italian '68. Manni invites us to consider how the Italian intellectual milieu was shaped by the deliberate erasure of one of the major figures of early twentieth-century philosophy: Benedetto Croce. Charting the anti-Croce campaign of the 1950s, he recounts how this set the scene for the arrival of a particular blending of youthful existentialism with Italian communism, producing an overarching ideology he refers to as 'Romantic Marxism.' The main features of this ideology are sketched out and the internal tensions it contains are revealed. More importantly, however, Manni claims that Romantic Marxism made possible its opposite extreme—versions of neo-fascism dominating Italian politics today, highlighting Italy's contemporary double bind. In this way, Manni argues, we can see that once the moderating influence of Croce's ethics and politics had been erased, the direction was set for years of Italian political life in which both left and right forgot that power corrupts.

19.

The next three chapters turn to post-'68 legacies of rights and freedom (and their distortions).

The first of these, Natasha Lushetich's 'On Ludic Servitude,' is critical of May '68's legacy of freedom. The chapter centres on the distinction between two conceptions of freedom (positive and negative), showing how they have become co-opted and intertwined. Focusing on the ludic inflection towards neoliberalism, Lushetich critically interrogates the legacy of 1968's ludicity (including practices such as situationist *détournement*) and relation to freedom, and how, today, positive freedom has become negativised, the difference trivialised. Lushetich refers to Estienne de La Boétie's notion of 'voluntary servitude'[102] to explore the dynamic that springs from the appearance of freedom, which she calls 'enslavement through (negative) freedom.' Drawing on '68's legacy of ludic practices, today's 'gamified capitalism' brings about only the illusion of long-lasting freedom and 'fair play.' Lushetich draws upon a variety of examples extending into the digital—from alternative performance and activism to alternate reality games and ludic apps—to examine gamification's persistence, even into labour (playbour), but also the possibilities of *détournement*.

Christos Marneros's chapter, 'Contrasting Legacies of '68: Deleuze and Human Rights,' partly refocuses attention away from the troubling extent of our contemporary impasses, through a twofold examination highlighting both the pessimism and optimism of '68. A key manifestation of the pessimistic legacy of '68, for Marneros, is the triumph of human rights discourses in the 1990s—understood by Marneros as a 'mode of being, thinking and doing politics'—because they erect a new transcendent morality. Human rights discourses emerged in the wake of '68 as a distorted expression of its resistance to all forms of power and oppression. In a way informed by the artistic critique and its neoliberal co-optation, human rights apply generic and universalist criteria extendable across global networks without friction, as opposed to the kind of concrete specificity associated with the social critique. Yet, Marneros identifies a contrasting legacy which reverses this priority. Gilles Deleuze's ferocious critique of human rights, which he explicitly associates with the ascent of a globalised capitalism, points towards an *ethos* which is radically immanent and non-dogmatic, focusing on concrete singularities not abstract generalities—this being a manifestation of '68 thought and its rejection of all forms of power including abstract totalities. For Marneros, this *ethos* is one of the legacies of '68 worth holding onto in order to think politically in the present, offering a potential way out of the double bind of human rights—where, for Marneros, neither what they oppose (oppression) nor the solution they offer is preferable.

Blanche Plaquevent's chapter "'68 and Sexuality: Disentangling the Double Bind,' goes further in the direction of optimism, to the extent that it questions the very notion that '68 sexuality was destined to be ensnared in the double bind of either repression or neoliberal co-optation. The chapter applies a repoliticising and historicising corrective to ahistorical views of 1960s sexuality that cast it as overly individualistic and all-too-readily co-opted by capitalism, restoring instead recognition of its revolutionary potential in relation to subjectivities in the everyday. In the intervening decades, commentators from across the political spectrum have argued that the 1960s sexual revolution has been recuperated by capitalism and selfish individualism. Focusing on the context of 1950s and 1960s France, Plaquevent challenges the fatalism of the double-bind narrative by distinguishing the 1960s' understanding of the sexual revolution from discourses that emerged later, showing how sexuality's co-optation was far from inevitable. Plaquevent conveys a sense of 1968's excitement, analysing expressions of sexuality (such as student slogans) that threw into question the boundary between public and private, and which reflected a sense of revolutionary fervour and agency. Moreover, the chapter explores some of the ways in which this legacy is still alive today.

20.

The final four chapters critically explore the conditions necessary for a genuinely progressive, practical and institutional construction of collectivity.

Iain MacKenzie's chapter, 'Two Kinds of Critical Pragmatism,' frames the double bind of neoliberalism in the form of a question: 'What do we do if we want to challenge a system that encourages us to do whatever we want?' The chapter explores this question through a brief history of the emergence of this double bind, before framing it as an expression of the philosophical problem of correlationism, as articulated by Quentin Meillassoux. While Meillassoux may have diagnosed the problem, MacKenzie argues that he has not yet proposed an adequate solution. The better approach to the double bind, it is claimed, can be found in critically informed pragmatist philosophy, of which there are two kinds: discursive and machinic pragmatism. The remainder of the chapter assesses these and comes down in favour of machinic pragmatism. The latter is considered to offer the possibility to think beyond the impasse of neoliberal individualism, whose political negative formed in its image—populist or folk politics—leads only to hyper-individuality as a localised collection of individuals impotently driven reactively by affect. Machinic pragmatism, theoretically rooted in the experience of May '68 and in the work of Deleuze and Guattari, appears to offer a way out of this impasse, and without requiring a return to an outmoded collective subject of history, made problematic after '68. However, machinic pragmatism offers such a solution only if read in terms of a rethinking of the nature of an engaged (as opposed to an escapist) critical practice, understood as a coming together of singularities breaking free from the shackles of post-'68 control institutions, and with a view to changing the world and not just the self.

Gabriela Hernández De La Fuente's chapter, 'May '68: An Institutional Event,' tackles the double bind of institutions head-on. If institutions were rightly critiqued during and after '68, what comes after institutions under neoliberalism is just as controlling. Yet, Hernández De La Fuente sees in the experimental University of Vincennes, opened in France in the autumn of '68 as a direct response to May, and in Félix Guattari's psychotherapeutic and militant practices centred on the La Borde psychiatric clinic, traces of a revolutionary conception of the institution, whose potentialities indicate a route out of our contemporary double bind. Hernández De La Fuente shows that, already in the 1950s, Guattari and his colleagues had been experimenting with the notion of a transversal institution understood as a horizontal relinking that does away with institutionalised hierarchies and rigid segmentations. This reflects the nonlinear temporality of the May '68 event, which was as much a set of potentials present in the milieu as it was a defined historical sequence, and thus potentially ripe for reactivation (this opens up a debate with Rosales's chapter). If '68 rejected the notion of a collective subject of history, it then did not for all that also do away with a rethinking of the institutions needed to coalesce collectives and give socioeconomic consistency to their desires. Marx's Thesis Eleven can thus be reformulated as follows: 'Philosophers have hitherto only interpreted the world in various ways; the point is to *create new institutions*,' and, indeed, new institutional events.

Also dialoguing with the book's first section, aylon cohen's chapter, 'Communist Guilt, Public Happiness and the Feelings of Collective Attachment,' addresses the practical construction of collectivity at the level of the riotous event itself. cohen's chapter serves as a rebuttal to Jodi Dean's claim that, without a leader, a revolt's collective energies cannot be prolonged beyond the event itself. Dean identifies such leaderless revolts with post-May '68 politics, and argues that the institution of the party is better able to regenerate the affects of collective unity experienced during a rebellion. However, for cohen, Dean's rendering of this process amounts to what they call an 'affective politics of communist guilt,' which is unable to meet the challenge of rekindling the cooperative relations needed for political struggle. Turning instead to Hannah Arendt and her concept of public happiness, cohen argues that the experience of 'political joy' is a better framework for understanding affects of collectivity occasioned by the rioting crowd. cohen considers the rioting crowd to establish a horizontal relational space in which 'riotous happiness' can prosper and propagate. cohen thus suggests how practices can give consistency to events independently of institutions, by working on affects directly. Hence, they indicate a way out of the supposed double bind of either the chaos of unformed energies, or their repression by the party-form.

The volume concludes with Ben Dunn's chapter, 'Community, Theatre and Political Labour: Unworking the Socialist Legacy of 1968,' which addresses the theory and practice of community building within the context of theatre and performance in Britain. Based on his field research with the performance company Glas(s) Performance, Dunn examines how collective performance can create a space in which the refusal of work need not also spell the end of community—indicating a way out of the supposed double bind of either community through work (socialism) or solitary creativity (neoliberalism). Dunn focuses on *Albert Drive*, a year-long arts and performance project in Pollokshields, Glasgow, arguing that it functions as a dramaturgical expression of what Jean-Luc Nancy calls the 'inoperative community.'[103] This is a community beyond work constructed through cultural activism. For Dunn, *Albert Drive* gives voice to an altermodernity that short-circuits the double bind of the socialist myth of progressive organised labour and the neoliberal ideology of the individual as work-in-progress, within whom the social and the economic, public and private, become blurred. This way, for Dunn, history is performatively rerouted through the indeterminacy of a collective becoming. As with cohen's chapter, the legacy of '68 is reflected in an understanding of disorder as no longer a pejorative designation, but as something capable of its own internal consistency.

This book therefore attempts to give some sense of the potential for a transmutation of failure into success, impasse into breakthrough, taking the full measure of both poles in order to better understand the possibility of revolution today.

NOTES

1. I would like to especially thank Krista Bonello Rutter Giappone for her careful reading of this chapter, and for her helpful comments and suggestions.

2. 2008 coincided with the fortieth anniversary of 1968, but it was its fiftieth anniversary in 2018 that seemed to reopen a door back to it, as the political fallout of 2008's economic crisis had by this stage become palpable. Consequently, 2018–2019 saw the appearance of a number of conferences and publications reflecting, more

urgently than before, on '68 and questions of resistance. For instance, '50 Years after May '68,' *Crisis and Critique* 5, no. 2 (2018), eds. Agon Hamza and Frank Ruda; 'La pensée dix-huit,' *La Deleuziana* 8 (2018), ed. Guillaume Collett; 'Restoration and Resistance,' *Pli*, 2019; and the conference that gave rise to this volume.

3. David Harvey, *A Brief History of Neoliberalism* (New York: Oxford University Press, 2005), 41–42.

4. Harvey, *Brief History*, 41.

5. Harvey, *Brief History*, 25.

6. Nancy Fraser, 'Feminism's Two Legacies: A Tale of Ambivalence,' *South Atlantic Quarterly* 114, no. 4 (2015): 700.

7. Fraser, 'Two Legacies,' 700.

8. Fraser, 'Two Legacies,' 700.

9. Robert Pfaller interviewed by Kamran Baradaran, 'Postmodernism: The Ideological Embellishment of Neoliberalism,' *Off Guardian*, 11 August 2019, https://off-guardian.org/2019/08/11/postmodernism-the-ideological-embellishment-of-neoliberalism/ (last accessed 17 August 2021).

10. On the 'refusal of work's theorisation in the French context and around May '68, see the introductory article 'Bring Out Your Dead,' from 'Preliminary Materials for a Balance Sheet of the Twentieth Century,' *Endnotes* 1 (October 2008): 2–19; on the North American experience, see Grégoire Chamayou, *The Ungovernable Society: A Genealogy of Authoritarian Liberalism* (Cambridge: Polity Press, 2021), 9–34.

The refusal of work would become a central pillar of the Italian radical left from the 1960s till the end of the 1970s. Writing in 1965, Mario Tronti states: 'The worker cannot be *labour* other than in relation to the capitalist. The capitalist cannot be *capital* other than in relation to the worker.' Mario Tronti, 'The Strategy of Refusal,' in *Autonomia: Post-Political Politics*, second edition, eds. S. Lotringer and C. Marazzi 31 (New York: Semiotext(e), 2007), 28–33. Emphasis in the original; Italian autonomism sought to struggle against labour itself insofar as it is capital. For more on this topic, see Daniel Fraser and Ben Dunn's chapters.

11. Luc Boltanski and Ève Chiapello, *The New Spirit of Capitalism*, trans. G. Elliott (London: Verso, 2018), 21; Eric Hobsbawm, *The Age of Extremes: The Short Twentieth Century, 1914–1991* (London: Abacus, 1995), 272–73; Paul A. Baran and Paul M. Sweezy, *Monopoly Capital: An Essay on the American Economic and Social Order* (London: Penguin Books, 1973), 150, 162–63.

12. Boltanski and Chiapello, *New Spirit*, xli; Harvey, *Brief History*, 25.

13. See Alex Williams and Nick Srnicek, '#ACCELERATE MANIFESTO: For an Accelerationist Politics,' *Critical Legal Thinking* (blog), 14 May 2013, https://criticallegalthinking.com/2013/05/14/accelerate-manifesto-for-an-accelerationist-politics/ (last accessed 18 August 2021).

14. Mariana Mazzucato, *Mission Economy: A Moonshot Guide to Changing Capitalism* (London: Penguin, 2021).

15. Philip Rucker and Robert Costa, 'Bannon Vows a Daily Fight for "Deconstruction of the Administrative State",' *Washington Post*, 23 February 2017, https://www.washingtonpost.com/politics/top-wh-strategist-vows-a-daily-fight-for

-deconstruction-of-the-administrative-state/2017/02/23/03f6b8da-f9ea-11e6-bf01-d47f8cf9b643_story.html (last accessed 2 August 2021).

16. Grace Blakeley, *The Corona Crash: How the Pandemic Will Change Capitalism* (London: Verso, 2020).

17. Silvia Federici, *Caliban and the Witch. Women, the Body, and Primitive Accumulation* (New York: Autonomedia, 2004), 115.

18. Karl Marx, *Capital: A Critique of Political Economy*, vol. 1, trans. B. Fowkes (London: Penguin, 1976).

19. Marx, *Capital*, 325; as Mario Tronti puts it: 'In the salary there disappears precisely every trace of the division of the working day into necessary labour and surplus-value. . . . The more that capitalist production develops and the system of its forces of production, the more the paid and non-paid parts of labour are confused in an inseparable manner.' Mario Tronti, 'Factory and Society,' *Operaismo in English*, 13 June 2013, https://operaismoinenglish.wordpress.com/2013/06/13/factory-and-society (last accessed 2 April 2021).

20. Marx, *Capital*, 1019.

21. Marx, *Capital*, 1039–40.

22. Tronti, 'Factory and Society.'

23. Paulo Virno, *Grammar of the Multitude: For an Analysis of Contemporary Forms of Life*, trans. I. Bertoletti, J. Cascaito, and A. Casson. (New York: Semiotext(e), 2004), 104.

24. Félix Guattari and Antonio Negri, *New Lines of Alliance, New Spaces of Liberty* (New York: Minor Compositions/Autonomedia, 2010), 35–36, 46.

25. Guattari and Negri, *New Lines*, 34; Hobsbawm, *Age of Extremes*, 264–66, 270.

26. We find this formulated most famously in the claim that the unconscious is a factory not a theatre, it produces rather than represents. Gilles Deleuze and Félix Guattari, *Anti-Oedipus: Capitalism and Schizophrenia*, vol. 1, trans. R. Hurley, M. Seem, and H. R. Lane (London: Continuum, 2004), 25, 62.

27. Guattari and Negri, *New Lines*, 34; see also Tronti, 'Strategy of Refusal,' 32.

28. Félix Guattari, *Molecular Revolution: Psychiatry and Politics*, trans. R. Sheed (London: Penguin, 1984), 66.

29. For Guattari, this was the result of the 'contradiction' between institutions' production of 'stereotyped models' of subjectivity corresponding to Fordist production, while demanding 'ever more complex units' of subjectivity due to the increasing involvement of continuous re-training, research and technological innovations. Guattari, *Molecular Revolution*, 212–13.

30. Kristin Ross, *May '68 and Its Afterlives* (Chicago: University of Chicago Press, 2002), 25.

31. For Jacques Rancière, politics as 'police' is precisely a matter of policing borders in an effort to divide and rule, contra the 'anonymous multitude [that] reaffirms the community of sharing' through dissensus, understood as a break with hierarchised categories. Jacques Rancière, *On the Shores of Politics*, trans. L. Heron (London: Verso, 1990), 58.

32. Ross, *May '68*, 25.

33. Still in his psychoanalytic phase, Guattari understands this as a 'transitional' or 'group phantasy,' a self-fictioning construction with real effects, temporarily shaking off the hold of the superego (on desire and inhibitions). Guattari, *Molecular Revolution*, 209, 211, 215.

34. Alain Badiou also emphasises the diagonal character of '68, though he understands this in terms of its 'evental' nature as lacking from its own place, i.e. its irreducibility to any one definable situation (such as the workers' strikes or student occupations). Alain Badiou, *The Communist Hypothesis*, trans. D. Macey and S. Corcoran (London: Verso, 2010), 41–100. Thus (like Rancière), he considers it as a specifically political event, rather than also in terms of its relation to historical shifts in capitalism.

35. The notion of intersectionality was first formulated within critical race theory in the early 1990s. See Kimberlé Krenshaw, 'Mapping the Margins: Intersectionality, Identity Politics, and Violence Against Women of Color,' *Stanford Law Review* 43, no. 6 (1991): 1241–99. Krenshaw's starting point is not that identity politics has failed to transcend its differences towards a theory of social justice, nor simply that identities themselves are functions of power designed to divide and rule, but that more attention needs to be paid to intra-group differences or intersections (of race, sex, gender and class), as the basis for an empowering reconstruction of our understanding of social identities. These are now to be seen as existing in a relational space pointing beyond siloed forms of oppression, to a web of oppression operating across identities if still by means of identity (1242).

36. Federici also notes capitalism's 'primitive accumulation of differences' (of gender, race and age) within the working class, as a set of hierarchies and power relations at the heart of the process of accumulation itself. Federici, *Caliban*, 63–64.

37. Around the same time, communisation theory also sought to think beyond the worker/capitalist dialectic's teleological focus, its promotion of the worker to the role of agent of history, and its submission of individual interests to those of the collective (see *Endnotes* in note 10). See Daniel Fraser's chapter for further discussion of this, as well as the chapters by Jose Rosales and Iain MacKenzie.

38. See the chapters by Christos Marneros and aylon cohen for discussions of similar themes.

39. Gilles Deleuze and Félix Guattari, *A Thousand Plateaus: Capitalism and Schizophrenia*, vol. 2, trans. B. Massumi (London: Continuum, 2004), 320–29.

40. 'May '68 was a becoming-revolutionary . . . becomings-children, becomings-women for men, becomings-men for women.' Claire Parnet interviewing Gilles Deleuze, in 'Gilles Deleuze: The ABC Primer / Recording 2, G to M,' *The Deleuze Seminars*, 4 February 1989, https://deleuze.cla.purdue.edu/seminars/gilles-deleuze-abc-primer/lecture-recording-2-g-m (last accessed 8 July 2020). For Deleuze and Guattari (2004), 'one becomes revolutionary' by 'using a number of minority elements, by connecting, conjugating them, one invents a specific, unforeseen, autonomous becoming.' They speak of 'masses' (rather than classes), understood as 'multiplicities of escape and flux,' that preexist the classes that structure them within a closed dialectic with capital. Deleuze and Guattari, *Thousand Plateaus*, 118, 519.

41. Deleuze and Guattari, *Thousand Plateaus*, 562–66. Already in 1954, Deleuze had emphasised the interdependence of instincts and institutions, institutions being

established through the organisation of instincts, instincts lacking their own principle of auto-synthesis. Gilles Deleuze, 'Instincts and Institutions,' in Deleuze, *Desert Islands and Other Texts: 1953–1974*, ed. D. Lapoujade, trans. M. Taormina (New York: Semiotext(e), 2004), 19–21.

42. 'Becoming-revolutionary remains indifferent to questions of a future and a past of the revolution; it passes between the two.' Deleuze and Guattari, *Thousand Plateaus*, 322.

43. aylon cohen's chapter further examines de-centred affectivity as a challenge to communist institutions.

44. Éric Alliez and Maurizio Lazzarato, *Wars and Capital* (New York: Semiotext(e), 2018).

45. Alliez and Lazzarato, *Wars*, 223–67.

46. Alliez and Lazzarato, *Wars*, 229–36, 264–66.

47. Alliez and Lazzarato, *Wars*, 265–67.

48. For a counterargument, see the passages below on Hardt and Negri, who see the expansion of the de-disciplinarised social factory as being more, not less, amenable to bringing about revolution.

49. See Deleuze and Guattari's conception of the 'mass' as ontologically and politically preceding class.

50. Deleuze and Guattari, *Thousand Plateaus*, 92.

51. Guattari, *Molecular Revolution*, 31.

52. Guattari, *Molecular Revolution*, 215–16 (translation modified). For the early Guattari, this is because 'The social contradictions to which the masses are subject do not strike them as a set of theoretical problems: they are experienced in the order of the imaginary' and worked on at the level of 'group phantasizing,' by which he means a 'transversal' becoming that seeks to break with dominant significations to establish a real subjective rupture (209). On Guattari's theories of transversality and revolution, see Janell Watson's *Guattari's Diagrammatic Thought: Writing Between Lacan and Deleuze* (London: Bloomsbury, 2009), 15–54, 166–81.

53. Jacques Rancière also views May '68 as pointing to an 'autonomous process of reconfiguring the visible, the thinkable, and the possible,' through the dissensual transgression of categories, 'and not the accomplishment of a historical movement bent by a political party to its will.' Jacques Rancière, *Moments politiques: Interventions 1977–2009* (Paris: La Fabrique, 2009), 195.

54. For further discussion of this topic, see Jose Rosales's chapter.

55. Guattari therefore saw Maoist-style guerrilla warfare in Paris as being premature, as it would have 'blocked off the possibilities' of developing a collective masochistic fantasy formation as an essential first stage. Félix Guattari, *Psychoanalysis and Transversality: Texts and Interviews 1955–1971*, trans. A. Hodges (New York: Semiotext(e)), 287. Deleuze and Guattari (2007) speak of May '68 as a 'visionary phenomenon, as if a society suddenly saw what was intolerable in it and also saw the possibility for something else' (234). Deleuze and Guattari, 'May '68 Did Not Take Place,' trans. H. Weston, in G. Deleuze, *Two Regimes of Madness: Texts and Interviews 1975–1995*, ed. D. Lapoujade (New York: Semiotext(e), 2007), 233–36; see also Ross, *May '68*, 31–33.

56. Guattari, *Psychoanalysis*, 287.
57. Guattari, *Molecular Revolution*, 65.
58. Deleuze and Guattari, *Thousand Plateaus*, 514–16.
59. Gabriela Hernández de la Fuente explores these 'transversal' institutions further.
60. Deleuze and Guattari, *Thousand Plateaus*, 238–39, emphasis mine. For further discussion of these points, see Iain MacKenzie's chapter.
61. Deleuze and Guattari, *May '68*.
62. Deleuze and Guattari, *May '68*, 234.
63. Maurizio Lazzarato, *Le capital déteste tout le monde: Fascisme ou révolution* (Paris: Éditions Amsterdam, 2019), 12, 176–78. Alliez and Lazzarato (2018) and Lazzarato (2019) consider '68 thought to develop its theory of revolution proper around the mid-1970s—as found in the works of Deleuze, Guattari and Foucault, where we find a conception of revolutionary strategy offering itself as an alternative to the theory of class war. These authors' works tend more towards the pole of negative freedom from around 1984 onwards (and, for Foucault, already in the late 1970s). Only in this sense can Deleuze and Guattari be described as representatives of what Boltanski and Chiapello (2018) call the 'artistic critique.'
64. Alliez and Lazzarato, *Wars*, 368.
65. Boltanski and Chiapello, *New Spirit*, 93, 118, 194, 250, 285, 314, 320, 360, 383, 443, 456, 515. For a 'philosophy of the firm' giving a more 'authoritarian' account of its role after '68, and its relation to the state, see Chamayou, *Ungovernable Society*.
66. Boltanski and Chiapello, *New Spirit*, 97, 122, 452.
67. Boltanski and Chiapello, *New Spirit*, 24, 58, 70–87, 86, 90, 93–94, 96.
68. Michel Foucault, 'Nietzsche, Genealogy, History,' in *The Foucault Reader: An Introduction to Foucault's Thought*, ed. P. Rabinow, trans. D. F. Bouchard and S. Simon (London: Penguin, 1991), 76–100; see also Gilles Deleuze, 'What Is a *Dispositif?*,' in G. Deleuze, *Two Regimes of Madness: Texts and Interviews, 1975–1995*, ed. D. Lapoujade, trans. A. Hodges and M. Taormina (New York: Semiotext(e), 2006), 338–48.
69. Michael Hardt and Antonio Negri, *Empire* (Cambridge, MA: Harvard University Press, 2000).
70. Michael Hart and Antonio Negri, *Commonwealth* (Cambridge, MA: Harvard University Press, 2009). For an instructive confrontation between Marxism and post-Marxism, see David Harvey, Antonio Negri and Michael Hardt, 'Commonwealth: An Exchange,' *Artforum* 48, no. 3 (2009): 210–21.
71. Hardt and Negri, *Commonwealth*, 325–60.
72. See also Wendy Brown, *Edgework: Critical Essays on Knowledge and Politics* (Princeton, NJ: Princeton University Press, 2005): 'How and when did sex and gender become essential objects of feminism rather than that which we aimed to overthrow? . . . what kind of feminism aims to conserve rather than reduce, eliminate, or at the very least diffuse sex and gender?' (99).
73. What makes identities revolutionary is therefore the becomings they can stage. This is missed by Slavoj Žižek, for whom class war is more fundamental than 'anti-

sexism and antiracism,' because while, for him, they seek recognition by the other, class alone aims for the other's 'annihilation' (quoted in Hardt and Negri, *Commonwealth*, 342).

74. Hardt and Negri, *Commonwealth*, 345, 355–57.
75. Boltanski and Chiapello, *New Spirit*, 37.
76. Boltanski and Chiapello, *New Spirit*, 38.
77. Boltanski and Chiapello, *New Spirit*, 169.
78. Boltanski and Chiapello, *New Spirit*, xliv, 223; see Natasha Lushetich's chapter for further discussion of this topic.
79. Boltanski and Chiapello, *New Spirit*, 435.
80. Boltanski and Chiapello, *New Spirit*, 435.
81. Boltanski and Chiapello, *New Spirit*, 3. This was further exacerbated by the collapse of the USSR in 1991 and the trenchant critique of communism voiced by the New Left ever since the 1960s.
82. For instance, the couple of years leading up to the international anti-globalisation protests of 1999, when the social critique fully re-emerged (1995 had already seen the largest general strike in France since May '68), saw a surge in iconic mainstream anti-capitalist film and music.
83. Boltanski and Chiapello, *New Spirit*, 89, 488. Chiapello later suggested that financialisation 'influence[s] the way social or environmental problems are defined and considered,' preventing the social critique from gaining any purchase on alternative solutions (xix).
84. Maurizio Lazzarato, *The Making of the Indebted Man: An Essay on the Neoliberal Condition*, trans. JD Jordan (New York: Semiotext(e), 2012), 8, 93–94, 108–9, 126–27. Lazzarato, *Fascisme ou révolution*, 25–27.
85. Lazzarato, *Indebted Man*, 93; Lazzarato, *Fascisme ou révolution*, 85.
86. As Yanis Varoufakis puts it: 'There is no capitalist logic to the developments that culminated on August 12 [2020]. For the first time, a widespread expectation of diminished revenues and profits led to—or at least did not impede—a sustained buying frenzy in London and New York. And this is not because speculators are betting that the UK or the US economies have hit bottom, making this a great time to buy shares. No, for the first time in history, financiers actually don't give a damn about the real economy.' Yannis Varoufakis, 'The Post Capitalist Hit of the Summer,' *Project Syndicate*, 31 August 2020, https://www.project-syndicate.org/commentary/covid19-and-postcapitalist-economy-by-yanis-varoufakis-2020-08 (last accessed 2 September 2021).
87. Yanis Varoufakis, 'Techno Feudalism Is Taking Over,' *Project Syndicate*, 28 June 2021, https://www.project-syndicate.org/commentary/techno-feudalism-replacing-market-capitalism-by-yanis-varoufakis-2021-06?barrier=accesspaylog (last accessed 7 September 2021).
88. Boltanski and Chiapello, *New Spirit*, 5, 129–31.
89. Tiziana Terranova, *Network Culture: Politics for the Information Age* (London: Pluto Press, 2004), 73–97; Vladan Joler and Andrej Petrovski, 'Immaterial Labour and Data Harvesting: Facebook Algorithmic Factory (1),' *Share Lab* (blog), 21 August 2016, https://labs.rs/en/facebook-algorithmic-factory-immaterial-labour-and-data-harvesting/#easy-footnote-2-996 (last accessed 2 April 2021).

90. Lazzarato, *Indebted Man*.

91. Brian Massumi, *Ontopower: War, Powers, and the State of Perception* (Durham, NC: Duke University Press, 2015).

92. We already see this phenomenon within neo-capitalism appearing in the early 1980s, with Reagan's Star Wars and Thatcher's Falklands War.

93. Hardt and Negri note neoconservatism's emphasis on maintaining identity, as opposed to neoliberal governmentality's use of identity as the starting point for developing networks that might give rise to social and economic fluxes productive of the multitude. Hardt and Negri, *Commonwealth*, 349. However, they do not consider that authoritarian capitalism can work hand-in-hand with economic liberalism by severing the connection between social and economic fluxes, or between labour and capital.

94. Guy Standing notes how, post-2008, 'income differentials went on widening,' rather than narrowing as is typically the case after a major recession. Guy Standing, *The Precariat: The Dangerous New Class* (London: Bloomsbury, 2011), 58.

95. Michel Foucault, *Discipline and Punish: The Birth of the Prison*, trans. A. Sheridan (London: Penguin, 1977).

96. See Alliez and Lazzarato, *Wars*; Lazzarato, *Fascisme ou révolution*.

97. Alliez and Lazzarato refer to this as the 'governmentality of war.' As they explain: 'governmentality does not replace war. It organises, governs and controls the reversibility of wars and power.' Alliez and Lazzarato, *Wars*, 26, 282. Arguably, governmentality can still be a preferred solution even at a solely political level, since its power is more insidious than is authoritarianism, but for Alliez and Lazzarato it in turn becomes a means to organise its own degree of authoritarianism to suit the political conditions.

98. Boltanski and Chiapello, *New Spirit*, 8–9, 19, 36–37.

99. Antonio Negri, 'French Insurrection: Antonio Negri on the *Gilets Jaunes* and the New Wave of Protests in France,' *Verso* (blog), 8 December 2018, https://www.versobooks.com/blogs/4158-french-insurrection (last accessed 2 August 2021).

100. By contrast, and within the lineage of '68 thought, Alliez has recently questioned the notion that becomings-revolutionary are capable in principle of providing intersectional solutions to emancipatory demands, due to the different strategies and objectives of these interest groups (38). Thus, Alliez replaces Deleuze's ontological prioritisation of becoming-revolutionary (or affective resistance) over history, with that of strategy understood as generalised civil war (47). Éric Alliez, '1968–2018, or from the "Revolution Impossible" to the Impossibility of Revolution? Variations on the *objet petit s*,' *Crisis & Critique* 5, no. 2 (2018): 31–50; see also Lazzarato, *Fascisme ou révolution*, 84–91. If Hardt and Negri (2009) wish to revitalise identity politics through the notion of the commons, Alliez and Lazzarato's approach is more in keeping with Foucault's mid-1970s work, in seeing identities under capitalism as irreducibly conflictual strategies.

101. Srnicek and Williams risk falling into this trap, by opposing their technological vision of a left modernity to the local and affective ('folk politics'), rather than trying to immanently bridge the two. Nick Srnicek and Alex Williams, *Inventing the Future: Postcapitalism and a World Without Work* (London: Verso, 2015).

102. Estienne de la Boétie, *Discourse on Voluntary Servitude*, trans. J. B. Atkinson and David Sices (Indianapolis: Hackett Publishing Company, 2012 [1576]).

103. Jean-Luc Nancy, *The Inoperative Community*, trans. P. Connor, L. Garbus, M. Holland, and S. Sawhney (Minneapolis, MN: University of Minnesota Press, 1991).

Part I

1968 AND MARXISM

Chapter Two

Communism as the Riddle Posed to History

Jose Rosales

On 24 May, we admired on television the impressive Paris demonstration called by the central CGT trade union. Throughout the country were other demonstrations. We were jubilant. If the most important workers' union embraced the movement, we had an avenue for hope! We saw proof of this in President General de Gaulle casting his bait on television: he announced the organisation of a June referendum on participatory decision-making for workers in enterprises and for students in the universities. We feared seeing students fall into the trap set, but not much effort was needed to avoid potential demobilisation. We learned that the response to the chief of state's proposal was another demonstration in Paris, with new barricades and, nec plus ultra, the burning of the Bourse!

On 25 May, at the Ministry of Labour in Paris, negotiations began between the trinity of trade unions, employers and the government.

On 27 May, we learned the epilogue. The content of the so-called Grenelle agreement: increased unemployment benefits and base wages, the workday gradually reduced to forty hours a week, the age of retirement lowered, revised collective agreements, recognition of trade union sections in enterprises and increased trade union rights. To the horde of hungry dogs, the owners threw some bones to chew on. Some affordable employer concessions to suffocate social change aiming to eliminate ownership itself.

The following day, there was Francois Mitterrand, who announced his candidacy for the presidency.

The next day, we learned that the secretary-general of the CGT, Georges Séguy himself, went to Renault factories in Boulogne-Billancourt. He presented the agreements to the strikers. Against his expectation, they voted to pursue the strike.

All of this was coming about without elections, without 'palace' manoeuvres, without an armed *coup d'état*, without a Day of 10 August 1792, against the Tuileries, without an attack on the Winter Palace, without a Bolshevik 'avant-garde Party,' and without a long Maoist grassroots war. This is how the slogan 'Be realistic, demand the impossible!' became a reality. Alas! Those who pretend 'genuinely' to represent working people, the leaders of the 'communist' party and the CGT trade union, took fright at the liberation struggle of the same working people.[1]

INTRODUCTION

Rather than some set of solutions or revolutionary program, May '68 appears to persist in the form of a problem. For someone like Alain Badiou, this problem of '68 belongs strictly to the order of *politics* insofar as the era was defined by and preoccupied with the question, '*What is politics?*.'[2] While for those like Félix Guattari, '68's problematic was *socioeconomic* in essence, with 'one specific battle to be fought by workers in the factories, another by patients in the hospital, yet another by students in the university. As became obvious in '68, the problem of the university is . . . the problem of society as a whole.'[3] And for others still, such as Jean-Luc Nancy, the problem of May '68 reveals itself to be decidedly *metaphysical* in nature ('Democracy is first of all a metaphysics and only afterwards a politics').[4] Thus it seems that the fate of May '68 is to remain an eternal site of contestation, always irreducible to any single sequence of events. Hence the suggestion that 'the meaning of May' signifies less a resolution of contradictions and more the formulation of a set of problems—the effect of which was a critical interrogation of the inherited figures and institutions of the workers' movement, which thereby altered the very meaning of communism as such. Perhaps the most significant outcome of the struggles of '68 stems from these confrontations between the emergence of new social movements on the one hand, and the unions and party of the left, on the other.

As the main institutions and organisational forms inherited from previous cycles of struggle, both the union and the party were either unwilling or unable to advocate for the political and economic demands of an emergent, collective, political subject. That is, if '68 achieved anything, it succeeded in giving a new meaning to struggle itself: a vision of struggle no longer subordinate to any party line, no longer in want or need of recognition from the established institutions of the left, and no longer faithful to a notion of revolutionary agency confined to the point of production. From this dual rejection of the classical identification of the industrial worker with the locus of revolutionary potential and the union and party as inherited organs of proletarian struggle, emerged an insurrectionary *praxis* aimed at overcoming the limitations of the union and party as the forms of organisation inherited by '68.[5]

What this means from the vantage point of the current conjuncture, however, is an altogether different matter. In other words, while it was the failure of the 1848 revolution that established the aim of seising state power for an organised working class anticipating 1910 (Mexican Revolution) and 1917 (Bolshevik Revolution), the theoretical and practical effects that were born out of '68 left its contemporaries uncertain regarding the potential actualisation of the possible futures implicated within that year:

> After 1848, the world's old left were sure that 1917 would occur. They argued about how and where and when. But the middle-range objective of popular sovereignty [i.e. seising State power] was clear. After 1968, the world's antisystemic movements—the old and the new ones together—showed rather less clarity about the middle-range objective. . . . We have no answer to the question: 1968, rehearsal for what? In a sense, the answers depend on the ways in which the worldwide family of antisystemic movements will rethink its middle-run strategy in the ten or twenty years to come.[6]

At the very least, '68 still merits the title of an event insofar as it refers to a political sequence whose refusal of capital as the structuring principle of social existence opened up new fields of the possible. It marks a period when a generalised antagonism proved itself capable of wresting back what was determined as impossible, via the counter-actualisation of its present—thereby initiating an experiment in constructing an anti-state communist form of life adequate to the task of establishing a new norm regarding the relation of the economic and the social.[7] And yet, all that was promising in the specific reorganisation of forms of everyday life that were obtained during '68 eventually became too many revolutionary breaks with history to produce a determinately anti-capitalist future. Thus, if, in 1844, Marx could still confidently write that 'Communism is the riddle of history solved . . . and knows itself to be this solution,'[8] after '68 and no longer certain of itself, *communism now appears as the riddle posed to history*.

That said, it is still necessary to ask whether or not we remain its contemporaries fifty years on. In other words, this is to ask whether the problem that has come to preoccupy the left of today is still the search for the forms and organisation of political subjectivity capable of ushering in a qualitative transformation of capital. For as Badiou suggests, today 'we have the same problem and are the contemporaries of the problem revealed by May '68: the classical figure of the politics of emancipation was ineffective.'[9] In what follows, I would like to propose that our relationship to May '68 is more complicated than any straightforward affirmation or rejection of our contemporaneity with the political sequence that bears its name and date. Moreover, it is only by understanding why we cannot simply affirm or reject all that is implied in Badiou's assertion of a singular problem as that which binds us to '68 that we are able to grasp how our relationship to '68 involves, by necessity, both responses. While it may be the case that what we share with '68 is our search for an answer to a singular question: *What form will collective subjectivity take such that it is adequate to the abolition of itself and its present state of affairs?* What is also made clear is that both the context and possible solutions this question solicited in 1968 are substantively different from the context and solutions that are currently in existence.

In this way, we are forced to recognise that if there is a double bind proper to '68, it is of an altogether different nature than the properly dialectical trap, which confronts us today. Inasmuch as '68's double bind was marked by a 'becoming-revolutionary without a revolutionary future,'[10] what defines the double bind of the current conjuncture is the left's division within itself, between those who call for a reinvestment in the party-form and parliamentary politics and those who reiterate their commitment to the recomposition and furthering of extra-parliamentary struggle. That is to say, unlike the movements of '68, the current cycle of struggles no longer finds itself in a condition solely defined by the existence of a revolutionary process that lacks an attendant, and emancipatory, future. Rather, contemporary social movements are circumscribed by the temptation of engaging in either a melancholic reflection on the past, but in the form of the grounds for revolutionary struggle in the present, or engaging in a farcical repetition of this past, pure and simple. And so, the concluding section of this chapter will demonstrate how it was Blanchot, rather than Badiou, who best captured the double bind that serves as the political horizon for '68's contemporaries: the dialectical trap of *melancholic reflection* and *farcical repetition*.

No longer simply bearers of a shared problem, to be a contemporary of '68 is to think and act against the temptation of the former—which substitutes an historical materialist analysis of the present for the derivation of 'lessons' that are said to be immediately applicable in the present (an approach that incorrectly presupposes an unchanged composition of the relation between Capital and Labour)—while rejecting the parochialism of the latter—which 'anxiously conjure[s] up the spirits of the past to their service, borrowing from them names, battle slogans, and costumes' whilst failing to produce a 'new scene in world history.'[11]

BADIOU'S 'FOUR MAYS'

'I would like to begin by asking a very simple question: why all this fuss about May '68 . . . 40 years after the event? There was nothing of the kind for the thirtieth or twentieth anniversary.'[12] Thus begins Badiou's reflections on the fortieth anniversary of the events of '68. And not without justification, for it is indeed strange that May '68 becomes worthy of national commemoration only once forty years of silence have passed. Beginning with this question, Badiou identifies two dominant modes of responding to this question. On the one hand, there is a set of answers that can be said to be pessimistic, which suggest that it is possible to commemorate May '68 precisely because it no longer has any socio-political influence on the present.[13] In other words, such a view holds that commemoration is possible precisely because what was really achieved through the events of May was the establishment of the conditions of possibility needed for neoliberalism to emerge.[14] On the other hand, there are those answers that are decidedly optimistic—ranging from arguments that view this commemorative moment as looking towards the past for the inspiration needed to change the present, to those who still hold on to a certain image of insurrectionary politics, which is said to contain the promise that another world is indeed possible.[15]

Contrary to these positions, and emphasising what he takes to be May '68's irreducibly complex character, Badiou argues that there are not *two* but *four* different Mays:

> [T]he reason why this commemoration is complicated and gives rise to contradictory hypotheses is that May '68 itself was an event of great complexity. It is impossible to reduce it to a conveniently unitary image. I would like to transmit to you this internal division, the heterogeneous multiplicity that was May '68. *There were in fact four different May '68s.* The strength and the distinctive feature of the French May '68 is that it entwined, combined and superimposed four processes that are, in the final analysis, quite heterogeneous.[16]

In place of both optimistic and pessimistic mystification, says Badiou, the reality of 'May 1968' was that of a political sequence whose realisation was due to the coordination and combined effects of (i) the student/university uprising, (ii) the general and wildcat strikes organised by workers and (iii) the protestations, which arose most notably from young people, oppressed social groups and cultural workers. Hence, Badiou continues, it is precisely for this reason that it comes as no surprise that the symbolic sites of '68 are 'the occupied Sorbonne for students, the big car plants (and especially Billancourt) for the workers, and the occupation of the Odéon theatre.'[17]

While each of these segments of '68 correspond to the first three iterations of May, what is it that constitutes the supposed 'fourth' May? And what is its relation to the university, factory and struggles over everyday life? According to Badiou, this 'fourth May' is nothing other than the generalisation of what one could call an 'absolute refusal' or 'absolute rejection' of the movements of '68 and their relation to previous cycles of revolutionary struggle. This was a form of collective refusal, which centred on two elements that, historically, have been seen as theoretical and/or practical givens regarding the question of how best to achieve revolutionary transformation: *the classical model of how revolutions are to proceed* and *the subject of history*.

As regards the classical model, the fourth May embodied a shared rejection of the Leninist outline of revolution (or what Badiou, in his essay on Sylvain Lazarus, calls 'the Bolshevik mode of politics')[18] across these various social movements: a vision of revolution that proceeds via workers' parties, backed by labour unions, all while professional revolutionaries organise the masses in the bid to seise state power.[19] For Badiou, it was this rejection of revolutionary orthodoxy—which was characteristic of the fourth May—that ultimately laid the grounds for the unification of the student, worker and cultural struggles active during '68. And it is for this reason that Badiou will go on to define this fourth May as a collective attempt to construct 'a vision of politics that was trying to wrench itself away from the old vision . . . [a politics] seeking to find that which might exist beyond the confines of classic revolutionism.'[20]

In addition to this collective rejection of 'classic revolutionism,' the other defining characteristic of this fourth May was its rejection of working-class identity as being the sole determinant of one's revolutionary potential. For Badiou, this rejection, founded upon the idea that 'the classical figure of the politics of emancipation' was 'ineffective,' had its validity confirmed by his own experience of factory workers welcoming him and his university colleagues during a march to the Chausson factory in Reims:

> What happened at the gates of the Chausson factory would have been completely improbable . . . a week earlier. The solid union and party *dispositif* usually kept workers, young people and intellectuals strictly apart. . . . The local or national leadership was the only mediator. We found ourselves in a situation in which that *dispositif* was falling apart before our very eyes. This was something completely new. . . . This was an event in the philosophical sense of the term: something was happening but its consequences were incalculable. What were its consequences during the ten 'red years' between 1968 and 1978? Thousands of students . . . workers, women . . . and proletarians from Africa went in search of a new politics. . . . A political practice that accepted new trajectories . . . and meetings between people who did not usually talk to each other. . . . At that

point, we realised . . . that if a new emancipatory politics was possible . . . it would turn social classifications upside down [and] would . . . consist in organising lightning displacements, both material and mental.[21]

Thus, says Badiou, to commemorate and reflect upon the events of '68 means to necessarily confront and understand it as a political sequence that was realised only because students, workers, cultural producers and historically marginalised identity groups (the youth, women, Algerians, etc.) shared one and the same horizon of struggle—replete with its dual rejection of the politics of parliamentarianism, party-led unions and transitional programs, and the figure of the worker as the sole bearer of revolutionary potential. Reflecting upon his own text written in the later months of 1968, Badiou would go on to write, 'the obsolescence of a strict Leninism centred upon the question of the party, which, precisely because it is centred on the party, continues to subordinate politics to its statist deviation. It is clear that the question of organisation . . . is indeed central to the lessons of May '68.'[22] Moreover, it was a political sequence whose guiding question was the following: 'What would a new political practice that was not willing to keep everyone in their place look like?'[23] It is precisely in this sense that 1968 is said to mark the birth of a political subjectivity defined by a defiance of the social positions ('places') allotted to it by capital. Or as Kristin Ross writes, and in a manner similar to a Badiouian theory of the subject:

May was a crisis in functionalism. *The movement took the form of political experiments* in declassification, *in disrupting the natural 'givenness' of places;* it consisted of displacements that took students outside of the university, meetings that brought farmers and workers together, or students to the countryside. . . . And in that physical dislocation lay a dislocation in the very idea of politics—*moving it out of its . . . proper place, which was for the left at that time the Communist Party.*[24]

And so, despite the postwar ascendency of communist parties throughout Western Europe in general and France in particular—a period when parties achieved a number of their intermediate objectives, such as the 'full organisation of the industrial working class and a significant rise in their standard of living, plus accession to a place in the state political structure'[25]—the early 1960s began to reveal the party as an institution that had outlived its utility. That is to say, insofar as it proved itself incapable of responding to the demands of a shifting composition of the working class (whether concerning the demands of the feminist and gay liberation movements or regarding France's ongoing colonial campaigns in Algeria). From the vantage point of party politics, demands such as these were viewed as secondary or tertiary concerns (at best) relative to those of the industrial working class.

To make matters worse, whatever symbolic gestures of solidarity the PCF gave domestically, it nullified internationally. Ever since the Charonne massacre in 1961, where an estimated two hundred Algerians were killed at the hands of the Paris police, the French Communist Party has continuously 'referenced ... the deaths at the Charonne metro, as well as to the martyrdom of Audin and Alleg, or the sacrifices of Iveton and Maillot, to bear witness to its anticolonial engagement.'[26] But for all of the authenticity contained in the party's bearing witness to these massacres, it was future socialist president François Mitterand, who in 1954, while serving as interior minister, summarised France's position regarding Algerian Independence in the following terms: 'Algeria is France. The only possible negotiation is war.'

What is more, in a series of critical reflections on the PCF's ongoing ambiguity regarding anticolonial struggle, and whose publication would earn him expulsion from the PCF, Balibar writes: 'There is no question that in the years between 1958 and 1962, no opposition to the colonial war could have triggered a historically effective mass mobilisation without the CGT, without the Communist Party.'[27] Any domestic mobilisation against French colonisation could not take place without the support and means of a Communist Party, whose underlying nationalism made it a 'surprising concentration of contradictions in which the legacy of the working class's patriotic role in the anti-fascist resistance and the worst "great power" (or medium power) chauvinisms, cemented by the influence and mimicking of Soviet nationalism, are mixed together.'[28] In the end, it was due to the PCF's hesitation in formulating a clear position regarding the struggle waged by the Algerian National Liberation Front (FLN), that an opportunity for furthering the aspirations of internationalism was ultimately missed:

> The opportunity was missed to forge an organic unity in struggle between French workers and immigrant workers. For both, internationalism remained ... a calculus of convergent interests, not a common practice in which one learns little by little to know each other, to overcome contradictions, to envisage a shared future.[29]

Errors such as these came to be viewed *neither* as accidents *nor* as aberrations, but as the actual functioning of a party-based strategy of vying for state power. That is, if the missed opportunity for building a really existing internationalist tendency is as grave an error as it appeared to have been, it is only because this jettisoning of internationalism is not simply one error among others; rather, it was the founding gesture of the PCF at the very moment of its ascendency: on 8 May 1945, just as France celebrated the liberation of Paris from Nazi occupation, French colonial soldiers massacred Algerians who were out demonstrating for liberation to reach them not only in Algiers but in Sétif and Guelma, as well. Reversing Marx and Engels's dictum that the proletariat 'has no country,' and in the aftermath of the Second World War, it is no exaggeration to claim that both Mitterrand and the PCF 'defended the interests of the working class' in decidedly nationalist terms.

Showing that this was no longer a party in opposition to the capitalist mode of production and to its cycles of so-called primitive accumulation within its colonies, experiences such as these would serve as the material basis for the 'fourth May's' analysis of the PCF and its unions as having effectively substituted class struggle for class collaboration. Thus, it is no surprise that, in light of de Gaulle's call for a referendum alongside public assemblies for workers and students, respectively, Paris saw both immigrant workers and students respond by sacking the Paris stock exchange (the Bourse) and erecting a new series of barricades: 'We feared seeing students fall into the trap set by . . . de Gaulle. But not much effort was needed to avoid potential demobilisation. We learned that the response to the chief of state's proposal was another demonstration in Paris, with new barricades, and . . . *nec plus ultra*, the burning of the Bourse!'[30]

Viewed in this light, the notion of there having been not two, but 'four Mays,' retains its analytical usefulness insofar as it allows us to conceive of '68 on its own terms: as a form of politics whose horizon of struggle was one that rejected past and present iterations of left-wing politics and gave consistency to a collective subjectivity via the fourth-May-as-diagonal 'that links the other three [Mays].'[31] Thus, in following Badiou we are necessarily led to the conclusion that it was only by virtue of the diagonal function of the fourth May that '68 succeeded in giving a new meaning to struggle itself: a vision of struggle no longer subordinate to any party line; no longer in want or need of recognition from the established institutions of the left; no longer faithful to a notion of revolutionary agency confined to the point of production—thereby making it possible to (briefly) live in reality what we have long been promised to be in truth: *non-alienated, collective* and, thus, *free*.

1968 TO ?

Today, however, things do not seem as clear as they did during 1968. The beginning of the year marked by a failed right-wing coup composed of various currents belonging to the renewed white supremacist currents at the heart of the history of the United States; and thereby further exacerbating the radical left's (at least in the United States and UK) difficulty in confronting its internal split between (i) that portion of the left that has invested its energies and belief in progressive change in candidates and parties on the parliamentary left, and (ii) the extra-parliamentary portion of the left, which remains ever-sceptical of achieving the radical transformation of our social totality via presently existing political institutions and organisations.[32] This alone is already a significant divergence from Badiou's assessment of our relation to the legacy of '68. For if we are the contemporaries of '68—and if '68 were truly defined by the diagonal function of this 'fourth May,' which united various social movements via their shared rejection both of the party-form with its unions and of the electoral process—then, from the vantage point of the present, this consensus forged during '68 has now been put into question.

That said, such an analysis was already put forward in 2015 by Plan C's Keir Milburn. In his article, 'On Social Strikes and Directional Demands,' Milburn notes how one of the key contributing factors that has led to this impasse is the failure of the movements of 2011 to bring about the desired and/or expected level of change. As he puts it, 'an impasse was reached in both the pure horizontalist rejection of representative politics and the initial attempts to address the crisis of social reproduction autonomously from the State and capital.'[33] Reflecting upon SYRIZA and the limitations of a straightforwardly parliamentarian approach to radical change, Milburn, correctly, underscores the fact that electing various left-leaning parties into power reveals what is inherently limiting about this reinvestment of the party-form. These limitations are due either to compromises made between the elected government and the EU or by the EU, IMF and World Bank's isolation of said government, in order to elicit the desired set of austerity measures, thereby rendering it amenable to the demands of the market: 'Neoliberalism . . . seeks to either replace points of democratic decision with pseudo-market mechanisms or, where this isn't possible, insulate points of political decision from pressure and influence from below.'[34]

If it is precisely the 'fourth May's' shared anti-state, anti-party and anti-parliamentarian orientation that is lacking and whose absence is felt in the left's current division within itself, the solution cannot simply be further calls of support for a 'diversity of tactics.' This is precisely because when the parties of the left have ended up in power, what we have seen in the past, and may see again in the near future, is the repression of all those extra-parliamentary groups' struggles, even though the very existence of these groups has helped to build a political climate favourable to the left as a whole. This was a tendency that realised itself in post-'68 France, though the best-known example is that of the Italian Communist Party's 'historic compromise.' In the recent years leading up to 2021, we have also seen echoes of this from Corbyn's Labour Party. For instance, in Labour's 2017 manifesto, one reads that the Labour Party will promise to rectify the damage done by Theresa May's cutting of funds to police and emergency personnel.³⁵ This rectification of the austerity imposed by Conservative leadership, however, is no less compromised in terms of its 'socialist' principles insofar as its proposed solution is the addition of ten thousand more police officers on the streets to, ostensibly, 'keep our communities safe.' And all of this while Corbyn was meeting with well-known grime MCs (e.g. JME), all of whom come from communities that are at the highest risk of being harassed, beaten, wrongfully stopped and searched, verbally and physically assaulted, or worse, by the police themselves. So, what are we to take away from all this?

(i) ΣΥΡΙΖΑ is Greek For Despair

In terms of a collective subject whose consistency is drawn from a shared horizon (consisting of principles, analyses and strategies), it would be more accurate to say that today, we are witnessing the undoing of the 'fourth May's' unifying function, which can be seen in the internal split between electoral and extra-parliamentarian approaches. And just as 'we must not forget . . . that May '68's last slogan was élections *piège à cons* [elections are a con],'³⁶ one possible slogan that captures the parliamentary left's rehabilitation of electoral politics—Pablo Iglesias's PODEMOS in Spain, to Alex Tsipras's ΣΥΡΙΖΑ in Greece and Bernie Sanders's bid for heading the Democratic Party in the US, and the UK Labour Party previously led by Corbyn—is the idea that 'elections are a mode through which class struggle *can again* be waged.' Viewed from the present, however, 2021 appears to mark the failure of the parliamentary left's consolidation of power in the wake of the Arab Spring, the 15-M Movement and so on. What is more, nation-states have enacted the policies of increasingly authoritarian regimes, whether the Chinese Communist Party's passage of the security bill effectively eliminating the long-standing 'one country two systems' policy regarding Hong Kong, or the passage of the 'terror bill' effectively criminalising public dissent by the Duterte-led Philippine Democratic Party (PDP–Laban).

It is in the wake of social democracy's defeat in its bid for state power, and in light of the anti-police uprisings that began as a response to the police murders of George Floyd and Breonna Taylor in the US, that the parliamentary left has reorganised itself at the local level, targeting city politicians while identifying possible seats that can be assumed within local office. In contrast to the rights-based and juridical character assumed during the initial formation of the Black Lives Matter movement (which demanded for the state's upholding of formal equality regardless of race in light of the policing of black and brown lives) the George Floyd Rebellion reoriented public discourse around an explicitly abolitionist character, calling either for the abolition of the police *tout court*. Moreover, unlike its previous rights-based iteration, both the gains and setbacks of the rebellion differed from city to city and state to state due to its confrontation with a police force that has grown increasingly explicit in its white supremacist function (e.g. police officers openly displaying blue lives matter and far-right symbols on their persons), a state ill-equipped to deal with the COVID-19 pandemic, and the various attempts by liberal 'organisers' to neutralise the rebellion's revolutionary aspirations by supplanting the language of abolition for that of 'defunding.'

As many experienced on the streets and read about in the various independent media outlets of the left, what appears as the reaffirmation of their fidelity to 'grassroots organising' on the part of the liberal organisers whose true function is to reinforce statist capture is but the worst form of localism since this strategy's function, and overall effect, is that of directing popular support for increasingly militant forms of struggle away from the struggles themselves and towards the voting booth. To take but one recent example, at a moment when 54 percent of Americans[37] felt that the extra-parliamentary act of burning down the third police precinct was a *justified* response to the police murder of George Floyd, organising efforts aimed at winning local elections hindered, rather than furthered, the development of a degree of popular support for a direct attack against the state, the likes of which has not been seen in the United States in at least fifty years. And yet, this reorientation of electoral campaigns with an eye on potential gains at the municipal and/or city level misses the problem posed by questions of *autonomy*—whether from traditional leftist institutions, or from currently existing political parties committed to a strategy of dual power.

Understood on their own terms via the immanent criteria proper to the political upheaval that conditioned their unfolding, the tactics and experiments in *autonomous* forms of increasingly militant organisation employed during May '68 in France, or between 1969 and 1978 in Italy, were not a set of solutions to the problem of an exhausted and impotent image of revolutionary politics. More than anything, they inaugurated the left's decades-long search for a solution. Thus, we are compelled to say that the post-workerist conception of *autonomy* cannot serve as a substitute for the actualisation of novel forms of the composition and organisation of struggles, if for no other reason than the fact that what autonomy achieved during this period was a rupture, or qualitative difference, established with the classical vision of revolution as such. This rupture enacted a ruthless criticism of the left at a moment when leftists felt trapped by the false choice between the capitalism of the US and the Stalinism of the USSR, without determining the strategies and organisational forms of the politics to come. To say this, however, is not to denounce *autonomia* or autonomist organising as such, but to acknowledge what current leftist movements should reasonably expect from the struggles we have inherited. Or, as Gilles Dauvé puts it:

> All previous unrest or insurrectionary periods had resulted in the creation of new forms, whether party, union, or autonomous body. In the West and in Japan, since the demise of the Spanish Workers' Party of Marxist Unification (POUM) in 1937, no far-left party with strongholds in the workplace has been founded and has managed to fight on. Nothing comparable to early twentieth-century social democracy, Stalinist parties, or the 1930s CIO. Syriza is just about capable of moderating unrest in Greece: it proves incapable of putting forward a platform alternative to mainstream bourgeois politics.[38]

Absent those forms of organisation required for the construction of a revolutionary horizon, the trap laid for both the parliamentary and extra-parliamentary left is the treatment of the *problems* that previous cycles of struggle posed to themselves as the *solutions* to the crises of the present. Autonomy presents itself as a problem and not as the practical resolution of the problematic already discovered in '68 ('the classical figure of the politics of emancipation was ineffective') and taken up again during the 1970s in Italy, such that the problem of autonomy today remains a problem of constructing forms of collective subjectivity adequate to the demands of abolition. 'What new forms of political organisation are needed to handle political antagonisms? As in science, until such time as the problem has not been resolved, you have all sorts of discoveries stimulated by the search for a solution.'[39]

(ii) The Fetish for Organisational Form

While the problem of the organisational forms assumed by current struggles relative to the organic composition of capital remains as urgent as it was in 1968, attempting to resolve these issues by specifying a particular figure or subject-position is, in fact, an insufficient ground upon which to establish contemporaneity, since this was a problem that every historical period had to pose and answer for itself—even if the solutions to this problem assumed different names such as *sans-culotte*, the peasant, the slave, the colonised and, of course, the worker. That said, what continues to bind us to the events of 1968 is the fact of a shared problem: What form of organisation must struggles take in order to carry out a qualitative transformation of capitalist social relations while constructing social relations that are communist in substance? A problem made all the more urgent since it implies that the kinds of organisation inherited from the workers' movement are not only ineffective, but must be left behind altogether; and it was precisely this rejection that rendered the struggles of '68 capable of establishing a break with its own history. Just as with the movements of '68, the current conjuncture presents the left with the task of constructing forms of struggle that aid and further the construction of anti-state communist social relations as well.

However, with regard to the problem posed by questions of organisational forms, of equal importance is the need to address what one might call the *fetish for organisational form*, which refers to thinkers and positions that, despite theoretical and/or practical differences, give primacy to (i) the *forms* assumed by struggles in the course of their unfolding, to the detriment of developing analyses of the shifting compositions of collective subjectivity, which serve as its content, or (ii) to the analytic and logical *forms* required for providing a materialist account of the current status of the capital-labour relation. Regarding the former, it is in the midst of Sergio Bologna's reflections on the virtues and limits of the Italian cycle of struggle spanning from the 1960s to the late 1970s, that he inadvertently provides us with an exemplary case of one variant of this fetishism of form:

> Despite having apparently left a void in its wake, despite having apparently only laid bare the crisis of political forms, including the crisis of the party-form, 1977 has to be considered one of the greatest anticipations of the forms and contents of political and social life seen in recent years. After 1977 there is no turning back, despite all the errors committed . . . *1977 was a year in which the wealth and complexity of problems was such that the political form able to contain and organise them all adequately could not be found.*[40]

Interestingly enough, even Badiou himself asserts the primacy of organisational form, rather than embarking on the development of the theoretical categories necessary to account for the ways in which the historically specific content of antagonism and anti-capitalist activity renders equally novel forms of organisation possible. As he puts it: 'the question of organisation . . . is indeed central to the lessons of May '68.'[41] In terms of the present moment, addressing this formalist fetish appears to be one more problem inherited by (or one more lesson to be learned from) the contemporaries of May. And yet, this formalist fetish had already been criticised in the years immediately following these events.

In his 1972 reflections on the limits proper to the Student-Worker Action Group at Censier, François Martin explains his assessment of the group's eventual re-centring around questions of labour and worker-identity as a regression: 'the unions represent labour power which has become capital. . . . The representatives of variable capital, of capital in the form of labour power, sooner or later have to associate with the representatives of capital who are now in power.'[42] For Martin, this reaffirmation of labour and worker-identity was a regression precisely because the very forms of struggle available to collective actions were limited to a concern with the rights of labour, which gave rise to a form of organisation—the union—that forecloses any possibility of communism as that 'positive transcendence of private property and human self-estrangement.' Martin's conclusion: 'There is only a capitalist, namely "unionist", organisation of the working class.'[43] Thus, the problems that structure the present of May's contemporaries is a rejection of the two-fold structure of the formalist fetish: a refusal to treat logical and theoretical forms of analysis as concretely revealed in practice, and a refusal of the various attempts at rehabilitating inherited forms of struggle that have outlived their usefulness in the present.

However, if both Badiou and Bologna fell prey to this fetishism of forms of organisation, it is in the recent work of thinkers such as Joshua Clover—despite its inestimable value in having provided a systematic and historical account of the development of riots into strikes (and back again)—that one finds the best example of the other side of this formalism, concerning the status of the relationship between epistemic forms of analysis and the phenomena under investigation. Regarding the current relation of capital's socio-economic structure to the possible existence of the long sought-after agent of abolition, the prospect of the left's present and future capacity regarding the self-determination of both the form and organisational structure assumed in the course of a struggle's unfolding is perhaps even more urgent than in 1968. And it is within such a context that we must begin by emphasising what Clover so carefully lays out: the strike and the riot continue to be, in large part, overdetermined by the accumulation and production of value—and this, in spite of everything that is redeeming in Marx's notion of the 'multiplication of the proletariat,' which refers to the process that follows from capital's increasing turn away from production and towards circulation and consumption (reproduction) for the extraction of value.[44] That is, the multiplication of the proletariat, for both Marx and Clover, is still a process of generalised precarity rather than the generalisation of a collective and antagonistic subject.

And it is precisely because of this generalised precarity that Clover rightly speaks of 'surplus rebellions,' 'circulation struggles' and 'riot-prime' as novel forms of struggles given their position within the arc of capital accumulation. Neither a revival of previous forms of rioting (e.g. bread riots) nor a faithful reproduction of prior instances of rebellion waged by social groups that maintain an indirectly market-mediated relation to a wage, what distinguishes surplus rebellions and circulation struggles from these prior iterations is precisely the fact that they are practical attempts at resolving the issues of social reproduction within the sphere of circulation as the site both of consumption and of capital's current means of self-valorisation. That said, these are not forms freely chosen and constructed by surplus populations but, as we are told, are the products of the value-determination and overdetermination of contemporary struggles. Their novelty, then, appears to come not from the self-determination of surplus populations but from the overdetermination of the value-form itself. It is for this reason that, just as the history of the workers' movement failed in staving off a capitalist form of self-organisation via the union, surplus rebellions and circulation struggles, too, find themselves assuming organisational forms determined by cycles of value accumulation rather than by the modalities of (lumpen)proletarian agency.

Thus we are compelled to ask: If, as Clover has painstakingly shown, an adequate theory of the riot is necessarily a theory of crisis, such that it is only by understanding the shift of capital flow from production and trade to finance and circulation that one can grasp what is essential in the riot as the way in which struggle manifests today, to what extent is this an already foreclosed or overdetermined image of the nature of the ongoing cycle of struggle today? For, as Clover writes, '*The riot*, for all its systematically produced inevitability . . . *is the form* of struggle *given to surplus populations*, already racialised . . . *whose location* in the social structure *compels them to some forms of collective action rather than others.*'[45] If *riot prime* as the political form surplus rebellions assume in the current conjuncture is determined by the forms of value to which it is indexed by its 'location in the social structure,' how, then, is this not a theory of the riot that results in an understanding of *riot prime* (circulation struggles) as an instance of value-determination, as opposed to a counter-determination of capitalist social relations by surplus populations themselves? Interestingly enough, one possible beginning towards addressing this problem is to be found in Clover's own articulation of the correspondence between the form of struggle and cycles of accumulation:

> *strike* as the form of collective action that struggles to set the price of labour power, is unified by worker identity, and unfolds in the context of production; *riot*, struggles to set prices in the market, is unified by shared dispossession, and unfolds in the context of consumption. Strike and riot are distinguished further as leading tactics within the generic categories of production and circulation struggles. We might now restate and elaborate these tactics as being each a set of practises used by people when their reproduction is threatened. Strike and riot are practical struggles over reproduction within production and circulation, respectively. . . . They make structured and improvisational uses of the given terrain, but it is a terrain they have neither made nor chosen. The riot is a circulation struggle because both capital and its dispossessed have been driven to seek reproduction there.[46]

What is striking in this passage is that what comes to define both the strike and the riot is not simply their position within the circuit of capital, but how their primary concern is one of resolving issues of reproduction while only conditionally unfolding as struggles of circulation or production. And this is precisely what is demonstrated here with the definition of strikes and riots as tactics employed in struggles over reproduction. However, to say, as Clover does, that 'a theory of riot is a theory of crisis'[47] obviates this analytic separation between struggles and their conditions such that crisis *acts* through riots. If nothing else, it is by maintaining (if not deepening) this antagonism and separation between struggles and their 'terrain' that one can avoid conflating determinations of value with determinations of social movements / uprisings / and so on. A separation between determining condition (production-circulation) and determining-agent (proletariat, surplus populations) such that, despite their limitations, the particularly promising content of riots and strikes is not simply equated with the compulsion of value. That is to say, if the reproduction of labour power and the self-valorisation of capital simply name 'the same activities . . . seen from different positions,' it is also the case that struggles over reproduction can be more or less reproductive of value, and suggests the possibility of a mode of struggle that reproduces itself without reproducing the value relation itself.

Interestingly enough, it is here that Clover nominates the commune as the form of life to come, where 'both production and circulation struggles have exhausted themselves.'[48] Unlike its more historically frequent siblings in the riot and strike, the commune appears as a privileged form due to its capacity for reproducing non-valorising modes of struggle that do not entail the reproduction of the value relation as its necessary precondition: 'Alongside these classic circulation struggles, it can be no surprise that Occupy Oakland centred on a communal kitchen signalling the centrality of surplus population to the encampment.'[49] And yet, on this account, what gives rise to the commune as the future form assumed by struggles over reproduction is not any number of social movements or variations of heterogeneous collective subjects, but 'a spreading disorder . . . that now seems to belong not to riot but to the state, to what had previously been itself a violent order. Against this great disorder, a necessary self-organisation, survival in a different key.'[50]

No longer able to satisfy even the least of life's reproductive requirements within the production or circulation process, the commune, as presented here, emerges as a form of self-organised survival whereby an individual's own reproduction can no longer be had whether via the state or the market. This, however, is an image of the commune as indiscernible from the realisation of increasingly severe capitalist crises, where the realisation of the commune is identical to the realisation of capitalist immiseration made absolute. And so, it is by insisting upon the separation of struggles from their conditions that strikes and riots will no longer be defined by their place within capitalist society. By acknowledging the riot and the strike as reproduction struggles, we can, at the very least, begin to develop an account—not simply of the ways in which capital establishes the boundaries of a given dispute—that differentiates between the determinations of capital and the determinations of collective subjectivities that avoid reproducing both labour and value in the process.

Without noting this difference, it is difficult to see how the commune can be said to be 'the political form at last discovered under which to work out the economical emancipation of labor,'[51] since it is only when productive labour ceases to be a class attribute and an attribute of society as a whole that our collective activity is concretised as a classless form of social reproduction. Hence, this claim that circulation struggles necessarily give rise to the riot as their dominant mode of antagonism, which implies that the determining agent of the riot is not its participants but the socioeconomic preconditions for the accumulation of value helpfully clarifies the problematic equivalence at the heart of Clover's dictum: 'a theory of riots *is* a theory of crisis.' For what is achieved by means of this 'analytical correlation between the present shape of accumulation and the leading tactic of action is not the delineation of 'the contours of a "leading subject" or organisation, but precisely its impossibility,'[52] such that it is neither surplus populations nor a recomposed (lumpen) proletariat but *value* that riots in the streets.

« *UNE AUTRE FIN DU MONDE EST POSSIBLE* »

Given the preceding analysis, it would seem that there is good reason to agree with Badiou's claim regarding our contemporaneity with '68, insofar as ours is a time defined by a search for an adequate resolution to the problem discovered in occupied universities and barricaded streets (i.e. the classical figure of revolutionary subjectivity has been found to be ineffective). That said, what is perhaps the more interesting and relevant point to underscore is that despite Badiou's best efforts, the 'double bind' characteristic of '68's cycle of struggles and of which we are the contemporaries, is of a qualitatively different kind than that which characterises the historical and political-economic situation of today. And it is precisely on this issue of acknowledging what continues to bind us to, while distancing us from, '68 that the political writings of Maurice Blanchot become relevant.

Writing in December of '68, Blanchot articulated what Badiou would only come to argue forty years after the event.[53] Namely, that the problem confronting the movements of '68 was the question of developing novel forms and organisations of struggle that would adequately resolve the crisis experienced in the face of the notion of revolutionary subjectivity born out of 1917:

'*May, a revolution by idea*, desire and imagination, risks becoming a purely ideal and imaginary event if this revolution does not renounce itself and yield to new organisation and strategies.'[54] Given the benefit of our vantage point it would not be controversial to say that the movements of '68 largely failed to develop the forms that struggle must take relative to the historical and material conditions of the 1960s. This is not to say that May '68 was itself a failure, for its singular achievement was to reconceive the political horizon of future struggles to come. This being the case, we can say that the double bind proper to '68 is characterised by the realisation of a 'becoming-revolutionary without a revolutionary future.'[55] That is, '68's achievement was its recognition of the inefficiency and impotence of a certain dogmatic image of revolutionary thought, and its demonstration of this historical break through the collective practises embodied by each of the 'four Mays.' That said, and in addition to the prescience of his analysis, Blanchot's reflections gain further significance with respect to the task of determining whether or not our contemporaneity with May extends beyond this shared problem and includes the same double bind.

Towards the end of the very same series of reflections, Blanchot provides his analysis of what, in the wake of '68, it will mean to participate in, and organise on behalf of, the ruptures, insurrections and revolutions to come. In light of the theoretical contribution of what we could call Badiou's 'contemporaneity thesis' (i.e. the seeking out of new forms for political subjectivity and its attendant organisations that would ensure its reproducibility), Blanchot's contribution is that of highlighting two particular dangers, or threats, that await revolutionary politics after '68. Politics after '68, says Blanchot, finds itself confronted by:

a) *The temptation to repeat May*, as if May had not taken place or as if it had failed, so that it might someday reach its conclusion. Thus, we see the same tactics of agitation that had meaning and effect in February-March-April poorly and painfully retried.
b) *The temptation to continue May*, without noticing that all the force of originality of this revolution is to offer no precedent, no foundation, not even for its own success, for it has made itself impossible as such . . . everything is posed in other terms, and not only are the problems new but the problematic itself has changed. In particular, all the problems of revolutionary struggle, and above all of class struggle, have taken a different form.[56]

By virtue of Blanchot's diagnosis, we too arrive at what distinguishes the political condition of 1968 from that of our present. Unlike '68's double bind of a really existing revolutionary process devoid of a revolutionary future, it is these two temptations that form the double bind proper to our present, which is that of a dialectic between *melancholic reflection* and *farcical repetition*. So if we are to claim the existence of a double bind proper to our present, it is not defined by the logic of a 'becoming-revolutionary without a revolutionary future'—for what can be said about the current composition of the progressive and radical left is that, at the very least, each segment offers some vision of an emancipated future world (and this is true regardless of the degree to which their respective proposed futures have been more or less theorised). Rather, what we are seeing today is a left caught between the temptation to prolong a political sequence that in reality has already come to pass, or to faithfully emulate the images of struggle that became associated with '68 as a whole. Moreover, and to perhaps make matters worse, the double bind of melancholic reflection and farcical repetition is one that pertains to *both* the parliamentary *and* extra-parliamentary segments of the present-day left (whether this be in the guise of a nostalgic reinvestment of the party-form as object of the desire for revolution, or as embodied in the mass mobilisations whose form and organisation simply repeat the past in the present).

However, unlike the fetishisation of organisational form that persists throughout Badiou's critical reflections of this period, and by recognising the existence of a problem proper to struggles that persist beyond '68 as something distinct from its characterisation as a problem of the exhausted figure of revolutionary subjectivity at the moment of its revolutionary-becoming à la Badiou, Blanchot is able to critically reconceive the necessity of developing new forms of political organisation alongside novel modalities of praxis. For this is what is at issue with Blanchot's warnings regarding the double bind of political struggle in the wake of '68. In other words, Blanchot's identification of the melancholic and farcical dimensions of the cycle of struggles post-'68 is simultaneously a critique of a period of which he is a part: a critique of the content of struggle and, only subsequently, a critique of misguided attempts at rehabilitating what are essentially obsolete strategic and practical forms. Thus, to affirm the truth of Blanchot's insight is to acknowledge that to be a 'contemporary' of '68, in the Badiousian sense, is to remain caught within the double bind of melancholic reflection and farcical repetition. What is more, not only does one's contemporaneity with '68 signal the manner by which one remains tied to a past, whose material conditions and modes of composition are no longer capable of affecting the present conjuncture; for contemporaneity is itself a sign that the problem that shapes and gives meaning to revolutionary struggles today has been poorly posed.

If the problem identified by Badiou is an insufficient ground for establishing contemporaneity, it is because it presupposes a shared, intuitive or common-sense understanding of the very definition of communism as such. It is as if everybody knows that it is only by abolishing capital that the freedom of some will no longer require the immiseration of others, and thus no one can deny that, after '68, we still remain communists via a fidelity to communism as an Idea, as opposed to maintaining a party line defined by a dogmatic belief in a historically validated program. And yet, it is the very existence of a shared understanding (common sense) of the very idea of communism, let alone the possibility of its real existence, that '68 has shown to no longer be certain. It is in this sense that Badiou's 'contemporaneity thesis' remains a poorly posed problem, since it takes the rupture effected by '68, which suspended one's ability to treat terms such as communism as an idea that is as clear and distinct as it is self-evident, as the very grounds for the question that guides theoretical and practical activity. To say that the absence of novel organisational forms necessitated by the historical and material conditions of 1968 is a poorly posed problem is not to dismiss the relevance of the forms that struggles can and may assume. Rather, it is to acknowledge the manner by which this formulation of the problem proper to the reality of communist struggle presupposes the primacy of the form of organisation over the content of self-organising activity.

Interestingly enough, Badiou briefly recognises this aporia as one of the defining experiences of the French left in the midst of '68 itself: 'the secret truth, that was gradually revealed, is that this common language, symbolised by the red flag, was dying out. There was a basic ambiguity about May '68: a language that was spoken by all was beginning to die out.'[57]

Insofar as Badiou is right to claim that May '68 marked a qualitative break with the PCF and CGT as twin personifications of communism ('May '68 . . . posed a huge challenge to the legitimacy of the historical organisations of the left, of unions, of parties and of famous leaders'), our problem is not simply a question of undoing the conflation of the proletariat with the figure of the industrial worker. Rather, it is a question that enquires into the existence and meaning of a communism shorn of the theoretical and practical dogmas of the 'historical organisations of the left,' raised to the level of orthodoxy. And yet, if our problem is one of discovering a new figure of revolutionary subjectivity, what remains unclear is the manner by which this definition of politics can be said to belong to the continuum of Events constitutive of what Badiou, quite seriously calls, the 'Idea of Communism.'

It is for this reason that we maintain that, after '68, we are confronted by the fact that the answer to the question 'what is the meaning of communism?,' or 'What is communism?,' can no longer take a self-evidentiary form.[58] Moreover, the very absence of a self-evidentiary reply signals to us that, today, communism presents itself in the form of a problem; a problem that is itself the ground for reinventing, redefining or renewing the search for the political process that remains incommensurable and mutually excludes the logic of both capital and 'really existing socialism.' To affirm Blanchot's dictum that, after '68, 'all the problems of revolutionary struggle . . . have taken a different form,' is to acknowledge the fact that communism, too, has taken a different form. No longer the solution to the riddle of history that knows itself to be such, and after '68, communism appears as the very riddle posed to history.

NOTES

1. Kadour Naïmi, *Freedom in Solidarity: My Experiences in the May 1968 Uprising*, trans. David Porter (Oakland, CA: AK Press, 2019), 86–94.
2. Alain Badiou, *Communist Hypothesis,* trans. David Macey and Steve Corcoran (London: Verso, 2010), 39–40.
3. Félix Guattari, *Molecular Revolution: Psychiatry and Politics*, trans. David Cooper (London: Penguin Books, 1984), 66. Or as Guattari says further on,
"Significantly, after May '68, most revolutionary movements failed to grasp the importance of the weak link that had become apparent during the student struggle. Quite suddenly, students and young workers 'forgot' the respect that was due to the superior knowledge and power of teachers, foremen, managers, etc. They broke away from the old submission to the values of the past and introduced an entirely new approach. But the whole thing was labelled spontaneism, in other words a transitional manifestation that must be left behind for a 'superior' phase, marked by the setting-up of centralist organisations. Desire surged up among the people; it was noted, but expected to quieten and accept discipline. No one realised that this new form of revolt would in [the] future be inseparable from all further economic and political struggles."
4. Jean-Luc Nancy, *The Truth of Democracy*, trans. Pascale-Anne Brault and Michael Naas (New York: Fordham University Press, 2010), 34. Or as Brault and Naas write in the translators' foreword, 'Democracy must therefore be thought as the incommensurable sharing of existence that makes the political possible but can in no way be reduced to the political. As such, it is first of all a metaphysics and only afterwards a politics. It was May '68, Nancy argues, that demonstrated all this in an exemplary way and so deserves to be not simply remembered and commemorated but rethought and renewed' (xi).
5. While not an outright rejection and abandonment of working-class struggles, this critique of unions, the party-form and the status of worker-identity as that which determines one's revolutionary potential, has led to various, and often radically different, conclusions regarding the future of communist politics in a post-'68 era. Most notable among these are those from ex-members of *Socialisme ou Barbarie*, Cornelius Castoriadis and Jean-Francois Lyotard:
"Some of the most acute theories of class dilution originated from lapsed Marxists, precisely ex-luminaries of *Socialisme ou Barbarie*: Cornelius Castoriadis . . . Jean-Francois Lyotard. They were among the first to come up with a *post-worker* doctrine. When Lyotard warned us in 1979 against the totalitarian risks involved in *grand*

narratives, he did not mean the Bible or the Quran; he targeted the master narrative of the historical mission of the proletariat. The ascending bourgeoisie had claimed to bring prosperity, peace, and freedom, and we know what it meant. Likewise, so Lyotard argued, the proletarian pretension of emancipating humankind is a fraud. Marx's dream has led to a Stalinist nightmare. All we can do is hope for small narratives—fragmentary partial reforms. Castoriadis and Lyotard excel at debunking the idea that the proletariat could and should replace the bourgeoisie: this was the only communist theory they ever knew."
Gilles Dauvé, *From Crisis to Communisation* (Oakland, CA: PM Press, 2019), 19.

    6. Giovanni Arrighi, Terence K. Hopkins and Immanuel Wallerstein, *Antisystemic Movements* (London, UK: Verso, 1989), 115, emphasis mine.

    7. Andrew Culp's notion of 'virtual communism' is instructive here with respect to *counteractualisations* enacted via mass mobilisations:

"[I]f communism is 'not a *state of affairs* which is to be established' or 'an *ideal* to which reality [will] have to adjust itself,' then communism may still be on the horizon—not as the communism of capitalism, but as a revolution that 'abolishes the present state of things.' Furthermore, this virtual communism is a fresh set of problems posed by life itself and not an ideal state or a pure politics. . . . Virtual communism thus proceeds by opening 'a space for political construction and experimentation' that creates a rupture, not by reactivating a potential that has been limited by capital but 'by retraversing and reconfiguring the economic, the social, the political, and so on.'. . . While virtual communism does not hold the certainty of historical passage held by those theorising the commons emerging within capitalism, it does map out a terrain of struggle for forms of life that already believe in this world."
Andrew Culp, 'Philosophy, Science, and Virtual Communism,' *Angelaki: Journal of the Theoretical Humanities* 20, no. 4 (December 2015): 91–107, 103.

    8. As Marx writes in his 1844 Manuscripts,

"*Communism* as the *positive* transcendence of *private property* as *human self-estrangement,* and therefore as the real *appropriation* of the *human* essence by and for man; communism therefore as the complete return of man to himself as a *social* (i.e. human) being—a return accomplished consciously and embracing the entire wealth of previous development. This communism, as fully developed naturalism, equals humanism, and as fully developed humanism equals naturalism; it is the *genuine* resolution of the conflict between man and nature and between man and man—the true resolution of the strife between existence and essence, between objectification and self-confirmation, between freedom and necessity, between the individual and the species. *Communism is the riddle of history solved, and it knows itself to be this solution.*"
Karl Marx, *Economic and Philosophical Manuscripts of 1844*, The Marx-Engels Reader, ed. Robert C. Tucker (New York: W. W. Norton & Company Inc, 1972), 84, emphasis mine.

    9. Badiou, *Communist Hypothesis*, 47.

    10. Gilles Deleuze and Claire Parnet, *L'abécédaire de Gilles Deleuze. de G comme Gauche à M comme Maladie 2*. DVD. Paris: Vidéo: Editions Montparnasse, 2004.

    11. Marx, *The Marx-Engels Reader*, 595.

12. Badiou, *Communist Hypothesis*, 43.

13. 'We can now commemorate May '68 because we are convinced that it is dead. Forty years after the event, there is no life left in it.' Badiou, *Communist Hypothesis*, 47.

14. 'The libertarian ideas of '68, the transformation of the way we live, the individualism and the taste for *jouissance* have become a reality thanks to post-modern capitalism and its garish world of all sorts of consumerism ... Sarkozy himself is the product of May '68, and to celebrate May '68 ... is to celebrate the neoliberal West.' Badiou, *Communist Hypothesis*, 33–34.

15. 'This commemoration ... may mask the vague idea that a different political and societal world is possible, that the great idea of radical change, which for 200 years went by the name of "revolution" ... is still quietly spreading, despite the official pretence that it has been completely defeated.' Badiou, *Communist Hypothesis*, 45.

16. Badiou, *Communist Hypothesis*, 34–35, emphasis mine.

17. Badiou, *Communist Hypothesis*, 39.

18. Alain Badiou, 'Politics as Thought: The Work of Sylvain Lazarus,' *Metapolitics*, trans. Jason Barker (London: Verso, 2005), 26–57, 39.

19. Or as Badiou recounts from his own experience of May,
"At the time we assumed that the politics of emancipation was neither a pure idea, an expression of the will nor a moral dictate, but that it was inscribed in, and almost programmed by, historical and social reality. One of that conviction's implications was that this objective agent had to be transformed into a subjective power, that a social entity had to become a subjective actor. For that to happen, it had to be represented by a specific organisation, and that is precisely what we called a party, a working-class or people's party. That party had to be present wherever there were sites of power or intervention. There were certainly wide-ranging discussions about what the party was. . . . But there was a basic agreement that there was a historical agent, and that that agent had to be organised. That political organisation obviously had a social basis in mass organisations that plunged their roots into an immediate social reality. . . . This gives us something that still survives today: the idea that there are two sides to emancipatory political action. First there are social movements. . . . Then there is the party element, which consists in being present in all possible sites of power, and of bringing to them . . . the strength and content of the social movements."
Badiou, *Communist Hypothesis*, 40–41.

20. Badiou, *Communist Hypothesis*, 43.

21. Badiou, *Communist Hypothesis*, 45.

22. Badiou, *Communist Hypothesis*, 53.

23. Badiou, *Communist Hypothesis*, 53.

24. Kristin Ross, *May '68 And Its Afterlives* (Chicago: University of Chicago Press, 2002), 25, emphasis mine.

25. Arrighi, Hopkins and Wallerstein, *Antisystemic Movements*, 85–88.

26. Étienne Balibar, 'From Charonne to Vitry (1981),' *Viewpoint Magazine*, 1 February 2018, https://www.viewpointmag.com/2018/02/01/charonne-vitry-1981/ (accessed on 3 August 2020).

27. Balibar, 'From Charonne to Vitry (1981).'

28. Balibar, 'From Charonne to Vitry (1981).'
29. Balibar, 'From Charonne to Vitry (1981).'
30. Naïmi, *Freedom in Solidarity*, 86.
31. Badiou, *Communist Hypothesis*, 44.
32. As Jason Smith aptly put it, rightly summarised,

"Far from meshing together in a seamless continuity, or mutually reinforcing one another in friction-less feedback, socialists in the US (and the UK) will have to start again, this time from the structural and radical incompatibility or contradiction between these two forms of power [mass movements and electoral politics]. With the defeat of Sanders (and Corbyn), and with the necessary historical and strategic considerations that such defeats compel, they will most likely have to renounce the assumptions that permitted their participation in these failed electoral campaigns to begin with. These campaigns did not bring into being a 'new politics,' one that reversed the order of historical effectivity, subordinating movements initiated by broad masses of people to the call and command of elected politicians. Reforms brought about in the political sphere will be imposed on the state by years and even decades of confrontations with movements that are willing to fight for themselves: at their own initiative, for objectives they themselves formulate. The current course of events, disturbing as it is, will provide ample opportunity for such efforts."

Jason E. Smith, 'Life Comes at You Fast,' Brooklyn Rail, https://brooklynrail.org/2020/04/field-notes/Life-Comes-At-You-Fast (accessed on 11 August 2020).

33. Keir Milburn, 'On Social Strikes and Directional Demands,' *Plan C* (blog), 7 May 2015, https://www.weareplanc.org/blog/on-social-strikes-and-directional-demands/ (accessed on 25 August 2018).

34. Milburn, 'On Social Strike and Directional Demands.' Of additional importance here is that of Yanis Varoufakis's anecdote regarding a conversation between himself and Christine Legarde (head of the IMF). As the story goes, after Varoufakis informed Legarde that it would be mathematically impossible for Greece to repay its debt according to the austerity measures proposed by the IMF, Legarde in fact agreed with his economic calculations but replied that the austerity package was something that *must* be done—a telling remark, as it reveals the function of the Troika as the set of institutions who secure the smooth running of neoliberalism regardless of the material needs of those who live in debtor countries.

35. UK Labour Party, *Manifesto* (2017), 46–47.
36. Badiou, *Communist Hypothesis*, 42.
37. Matthew Impelli, '54 Percent of Americans Think Burning Down Minneapolis Police Precinct Was Justified After George Floyd's Death,' *Newsweek*, 3 June 2020, https://www.newsweek.com/54-americans-think-burning-down-minneapolis-police-precinct-was-justified-after-george-floyds-1508452.
38. Dauvé, *From Crisis to Communisation*, 4.
39. Badiou, *Communist Hypothesis*, 63.
40. Sergio Bologna, cited in Steve Wright, *Storming Heaven: Class Composition and Struggle in Italian Autonomist Marxism* (London: Pluto Press, 2017), 184, emphasis mine.
41. Badiou, *Communist Hypothesis*, 53.

42. Gilles Dauvé, *Eclipse and Reemergence of the Communist Movement* (Oakland, CA: PM Press, 2015), 86.

43. Dauvé, *Eclipse and Reemergence of the Communist Movement*, 87.

44. As Clover writes,

"The long-term tendencies are apparent, and the signs we might expect to indicate a secular reversal nowhere to be seen. . . . In this context, class might be rethought in ways that exceed the traditional model . . . with its relatively static and sociologically positivistic 'working class' and accompanying forms of struggle. Given the relative dwindling of this form of labour, Marx must mean something else when, arriving at this conclusion regarding surplus populations, he proposes that 'accumulation of capital is therefore multiplication of the proletariat.'"

Joshua Clover, *Riot. Strike. Riot* (London: Verso, 2016), 159.

45. Clover, *Riot. Strike. Riot*, 168.

46. Clover, *Riot. Strike. Riot*, 46.

47. Clover, *Riot. Strike. Riot*, 1.

48. Clover, *Riot. Strike. Riot*, 191.

49. Clover, *Riot. Strike. Riot*, 179.

50. Clover, *Riot. Strike. Riot*, 187.

51. Karl Marx, *The Civil War in France: The Paris Commune* (Moscow: Progress Publishers, 1985), 60.

52. Alberto Toscano, 'Limits to Periodization,' *Viewpoint Magazine*, 6 September, 2016, https://www.viewpointmag.com/2016/09/06/limits-to-periodization/ (accessed on 4 September 2020).

53. This statement should not be taken as an implicit critique or some thinly veiled *ad hominem* at Badiou's expense. Badiou himself admits such a point in a moment of self-criticism in his reflections on the fortieth anniversary of '68: 'The fourth May '68 is seeking to find that which might exist beyond the confines of classic revolutionism. It seeks it blindly because it uses the same language as the language that dominated the conception it was trying to get away from. . . . They were—to use the beautiful, colourful language of the Chinese once more— "raising the red flag to fight the red flag." . . . What we failed to see at the time was that it was the language itself that had to be transformed, but this time in an affirmative sense.' *Communist Hypothesis*, 43.

54. Maurice Blanchot, 'On the Movement,' in *Political Writings, 1953–1993*, trans. Zakir Paul (New York: Fordham University Press, 2010), 106.

55. *L'Abécédaire de Gilles Deleuze*, see note 10.

56. Blanchot, 'On the Movement,' 108, emphasis mine.

57. Badiou, *Communist Hypothesis*, 55.

58. We would do better in taking up Joshua Clover's insight regarding the shifting terrain of struggle post-'68, since it is Clover, rather than Badiou, who is able to grasp the relevant problems and questions that define our present and will shape the struggles to come:

"the imagined course of capitalism→socialism→communism that has been with us at least since 'Critique of the Gotha Program,' and was a kind of common sense of the worker's movement a century ago, was premised on a historically concrete situation in which industrial production oriented social organisation, and worker control

of that sector gave onto total expropriation of the expropriators. Is that still true? Is there still a worker's movement in that way? Even if there were, does the hard limit of climate collapse mean that the unfettering of industrial production on which that particular vision of the emancipation from labour was premised is not survivable? To the extent that any of these questions have answers, they all point away from the promise of what we now call socialism as a program of emancipation. It seems more to be a progressive management strategy for capital. It will ease some misery. It will point itself toward managed competition and greater democracy in a fraction of workplaces. Those are all to the good. I honestly don't know if this contemporary iteration of socialism is, in addition to its limited gains, a blockage to movements that could meaningfully challenge capital. That is a serious and undervalued question.
. . . History has not been kind to the notion of a progressive, step-by-step shift that arrives at a qualitatively different social arrangement. The good news is that, if we take the logic of 'combined and uneven development' seriously, it suggests that there is no historical requirement to pass through the lower stage to get to the higher stage. If we no longer believe in a ratcheting, incrementalist motion that ends in emancipation, we have to sit with the knowledge that the leap down either course will mean forgoing the virtues of the other.

Joshua Clover, 'To Preserve the Possibility of Communal Life and Emancipation,' *Coils of the Serpent* 8 (2021): 169–85, 169–70.

Chapter Three

Workers and Capitalists

Two Different Worlds? Immanence and Antagonism in Marx's Capital

Daniel Fraser

The events of May 1968 precipitated a paradigm shift in the understanding and reception of Marx's work. In the wake of '68, and in the face of decades of neoliberal restructuring and deregulation, decomposition of class identity, globalisation and so on, Marxist thought has tended to move away from notions of the class subject and teleological progress, emphasising instead a political space of interruption and absence.[1] Temporalities of progress and post-capitalist horizons lost ground: the 'logics' of resistance, of meaningful struggle against capitalist domination, moved from the transitional to the negating, from the production of the future to the self-immolation of the present.[2]

In relation to this new terrain, the activity of May 1968 occupies a somewhat ambivalent position. On the one hand, the events were a catalyst for the emergence of these new understandings of Marx, constituting a time when breaks with Soviet orthodoxy (particularly in the wake of the horrific events in Hungary in 1956) had become galvanised, when new forms of resistance outside the 'Party' were burgeoning and there was a resurgence of revolutionary hope.[3] On the other, the recuperation and dissolution of the workers' movements in Europe by capital and the accompanying transformations of labour, reconfigured the principal antagonisms of '68 in ways that meant its revolutionary promise, and many of its forms of struggle, could no longer be relied upon. What came next had to 'let the dead bury their dead in order to arrive at its own content.'[4]

In some cases, the fallout from '68 and the struggles that followed, as well as the momentous decoupling of currency from the gold standard, led theory towards a valorisation of capital's tendency for flux (for revolutionising production without altering its primary relation). This tendency is evidenced in everything from Marshall Berman's picture of modernism / modernisation

Figure 3.1. *From the Depths.* Print illustration by William Balfour Kerr.

in *All That Is Solid Melts into Air* to the post-structuralism of Jean-François Lyotard and Jean Baudrillard, who identified in the totalising and disenchanting force of capitalism a potential inverted form of liberation, a dissolution in its exhilarating flow and flux.[5] This disenchantment, which lacks any horizon of truth or falsehood, bears resemblance to Debord's notion of the spectacle (particularly the idea of simulacrum in the work of Baudrillard), though one divorced from its material basis; becoming a merely 'self-referential system.'[6] In their collaborative work, Gilles Deleuze and Félix Guattari developed the notion of the tendency that had been a central component in the philosophy of György Lukács in his attempts to break away from Soviet orthodoxy,[7] reconfiguring it as the 'immanent radicalisation of capital's own dynamic of deterritorialisation.'[8] In these valorisations of dissolutive power are the beginnings of accelerationism.[9] Rather than the negation of the interruptive and disruption of absence, accelerationism engenders a kind of hypercapitalism, contending that such force can accelerate beyond capital, its delirious processes pushing social being, and any possible subject, beyond its own limits. Accelerationism absolves itself of the double bind of immanence-antagonism: it accepts capital's terms and seeks to immerse itself as deeply as possible, pushing them to the highest velocity.[10]

However, in the contemporary Marxist philosophical field, two heterodox schools of thought remain most prevalent. The first of these is the new-dialectical, Hegelian, value-form school, whose internal differentiations include members of the *Neue Marx-Lektüre* (new reading of Marx) group such as Hans-Georg Backhaus and Michael Heinrich, the *Wertkritik*, or value-critique theorists, that largely grew out of the German-language journals *Krisis* and *Exit*, including Robert Kurz, Norbert Trenkle and Roswitha Scholz, as well as Moishe Postone and Chris Arthur. The other current is the post-autonomist Marxism that developed through the early work of Antonio Negri, Mario Tronti and the Italian *operaismo* movement, whose focus is on command and struggle over the exploitation of labour, and the possibility for the working class to define itself outside of its role as labour-power.

The question of immanence and antagonism remains a vital problem in the interpretation of the political significance of *Capital* in both these methods of approach. The problem centres on the possibility of political struggle, of meaningful activity, against a social form which, seemingly, has no outside. That is, how to 'attempt to articulate a path beyond a capitalism that seems to have absorbed and recuperated all opposition.'[11] In general terms, those of the Hegelian logic school, for whom labour is internal to capital, deny the meaningful exteriority of class struggle, whereas conversely the post-*operaismo* positions seek to denote potential exteriorities which might yet prove revolutionary.

From the Depths depicts a world of plenitude, a gilded hall of bourgeois pleasure, held from beneath by the efforts of labour. The circa 1906 print, as a comment on wealth inequality in the United States, presents the very real weight of the history of the present on the backs and shoulders of the worker. To the alarm of those above, an anonymous fist breaks through from the world below, a symbol of rebellion and struggle, but also initiating a horror of recognition: a recognition of the fragility of the separation. Those who struggle are in the very depths of that which they struggle against. In this way the image potently illustrates what is at the core of these arguments: the contestation of the double bind of immanence and antagonism as it manifests in the dynamics of the capital-labour relation; the motive force by which the capitalist mode of production is continually formed and re-formed. Put simply, this double bind concerns the question of how to struggle against a system of relations when those engaged in the struggle are themselves an internal component, and actively constituting element, of those relations. My chapter shall seek to render explicit this relation and the problems for any political resistance this presents, emphasising the importance of primitive accumulation (defined by Marx as the 'historical process of divorcing the producer from the means of production')[12] as the ground upon which the capital-labour relation is founded and as a mode of violence which is continually reproduced within its motion.

Subsequently, this chapter will address the political import of this understanding of the class relation, turning to the work of the schools of heterodox Marxism that either emerged or intensified following '68, in order to demonstrate the centrality of the question of immanence and antagonism to the contemporary critical field. Further, this chapter will seek to argue that a thorough understanding of the capital-labour relation necessitates a critical theory of capital that both recognises the extent of capitalist subsumption and the failure of orthodox ideas of class consciousness, and does not abandon a class analysis through misguided attempts to dissociate an exoteric / esoteric Marx—that is, by attempting to de-couple the critique of abstract capitalist forms of sociality from their historical material content.

WORLDS APART

At first sight, one might find nothing more obvious than an affirmative answer to the question of whether the worlds occupied by worker and capitalist are entirely distinct. Empirical evidence would suggest that poverty, the subjection to wage labour in order to subsist and the reduction to being a mere organ for the production of surplus value were worlds apart from owning private property and the means of production, controlling and purchasing labour-power and the boundless drive for accumulated wealth. However, to do so would be to elide many of the complexities of Marx's arguments, in *Capital* and elsewhere, which show the capital-labour relation to be one whose principal elements are intrinsically bound up with one another. This has deeply rooted political implications for the pathways via which workers may resist or overcome domination.

Before attempting to understand the world(s) inhabited by the capitalist and the worker, one must outline the terms as they are deployed in *Capital*. Marx attests that: 'The characters who appear on the economic stage are merely personifications of economic relations; it is as the bearers of these economic relations that they come into contact with one another.'[13] The capitalist is 'only capital personified'[14]—that is, one who advances wealth and, through the purchase of labour-power and the ownership of means of production, produces surplus value and accumulates more wealth. The worker on the other hand, as labour personified, is one who sells their labour-power for a wage and whose labour is expended in the value-creation process over the course of a working day. As such, the capitalist and worker are concrete instantiations of the abstract processes in which they take part. The capitalist and the worker are the manifestations at the level of the activity, or history, of the systemic contradiction: that is the capital-labour relation: 'The struggle between capitalist and the wage-labourer starts with the existence of the capital-relation itself.'[15] When considered as totalities, as collective labour and collective capital, one arrives at the idea of the capitalist class and the working class.[16] In this sense, 'working class' simply refers to the collective bearers of variable capital and the capitalist class the collective bearers of capital in general:[17] class functions here as a structural category. The two form no part of a sociological stratification of multiple classes. Conceived of in this manner, the worker, as a member of the working class, is a 'critical concept.'[18] To be a productive worker is 'not a piece of luck, but a misfortune.'[19]

This complex of relations therefore involves both conceptual contradictions as well as historical, contingent conflicts. As a result, any elaboration of the world of the capitalist and the worker must address their antagonistic relationship at the levels of individual and class as well as in terms of whether there can be said to be a relation which stands above the class relation—that is, whether the contradiction between capital and labour is internal to the more fundamental contradiction of capital itself. Further, the extent to which a conception of class, and working-class struggle, may be identified beyond these confines, and potentially forge a path to a world beyond the capitalist mode of production, will have to be elaborated.

The sphere of law offers a way in to understanding these problems. Central to Marx's exposition of the capitalist mode of production is the necessity for a juridical framework of equality and freedom to exist for both capitalist and worker. The process of the sale and purchase of labour-power on the market must be performed by free proprietors and as such the capitalist and worker belong to the same juridical 'world.' The two meet in the market on equal footing, as owners of commodities, whose sole difference is that one is a buyer and the other a seller: they are equal before the law.[20] Their equality is vital for understanding that exploitation does not occur as a result of human 'cheating' or from unfair contracts but is endemic to capital's system of relations. The worker is paid the value of their labour-power. Their *exploitation* is as a result of the discrepancy between their wage and the quantity of value produced by their labour,[21] a discrepancy guaranteed by the wage form itself.[22] That a proportion of this labour is unpaid in no way contradicts the law of commodity exchange.[23] However, the freedom of the worker is double-edged. Workers are neither part of the means of production, as slaves and serfs are, nor do they own the means of production themselves. Underlying the capitalist mode of production then is a class relationship, one existing between a class of largely property-less but free workers and a class of property owners in possession of the means of production.[24]

This separation that compels the worker to sell their labour-power is the prerequisite for the relationship between capitalist and wage labourer.[25] It is a relation that has 'no basis in natural history' but rather is the result of historical development.[26] Nature does not simply produce owners of the means of production and commodities on the one hand and propertyless workers on the other with nothing but their own labour-power. Nor does this relation have a common transhistorical social basis: it has arisen through economic revolutions and entails 'the extinction of a whole series of older formations of social production.'[27] The process of capital accumulation presupposes the existence of 'masses of capital and labour-power in the hands of commodity producers.'[28] To get out of this otherwise never-ending circle, Marx posits a pre-capitalist mode of so-called primitive accumulation, which forms the capital-labour relation: an historical act of separation which is then maintained and reproduced on a 'constantly extending scale.'[29] This act of separation is undertaken by a pre-capitalist state which acts in the interests of the creation of the self-reproducing cyclical capitalist process itself. It is an exercising of state power / violence [*Gewalt*], the force that is the 'midwife of every old society which is pregnant with a new one.'[30]

In historical terms, primitive accumulation is the point of departure for capital, and 'plays approximately the same role in political economy as original sin does in theology.'[31] The narrative it presents is one of careful, hardworking merchants who saved and made good investments, and lazy, unproductive peasants who spent and ate all they had. The reality of course is much darker. The act of separation can be found in Britain in the Enclosure acts and clearances that helped provide proletarian workers for manufacturing, as well as in state violence and plunder of the non-European world. Indeed, Marx notes its 'chief moments' as colonial expansion, the 'extirpation, enslavement and entombment in mines' of indigenous Americans, the 'conquest and plunder' of India and the African slave trade.[32] The 'treasures captured outside Europe by undisguised looting, enslavement and murder flowed back to the mother country and were turned into capital there.'[33]

This separation, however, is not merely an historical concept but a systemic one. Its violence is an act that, in a different form, is repeated in the antagonism between classes which has been generated from it. The separation of the means of production from the worker is a precondition for capitalist social relations, maintained by its reproduction; it is the condition of possibility for the perverted forms of worker and capitalist.[34] The maintenance of the worker's separation from the means of production is the logic of transformation by which these means then confront the worker as an 'alien, commanding personification.'[35]

The separation of means of production from labourer that then confronts it as an independent power is essential to capital. This logic of separation 'constitutes the concept of capital and of primitive accumulation.'[36] This would seem to suggest that the capitalist and worker do indeed belong to separate worlds: that in fact the capitalist mode of production is both founded on their separation and constituted by the continual reproduction of this separation.[37] However, this break is also a suture, and binds the two in an immanent and dynamic relationship of antagonism.

WOUND AND SUTURE

The chapter on 'The Working Day,' with the subsequent examinations of manufacture and industry, presents one of the clearest expressions of the antinomic standpoints of capitalist and worker. The analysis of the capital-labour relation and its production of surplus value cannot at this point be understood merely at the level of social form. Rather, it is here that the voice of the worker arises 'which had been previously stifled in the sound and fury of the production process.'[38] The establishment of a norm with regard to the working day is the product of centuries of concrete historical struggle between the capitalist and worker.[39] This struggle, to make the length of the working day as long or as short as possible, does not contradict the law of commodity exchange guaranteed by juridical law but is a product of right against right and 'between equal rights, force decides.'[40] As is clear from the activities of factory inspectors within this violent establishing of a norm, the world of antagonism between the worker and the capitalist is continually mediated by state actors, beyond the guaranteed contract of commodity exchange. These state activities regulate certain destructive tendencies of the compulsion for ever-increasing valorisation in order to maintain labour-power, whilst simultaneously securing the conditions for the continued reproduction of capitalist social relations.[41]

The development of the productive forces through manufacturing, and the increasing division of labour and specialisation of the worker, revolutionises the mode of labour and enacts an anthropological change in the worker, rendering them a 'crippled monstrosity,' nothing other than an 'automatic motor in a detail operation.'[42] The worker's fragmentation, the limitation of their mental and physical capacities, results in their labour-power being only able to function within the environment which transformed it: the capitalist's workshop.[43] With the advent of machinery driving the extraction of relative surplus value,[44] the revolution in the instruments of labour revolutionises the world of the worker. Women and children are brought to the labour market as new members of the working class, the worker's agency is transformed and the 'free' contract with the capitalist is undermined. The worker sells their wife and child: they have 'become a slave-dealer.'[45] Further, the industrial process introduces a struggle, within the antagonism of the capital-labour relation, between the worker and the machine, the instrument of labour itself, as the material mode of capital's existence.[46] The machine is a direct competitor to the worker and renders a portion of the labour of the working class superfluous to the valorisation process. The estrangement from the conditions of labour and the products of labour, which are given by the capitalist mode of production to the worker, are developed into a complete and total antagonism.[47] The most powerful instrument for reducing labour time suffers a dialectical inversion and becomes 'the most unfailing means for turning the whole lifetime of the worker and his family into labour-time at capital's disposal.'[48] This is what Marx means by the following: 'The rule of the capitalist over the worker is the rule of the object over the human, of dead labour over living, of the product over the producer, since in fact the commodities which become the means of domination over the worker are . . . the products of the production process. . . . It is the alienation process of his own social labour.'[49] The dead labour of the machine supplants the living body of the labourer, 'the conditions of work employ the worker.'[50] The workers themselves produce their own means of domination by the capitalist. They, by their own labour, 'keep in existence a reality which enslaves them in ever greater degree.'[51]

In the process of capitalist accumulation, the capitalist is driven by the compulsion for the expansion of value and the competition between capitalists. This compulsion is accumulation for its own sake.[52] In tension with this compulsion to accumulate is the formation of surplus population. The worker is a *problem* for the capitalist: as the only source of surplus value, they are necessary for the production process; yet, the drive towards accumulation tends to expel labour from production through the introduction of machinery and technology, so necessary labour is a 'tendentially diminishing magnitude.'[53] At the same time, changes in composition such as increases in the scale of production may set larger numbers of workers into motion. As a result, there is an ever-shifting attraction and repulsion of workers in the production process precipitated by the accumulation of capital, which continually creates a surplus population: 'The working population therefore produces both the accumulation of capital and the means by which it is itself made relatively superfluous.'[54] The freedom of the worker confines them to pauperism. If the capitalist has no use for the worker's surplus labour, the latter are unable to perform their necessary labour and are therefore unable to continue to live as a worker: their labour capacity exists without the 'conditions of its existence.'[55] It is the means of employment and not of subsistence which categorises the worker as part of the overpopulation or not. The law of population is not abstract and ahistorical but multiple, and these laws are historically specific to the modes of production in which they operate.[56] Overpopulation is therefore a historically determined relation—one which, in the capitalist mode of production, governs the ability of the worker to subsist as a worker, setting it into a state of perpetual precarity, as the law of accumulation governs the ability of the capitalist to exist as capitalist.

The notion of the reproduction of society is one of the concepts by which the identity of the spaces occupied by capitalist and worker may be most clearly evidenced. The process of production is also a process of reproduction, the conditions of which are the same.[57] This process perpetually reconstitutes the capital-labour relation. Through the continued repetition of the capitalist production process, the wage-labourer and the capitalist reproduce one another. The worker 'constantly produces objective wealth' in the form of capital—'an alien power that dominates and exploits him.'[58] Similarly, the capitalist 'just as constantly produces labour power,' an abstract subjective form of social wealth 'separated from its own means of objectification and realisation.' The capitalist produces the worker as wage-labourer.[59] Though the laws that drive capitalist and worker may be different, they are mutually co-constitutive in the capital-relation. The world they occupy is one and the same. The idea of revolution, the bursting asunder of the capitalist integument,[60] is a question of the non-reproduction of the class relation. To reach beyond the horizon of capitalism is not for one class to triumph over the other; rather, the condition for the emancipation of the working class is 'the abolition of every class.'[61] The negative conception of the worker as an object (a character mask) representing, like the capitalist, a perverted form of social human practice, clearly demonstrates this fact.

INSIDE/OUTSIDE: HETERODOXY AND POLITICS

The question of the relationship between the capitalist and the worker, and their struggle as antagonistic classes, has remained one of the most vital questions in communist thought and has been developed along several trajectories seeking to ground meaningful political action. Of particular import is the question of subjectivity, more specifically: to what extent an idea of a 'revolutionary subject' can be derived from Marx's analysis. In addition, there are the questions of what forms of resistance the worker may undertake to the processes of capital, and whether any autonomy from its domination can be achieved.

Lukács, adopting Weber's articulation of modernity in terms of a historical process of rationalisation, seeks to show that this process is a function of capitalism and the proliferation of the commodity form. For Lukács, the working class attains a role that is different from the one of the capitalist. Though both are presented with the reality of an alienated world the capitalist endorses its facticity, their position is confirmed by the process of self-alienation, whereas the worker is unable to remain within this ideology. The working class is posited as the subject-object of history, that which generates its dynamics and may escape the shackles of reification.[62] The capitalist, therefore, belongs to a class-in-itself that can never become a class-for-itself, while the worker belongs to a class that, recognising (becoming conscious of) the antagonism at the level of totality, can become a collective subject-object of history.

The work of the value-critique school firmly identifies the capitalist and worker as belonging to the same world. In fact, such an identification is central to their attempts to re-affirm the critical nature of Marx's project, whilst recognising the large-scale failure of the revolutionary socialist movements of the twentieth century. It does so through a reactivated Hegelian reading of Marx's categories and the positing of a separation between an 'exoteric' and an 'esoteric' Marx. This 'break' identifies with the former the Marx of political activity, productive forces and class struggle, and the latter with a more fundamental Marx, who developed the radical critique of the categories of political economy. The former then is the Marx of orthodoxy and teleological overcoming, the one whose ideas have reached obsolescence as demonstrated by the warped authoritarianism of Russia and China, the failure of left-wing democratic electoral politics, the failure of trade unions to be anything other than a left-wing of capitalism and so on. Whereas it is only the latter, esoteric Marx, that in the value-critique interpretation is capable of theorising the genuine abolition of the capitalist mode of production.[63] It is the exoteric Marx whose worker and capitalist (under the aegis of value-critique) belong to different worlds, who stands as the root cause of the problems of orthodoxy and is therefore to be jettisoned.

This focus on the logical forms of Marx's analysis is bound up with a notion of crisis: Norbert Trenkle goes so far as to say that value-critique is 'in essence a theory of crisis.'[64] Crisis is here understood as the argument that, since the 1970's decoupling from the gold standard and subsequent deregulation, capitalism has been in irrevocable decline, having reached the historical limits of its own expansion (limits imposed by the contradiction inherent in capital's own logic and inscribed within the structure of its basic categories: abstract labour, money, commodities, value). The evidence of this crisis can be seen most clearly in the increasing superfluity of human labour to production, the prospect of environmental collapse of the species and the biosphere, and the destruction of the 'symbolic and psychological foundations of human culture.'[65] The teleology of overcoming is supplanted by a teleology of collapse, a negative teleology. The end of capitalist civilisation is brought about by the destructive tendencies of its inner logic. If Walter Benjamin wrote in the 1930s that the experience of that generation was 'that capitalism will not die a natural death,'[66] this lesson has been studiously unlearned in the crisis theory of the following generations, though the prophesised outcome is not a proletarian triumph but environmental-societal collapse and barbarism.

Though in some sense, following in the tradition of the Marxism of the Frankfurt School in their focus on the commodity structure and the tendential 'capitalisation' of the social forms of being, the fallout from the events of '68 and the following decade of struggles pushed the revived Hegelian readings of Marx to increasing focus on the capital relation.[67] That is, the automatic-seeming development of the forms of value, commodity money and then the increasingly financialised forms of value (interest-bearing capital). This purifying domination by abstraction intensified through the subsumption of forms of life into the motor schema of value-expansion, which became a self-creating objectivity outside human content determining social relations. Here, the struggle between capital and labour is construed as 'an immanent conflict between social and economic interests internal to capitalism.'[68] Value-form theory, like the debates around communisation in post-'68 France, were premised on the period's breaks with orthodox Marxism, the strikes and 'struggles and the revolutionary hopes they engendered.'[69] However, their comprehensive defeat in the radicalisation of neoliberal political economy could be seen as emblematic of the dissolution of the working class as collective subject, one whose struggle points beyond the capitalist horizon, and a catalyst for driving the focus on abstract domination and the distancing of class.[70]

The fullest account of this understanding of capitalism's internal logic is perhaps the one elaborated by Moishe Postone, whose work represents a North American counterpart to the Hegelian *Wertkritik*. Like Jappe, Postone pushes away from class, seeking to advance a notion of capitalism as a system of abstract domination which holds over any individuals within it, displacing the centrality of struggle in the process.[71] Postone develops a model drawing on Hegel's logic to expound the relations described by Marx in *Capital* as a series of form determinations, leading from the two-fold nature of the commodity and 'rising from the abstract to the concrete.'[72] All the systemic contradictions of capital are not between capital and labour because labour is immanent to capital, whose relation to itself as 'automatic subject' establishes the objective framework through which class struggles subsist.[73] This, he argues, makes the dynamic contradiction of capital quasi-independent from its constituting individuals. Rather, it is a contradiction that has the 'properties of an intrinsic historical logic.'[74] He argues that capital is a system of social, 'self-generated structural domination' that alienates both worker and capitalist despite their vastly unequal power and wealth. This abstract domination 'has no determinate locus' such as the concrete antagonism of classes or institutional agencies.[75]

Postone inverts Lukács's assertion of the proletariat as the subject of history, arguing that when Marx uses *Geist* in *Capital* it is to describe capital itself rather than the working class and that, as such, the former may be more accurately designated as the Subject of history.[76] Postone's position argues against a Hegelian model of history in Marx, removing the notion of a single category (for example a transhistorical conception of labour) coming to fruition through its own historical development. Instead of a dialectical realisation of the class of workers as Subject of history, it is by doing away with the Subject—the dynamic that continually constrains human agency—that human beings may become the subjects of their own history.

In stark contrast to this, positions which stress the subjective component of the class relation have mobilised the notion of autonomy to place struggle at the forefront of resistance. In doing so, they seek to outline methods by which workers may define themselves externally to domination by capital and reconfigure social forms in line with class interests. In his work as part of the *operaismo* movement, Mario Tronti sought to do this by drawing attention to the worker's refusal of the role assigned to it by capital, denying its existence as labour-power and gaining autonomy. The working class can be juxtaposed with labour-power. Capital seeks to incorporate the labourer merely as labour-power, but the working class may attempt to identify as a class-for-itself through struggles which 'rupture capital's self-reproduction.'[77] These questions of autonomy and class composition remained prevalent in analysis of the outcomes of the struggles in '68, as well as in the Italian factory strikes and struggles in the decade that followed.[78]

This re-framing of the fundamental contradiction of the capital-labour relation identified the potential for a revolutionary subject in the collective worker, understood as an internal element of capital (variable capital), through a refusal of work and the evasion of its function as productive labour.[79] Tronti develops the notion of the worker and capitalist classes as forms with 'opposed world views,' but with the 'same content': the struggle of the workers. The capitalist class seeks to use the will-to-struggle of the worker as a mechanism of development, whilst the working class may reform this mediation for their own tactical advantage. The working class 'is, at one and the same time, the *articulation* of capital, and its *dissolution*.'[80] In this way the working class can re-form the power relations it is subject to, tipping them towards its own interests against capitalist technology, forcing capital to change its composition. However, this position comes close to being a 'romantic invocation of the revolutionary subject's immediacy'[81]—one that externalises the subject from capital's structure and leads to a voluntarist position of subjectivity. Labour and the worker are conceived as external to their own mode of existence.

By focusing in particular on the standpoint of the worker, this analysis has repeated the 'mistake' Postone identifies in previous interpretations of Marx's texts.[82] However, objective approaches that describe the class relation as internal to the capital relation are continually in danger of replicating the fetishism of the capitalist mode of production, by reducing class struggle to an 'objective mechanism which merely mediates the reproduction of the capital-relation.'[83] This often becomes the mechanism for advancing the need for a party form to mediate the class relation in the worker's interest, eliding the human social content of abstract relations of domination; thereby overlooking that it is only the activity of the working class, the activity that co-constitutes the relations themselves, that may abolish its own conditions of reproduction. The subjective approaches of the autonomists conversely fail to recognise the immanence of the worker in relation to the capitalist, which often results in an uncritical fetishisation of production or a voluntaristic approach to the class relation, seeking to secede from the relation through the creation of spaces outside of capital. This is further problematised by the increased 'flexibilisation' and fragmentation of the workforce in recent decades, which has shifted the make-up of the capital-labour relation and made the self-identification of a person as a 'worker' less and less likely. Capitalism has continually dissolved sociological conceptions of class as it has universalised its own production.[84] Nevertheless, as with the invaluable insights about the perverted objects of social being in capital, and the domination of abstract forms to be gained from the likes of Postone and *Wertkritik* interpretations, the autonomist and post-autonomist positions provide important points of understanding. Their determined focus on struggle and class insurgencies, offers a perspective that refuses any logic of defeat and is often open to the search for new forms of organizing, recalibrating and resisting.[85]

Class, then, is both a structural category and a *relational* one. It is structural in that, on one level, 'working class' simply refers to the collective bearers of variable capital, which later only exists in a historically specific mode of production. In other words, a class *is* a class relation: a social relationship of struggle that is in continuous motion with the 'sheer unrest of life.'[86] Class then can be said to be structural, but this structure only occurs in and through struggle; it is a social relation of struggle composed and recomposed through struggle. Similarly, capital 'is constantly changing from one form into the other, without becoming lost in this movement.'[87] This is how it becomes 'transformed into an automatic subject.'[88] To assign this automatic subject the objective movement through which human social relations 'play out,' however, would be to fall prey to an objective delusion. The idea of capital as wholly 'self-determining substance,' as only self-valorising value, repeats the capital fetish by failing to see the human practice from and by which it is constituted.[89] The most developed perversion, the constituted fetish of capitalist society, is the relation of capital to itself, of a thing to itself.[90] The solipsism of capital's self-understanding as prime mover fails to understand the accidental, the chance of explosion that underlies the essential. The automatic is always a relationship of necessity and contingency. The Greek etymological root of 'automatic' (αυτόματο) connotes that which happens through both chance and certainty: value's self-automation is a speculative economy.[91] Dialectical reason operates in a tension between closed determination and radical contingency. It 'intervenes in the relation between determination and tendency,' subjectifying the logical-heuristic mediation, 'and imposes on it a qualification and historical dynamic.'[92] However, the material actuality of abstract social forms produced and reproduced by subjective human activity remains open to the future and cannot be entirely enclosed within any dialectical totality or logical unity.

Marx uses the dialectical process as an approach to analysing society as a totality. The objects of capital are all simultaneously raised and reduced to 'aspects of a dialectical process.'[93] Marx's dialectic is, he attests, (dialectically) exactly opposite to that of Hegel: the ideal world is 'nothing but the material world reflected in the mind of man.'[94] This inversion, which seeks the 'rational kernel within the mystical shell,' possesses revolutionary potential, for it simultaneously recognises the negation in that which exists (its destruction): it 'regards every historically developed form as being in a fluid state, in motion.'[95] This latent potentiality of negation within capitalist forms of social ontology is down to the struggle which underlies the capital-labour relation. Class is 'at once *praxis* and process,' that is both the structuring of life through struggle and the structuring of this same struggle by 'the patterns hitherto imposed—imposed through struggle' upon life.[96] Class struggle places 'at issue, in struggle, the mediations which give to that struggle its characteristic form or forms.'[97]

The value-critique positions which seek to delineate an exoteric/esoteric distinction, however useful they might be in their thoroughgoing critiques of Marxist orthodoxy, misconstrue class as a surface phenomenon rather than as a fundamental expression of the material activity by which the fetishised forms of capitalism are themselves formed. Capitalism is a system of production where the pervasive and most basic social relation is the capital-labour relation. This relation is a class relation. The creation of surplus value entails the reproduction of this relation that is the presupposition on which capitalist accumulation is predicated. That is, the fetishised modes of sociality that exist in capitalism are, at their most fundamental level, inscribed within the capital-labour relation: value and class are mutually implicated.

These two schools of thought articulate the complexity of the double bind. The bind which remains at the heart of the political questions facing Marxism after the events of May 1968: immanence and antagonism. A double entanglement of subjectivity, succinctly encapsulated by Adorno's remark that whilst it is true that the laws of motion in society abstract from 'individual subjects, degrading them to mere executors,' there would likewise be 'nothing without individuals and their spontaneities.'[98] The class relation is the activity-of-form [*Formtätigkeit*] as a form of activity. The performance of acts of exchange produces and reproduces the form of society. The subject can never be reified in its totality by capital: reification must 'be conceptualised in relation to the realm of resistance' which resides in the capital-labour relation itself.[99] The opening comes from the fact that the inverted and perverted world of capitalist social relations is continually being *re-formed*: Marx repeatedly insists on the 'structurally given crisis-ridden transformation of the historical forms of capitalist relations.'[100] The dynamic unity of accumulation does not eliminate labour and capital but 'rather continually pushes each mediation . . . to its point of contradiction and its supercession.'[101] The essential reproduction of the capital-labour relation and the accumulation of capital are continually in tension with the crisis-laden contradictory nature of the mediating forms of capitalist social ontology, whose composition is continually undergoing transformation through human action. Marx 'urges us to do the impossible,' simultaneously grasping progress and catastrophe 'without attenuating the force of either judgement.'[102]

CONCLUSION

The problem of the double bind of immanence and antagonism remains central to the question of meaningful anti-capitalist activity today. The mass social movement of '68 and the years that followed gave way to ever-increasing fragmentation, that has only been further exacerbated in recent years. The radical precarity of work, the flux of gig economies and the hyper-financialisaton of modes of life which the neoliberal model of governmentality establishes demonstrate the subsumptive power of capital to remodel not only labour processes, and existing forms of power-violence (*Gewalt*), such as racial oppression and sexual oppression, into 'modes of existence of itself,' but the most basic activities of life.[103] The passages in the *Grundrisse* in which Marx discusses the potential for the development of the individual,[104] and the natural transformation into a new kind of subject, do so through the capitalist tendency for the creation of *disposable time* as the antithesis to labour-time. This notion has been rendered untenable through the transformation of disposable time, through for example the culture industry, into a site for the continuing realisation of value.[105] The expansion of free time has left the freedom of time on the horizon. Free time is, as Adorno articulated, 'nothing more than a shadowy continuation of labour.'[106]

The extension of the logic of the market, of economics, to domains previously thought to be noneconomic, tends towards individuals as forms of 'human capital' (a term coined by economist Gary Becker): an entrepreneur of themselves, managing interests, revenue streams and becoming the producer of their own satisfaction.[107] Some, like Negri and Camatte who employ subsumption as a mode of historical periodisation, understand this process as a 'total subsumption of society,'[108] wherein capital *becomes* society.[109]

Ultimately, despite the fact that the experiences of the individuals occupying the two poles of the relation of capitalist exploitation are vastly different, the world they occupy is one and the same. The living contradiction of capitalism is one that, through its ceaseless drive towards accumulation, reproduces the antagonistic class positions of the actors which it requires. To return to the image presented in *From the Depths*, it is not a question of the worker being excluded and thus requiring revolution to break through into the world of the capitalist, to seize/reappropriate their wealth and their apparatuses of control, but of the complete negation of the mechanism which reproduces the difference to begin with. Recognising this, the question of resistance to capital and the subjectivity of the worker remain difficult problems to contend with.

The value-critique positions' strong analysis of the abstract forms of capitalist sociality and their dominance is vital for understanding the scope of capital's social ontology: that our very existence is a contradictory structure of capitalist social being.

However, abstracting away from class struggle, thereby uniting the capitalist and worker in a capital relation beyond their antagonism, risks becoming merely a critique of capital from the standpoint of the capitalist.[110] Further, the response to the paralysing immanence of such positions often involves the introjection of a quasi-theological Benjaminian messianic moment of rupture as the locus of transformation.[111]

The capitalist subject is the result of an 'unstable social process that is continually challenged by struggle and continually in need [of] be[ing] reaffirmed as "objective".[112] At the level of 'life-process in the realm of the social' there is an 'inversion of subject into object and *vice versa.*'[113] The object's subjectivisation and the 'objectivisation' of human relations are 'mutually dependent expressions of a perverted world.'[114] This process of alienation repeats the act of power-violence [*Gewalt*], separating labour from its means, which founds the 'specifically capitalist mode of production.'[115] Capitalist accumulation 'merely presents as a *continuous process* what in *primitive accumulation* appears as a distinct historical process.'[116]

Conversely, affirmations of the worker as worker, and class as class, oftentimes fail to recognise the immanence of collective resistance to the class relation, that class is not an object but a relation of struggle, otherwise it collapses into voluntarism. At the same time, though the negative conceptions of the worker avoid uncritically making the proletariat into an angel of history, whilst maintaining the class relation as the central contradiction of their analysis, one must be careful to re-affirm that it is only the mass of workers, in their struggle to survive the continual horrors of wage labour, whose activity contains the latent potentiality of capitalism's abolition.

NOTES

1. This tendency is apparent in the work of: *Théorie Communiste, Endnotes*, Gilles Dauvé and Karl Nesic, as well as groups like *Tiqqun* and *The Invisible Committee*.

2. In many ways, the centrality of the double bind of immanence and antagonism is indicative of this shift.

3. Most obviously in the case of France, the work of the Situationist International. For a good overview of the Situationists' role in 1968 and their legacy for Marxism, see Anselm Jappe, *Guy Debord*, trans. Donald Nicholson-Smith (Los Angeles: University of California Press, 1999).

4. Karl Marx, *The Eighteenth Brumaire of Louis Bonaparte*, trans. Saul K. Padover (1999 [1952]), https://www.marxists.org/archive/marx/works/1852/18th-brumaire/ch01.htm (last accessed August 2021).

5. See Marshall Berman, *All That Is Solid Melts into Air* (London: Verso, 2010 [1981]); Jean-François Lyotard, *Libidinal Economy*, trans. Iain Hamilton Grant (Bloomington: Indiana University Press, 1993); Jean Baudrillard, *The Mirror of Production*, trans. Mark Poster (New York: Telos Press, 1975).

6. Guy Debord, *The Society of the Spectacle*, trans. Ken Knabb (2002), https://libcom.org/library/society-of-the-spectacle-debord (last accessed February 2021). For a discussion of the relation between Debord and post-structuralism, see Jeppe, *Guy Debord*, 125–35.

7. See György Lukács, *History and Class Consciousness: Studies in Marxist Dialectics*, trans. Rodney Livingstone (London: Merlin Press, 1991).

8. See Gilles Deleuze and Félix Guattari, *Anti-Oedipus*, trans. Robert Hurley, Mark Seem and Helen R. Lane (Minneapolis: University of Minnesota Press, 1983), 239–40.

9. For an excellent summary of this shift, see Benjamin Noys, 'Apocalypse, Tendency, Crisis,' *Mute* (February 2010), https://www.metamute.org/editorial/articles/apocalypse-tendency-crisis (last accessed September 2020).

10. Outside the work of so-called Dark Enlightenment figures like Nick Land and the Cybernetic Cultures Research Unit (CCRU), perhaps the most well-known text is Alex Williams and Nick Srnicek, 'MANIFESTO for an Accelerationist Politics,' *Critical Legal Thinking* (May 2013), https://criticallegalthinking.com/2013/05/14/accelerate-manifesto-for-an-accelerationist-politics/.

11. Benjamin Noys, *Malign Velocities: Accelerationism and Capitalism* (London: Zero Books, 2014), xi.

12. Karl Marx, *Capital: A Critique of Political Economy*, vol. 1, trans. Ben Fowkes (London: Penguin, 1976), 875.

13. Marx, *Capital*, 179.

14. Marx, *Capital*, 342.

15. Marx, *Capital*, 553.

16. Marx, *Capital*, 344.

17. Variable capital refers to the wages paid for the production of a commodity. For a solid expanded definition of this term, see 'Variable and Constant Capital' in *Encyclopedia of Marxism* (1999–2018), https://www.marxists.org/glossary/terms/v/a.htm (last accessed February 2021).

18. Werner Bonefeld, *Capital, Labour and Primitive Accumulation* (July 2005), https://libcom.org/library/capital-labour-and-primitive-accumulation (last accessed April 2017).

19. Marx, *Capital*, 644.

20. Marx, *Capital*, 271.

21. This is not merely a Ricardian 'labour theory of value.' The measure of the value produced, as Marx states, is not the transhistorical category of useful labour common to all societies and social forms, but abstract labour. Where useful labour, or concrete labour, is an 'eternal natural necessity which mediates the metabolism between man and nature,' abstract labour is a historically specific category of homogenised labour abstracted from qualitative difference. The embodied value is not a measure of the individual labour of the worker but a 'congealed objectivity,' a representation of the peculiarly social abstract labour. See Marx, *Capital*, 133–42.

22. Marx, *Capital*, 769

23. Michael Heinrich, *An Introduction to the Three Volumes of Karl Marx's* Capital, trans. Alexander Locascio (New York: Monthly Review Press, 2004), 96.

24. Heinrich, *An Introduction to the Three Volumes of Karl Marx's* Capital, 91–92.

25. Karl Max, *Theories of Surplus Value*, part 3, trans. Jack Cohen and S. W. Ryazanskaya (Moscow: Progress Publishers, 1971), 89.

26. Marx, *Capital*, 273.

27. Marx, *Capital*, 273.

28. Marx, *Capital*, 873.

29. Marx, *Capital*, 874.
30. Marx, *Capital*, 916.
31. Marx, *Capital*, 873.
32. Marx, *Capital*, 915.
33. Marx, *Capital*, 918.
34. See Werner Bonefeld, 'The Permanence of Primitive Accumulation: Commodity Fetishism and Social Constitution,' *The Commoner*, no. 2 (2001): 1–15.
35. Karl Marx, *Grundrisse*, trans. Martin Nicolaus (London: Penguin Books, 1973), 452–53.
36. Marx, *Theories of Surplus Value*, part 3, 312.
37. Marx, *Theories of Surplus Value*, part 3, 422.
38. Marx, *Capital*, vol. 1, 342
39. Marx, *Capital*, vol. 1, 382.
40. Marx, *Capital*, vol. 1, 344.
41. Heinrich, *An Introduction to the Three Volumes of Karl Marx's* Capital, 207.
42. Marx, *Capital*, 481–82.
43. Marx, *Capital*, 481–82.
44. Absolute surplus value being that which is increased or decreased by the total length of the working day; relative surplus value being that related to technological advancements and changes to the production process that increase the ratio of surplus-labour to necessary labour within the working day. See Marx, *Capital*, chapter 16.
45. Marx, *Capital*, 519.
46. Marx, *Capital*, 553–54.
47. Marx, *Capital*, 558.
48. Marx, *Capital*, 532.
49. Karl Marx and Friedrich Engels, *Marx and Engels Collected Works*, vol. 34 (London: Lawrence and Wishart, 1994), 398.
50. Marx, *Capital*, 548.
51. Max Horkheimer, 'Traditional and Critical Theory,' trans. Matthew J. O'Connell, in *Critical Theory: Selected Essays* (New York: The Continuum Publishing Company, 1972), 213.
52. Marx, *Capital*, 742.
53. 'The Crisis in the Class Relation,' *Endnotes* 2 (April 2010), https://endnotes.org.uk/issues/2/en/endnotes-crisis-in-the-class-relation (last accessed April 2017).
54. Marx, *Capital*, 783.
55. Marx, *Grundrisse*, 609.
56. Marx, *Capital*, 783–84.
57. Marx, *Capital*, 711.
58. Marx, *Capital*, 716.
59. Marx, *Capital*, 716.
60. Marx, *Capital*, 929.
61. Karl Marx, *The Poverty of Philosophy*, trans. the Institute of Marxism-Leninism (Moscow: Progress Publishers, 1955 [1847]), https://www.marxists.org/archive/marx/works/download/pdf/Poverty-Philosophy.pdf (last accessed April 2017), 80.

62. Georg Lukács, *History and Class Consciousness*, trans. Rodney Livingstone (Cambridge: MIT Press, 1971), 145.

63. On this distinction, see Anselm Jappe, *The Writing on the Wall: On the Decomposition of Capitalism and Its Critics* (London: Zero Books, 2017), 23–27.

64. Norbert Trenkle, 'Value and Crisis: Basic Questions,' *Mediations* 27, nos. 1–2 (1998).

65. Jappe, *The Writing on the Wall*, 38.

66. Walter Benjamin, *Arcades Project*, trans. Rolf Tiedemann (Cambridge, MA: Harvard University Press, 1999), 948.

67. Though the beginnings of the *Neue Marx-Lektüre* emerged before the events of 1968, in the mid-1960s, intensification of value-critique Marxism occurred only afterwards, particularly the shift away from notions of class as revolutionary actor. See, for example: the Wertkritik school and the Krisis-Gruppe formed in 1986, Christ Arthur's *Dialectics of Labour: Marx and His Relation to Hegel* (Oxford: Basil Blackwell, 1986), and Alfred Sohn-Rethel, *Intellectual and Manual Labour: A Critique of Epistemology* (Leiden: Brill, 2021 [1970]).

68. Norbert Trenkle, 'Struggle without Classes: Why There Is No Resurgence of the Proletariat in the Currently Unfolding Capitalist Crisis,' *Mediations* 27, nos. 1–2 (2006), https://mediationsjournal.org/articles/struggle-without-classes (last accessed August 2021).

69. *Endnotes*, 'Communisation and Value-form Theory,' *Endnotes 2* (2010), https://endnotes.org.uk/issues/2/en/endnotes-communisation-and-value-form-theory (last accessed August 2021).

70. This raises an interesting question about theory/practice (another one of the key 'double binds' of Marx's work): namely, the potential for exogenous factors, like the revolutions of '68, to effect a transformation in an endogenous logic that subsequently denies them. The history of abstract domination always threatens to be de-historicising.

71. Moishe Postone, *Time, Labour and Social Domination* (Cambridge: Cambridge University Press, 1993), 30.

72. Marx, *Grundrisse*, 101.

73. Werner Bonefeld, 'Capital as Subject and the Existence of Labour,' in *Open Marxism 3: Emancipating Marx*, ed. Werner Bonefeld, Richard Gunn, John Holloway and Kosmas Psychopedis (London: Pluto Press, 1995), 187.

74. Moishe Postone, Viren Murthy and Yasuo Kobayashi, 'Rethinking Marx's Critical Theory,' in *History and Heteronomy: Critical Essays* (Tokyo: The University of Tokyo Center for Philosophy, 2009), 43.

75. Moishe Postone, 'Rethinking Marx (in a Post-Marxist World),' *90th Annual Meeting of the American Sociological Association* (Washington, DC: August, 1995), http://www.obeco-online.org/mpt.htm (last accessed April 2017).

76. Benjamin Blumberg and Pam C. Nogales, 'Marx after Marxism: An Interview with Moishe Postone,' *Platypus Review* 3 (March 2008), https://platypus1917.org/2008/03/01/marx-after-marxism-an-interview-with-moishe-postone/, (last accessed April 2017).

77. Harry Cleaver, *Reading* Capital *Politically* (Edinburgh: AK Press, 2000), 66.

78. On the events in Paris, see Mouvement Communiste, *May-June 1968: An Occasion Lacking Workers' Autonomy* (April 2008), https://mouvement-communiste.com/documents/MC/Booklets/booklet_may_68.pdf; for an excellent overview of workerism and autonomism in relation to class composition, see Steve Wright, *Storming Heaven: Class Composition and Struggle in Italian Autonomist Marxism* (London: Pluto Press, 2002).

79. Mario Tronti, 'Workerism and Politics,' *Historical Materialism* 18, no. 3 (2010): 187.

80. Mario Tronti, 'The Strategy of Refusal,' in *Italy: Autonomia: Post-Political Politics*, trans. Red Notes (Cambridge: Semiotext(e), 1980), 29.

81. Bonefeld, *Open Marxism 3: Emancipating Marx*, 189.

82. Postone, *Time, Labour and Social Domination*, 64.

83. Bonefeld, *Open Marxism 3: Emancipating Marx*, 191–92.

84. *Bordiga versus Pannekoek* (London: Antagonism Press, 2001), 25.

85. On this see Riccardo Bellofiore and Massimiliano Tomba, 'On Italian Workerism' (November 2008), https://libcom.org/library/italian-workerism?fbclid=IwAR0cWT65X2w5-CtzSlom5LV1TC5YxNPxAS-XhsuZnuIrEFtV3aEShe-1BuVs (last accessed August 2021).

86. G. W. F. Hegel, *Phenomenology of Spirit*, trans. A. V. Miller (Oxford: Oxford University Press, 1977), 27.

87. Marx, *Capital*, 255.

88. Marx, *Capital*, 255.

89. Werner Bonefeld, 'On Postone's Courageous but Unsuccessful Attempt at Banishing the Class Antagonism from the Critique of Political Economy,' *Historical Materialism* 12, no. 3 (January 2004): 112–13.

90. Marx, *Theories of Surplus Value*, part 3, 515.

91. Catherine Malabou, *The Future of Hegel* (London: Routledge, 2004), 160.

92. Negri, *Marx Beyond Marx*, 12.

93. György Lukács, *History and Class Consciousness: Studies in Marxist Dialectics*, trans. Rodney Livingstone (London: Merlin Press, 1971), 28.

94. Marx, *Capital*, 102.

95. Marx, *Capital*, 103.

96. Richard Gunn, 'Notes on Class,' *Common Sense*, no. 2 (July 1987): 17–18.

97. Gunn, 'Notes on Class,' 18.

98. Theodor W. Adorno, *Negative Dialectics* (London: Continuum, 1981), 304.

99. Peter Hudis, 'The Death of the Death of the Subject,' *Historical Materialism* 12, no. 3 (2004): 158.

100. Bonefeld, 'Open Marxism,' 34.

101. Negri, *Marx Beyond Marx*, 9.

102. Frederic Jameson, *Postmodernism, or, The Cultural Logic of Late Capitalism* (Durham: Duke University Press, 1991), 47.

103. Richard Gunn, 'Marxism and Mediation,' *Common Sense*, no. 2 (July 1987): 61.

104. Marx, *Grundrisse*, 708–12.

105. Peter Osborne, 'Marx and the Philosophy of Time,' *Radical Philosophy*, no. 147 (January/February 2008): 21.

106. Theodor W. Adorno, 'Free Time,' in *The Culture Industry: Selected Essays on Mass Culture* (London: Routledge, 1991), 194.

107. Adorno, 'Free Time,' 226.

108. Antonio Negri, 'Twenty Theses on Marx, Interpretation of the Class Situation Today,' in *Marxism Beyond Marxism*, ed. Saree Makdisi, Cesare Casarino Rebecca Karl (London: Routledge, 1996), 159.

109. Jacques Camatte, *Capital and Community* (London: Unpopular Book, 1988), 45.

110. *Aufheben*, 'Review: Moishe Postone's Time, labour and Social Domination–Capital beyond Class Struggle?,' *Aufheben* 15 (2007), https://libcom.org/library/review-moishe-postone-capital-beyond-class-struggle (last accessed April 2017).

111. Walter Benjamin, 'On the Concept of History,' in *Selected Writings: Volume Four, 1938–1940*, ed. Michael W. Jennings (Cambridge: Harvard University Press, 2003), 395.

112. Aufheben, *Moishe Postone's Time, Labour and Social Domination—Capital beyond Class Struggle?* (2007), https://libcom.org/library/review-moishe-postone-capital-beyond-class-struggle (last accessed August 2017).

113. Marx, *Capital*, 990.

114. Bonefeld, 'Capital as Subject and the Existence of Labour,' 191.

115. Marx, *Capital*, 775.

116. Marx, *Theories of Surplus Value*, part 3, 272, emphasis in the original.

Chapter Four

The Unfulfilled Promises of the Italian 1968 Protest Movement

Franco Manni

In 1968, Italy experienced widespread and long-lived student protests, to such an extent that the ritual of students occupying schools is commemorated every year to this day. From the 1970s to 2008, the Italian Communist Party (PCI) was probably the most successful communist party in Western Europe: it garnered 34.4 percent of the vote at the Italian Parliament elections in 1976 and, albeit under new name, secured twenty-seven out of eighty-one Italian seats at the European Parliament elections in 2008. While the party shifted its ideological affiliation from Soviet orthodoxy to Eurocommunism in the 1970s and then, after 1989, changed its name to the Democratic Party of the Left, it is notable that Italy is the only European country to have had a major party of communist lineage that consistently performed well in elections at national and European levels. It is tempting to think of the Italian '68 as the high point of a revolutionary fervour that spurred on this electoral success. There may be some truth in this, but as we look back from the vantage point of the 2020s the consequences of 1968 seem more complicated. In the 2018 national election, the largest number of seats went to the right-wing populist Five Star Movement. While the negotiations that followed this election were complex, it signalled a major shift in Italian politics such that, at the time of writing, the far-right Brothers of Italy (FDI) are snapping at the heels of the Five Star Movement and other right-wing parties, who they see as now part of the political establishment. The revolutionary spirit of '68, it would appear, has been overtaken by reactionary populist sentiment from the right. But why did this shift take place, and is it as straightforward as saying that 'the left is in retreat and the right is on the rise'?

Although we could look to understand this shift in many ways, the aim of the following reflection is to show that the intellectual context implied in this opening framing needs to be refined. As we look at the history of Italian ideas in the twentieth century, we can gather insight into tensions that shaped 1968 and its legacy up to the present political situation, in surprising ways. Charting these intellectual tensions, we need to consider debates that surrounded the work of the enormously influential Italian philosopher Benedetto Croce. On the one hand, there is the influence of Croce's work on two influential Italian intellectuals who did not welcome the events of '68: Norberto Bobbio and Pierpaolo Pasolini. On the other hand, there is the legacy of the debate about Croce's work within the intellectual circles of the left, signalled by the very different responses of Antonio Gramsci and Palmiro Togliatti—positive and negative, respectively. The exploration of these tensions in this chapter leads to the idea that '68 in Italy was informed by a form of 'Romantic Marxism,' the legacy of which was not just the electoral success of the PCI and its incarnations, but also the rise of the populist far-right in recent years. As such, it will be argued that the legacy of 1968 in Italy did not run out of steam with the decline of the left but that it is also evident in the rise of the populist right: these two aspects are in fact part of the same lineage.

THE STONE GUEST

Almost all Italian intellectuals (writers, artists, journalists) immediately fell in love with the 1968 protest movement. Only two notable intellectuals opposed it: Norberto Bobbio and Pierpaolo Pasolini. In many respects, the two men were quite different from each other. Bobbio was older and upper class; a renowned scholar, lecturer and writer of political philosophy; senator for life of the Italian Republic; married, a father of a large family; and a very reserved person. Pasolini, by contrast, was younger and middle class; a poet and, above anything else, a controversial film director; openly gay, artistic and libertine; and outspoken. However, despite these differences they shared some common characteristics. Most notably, during the Second World War they had both been members of the liberal resistance movement *Giustizia e Libertà* rather than any of the communist groups mobilising at the time. This shared commitment to liberal ideas led them both to question what they understood as the intellectual contradictions and moral distortions in the ideas and practices of the 1968 movement.

In June 1968, Bobbio was teaching at the University of Turin and published several articles on the student protests. In one particularly telling intervention, he called into question the idea of freedom motivating the protests:

> Today we know that freedom can be used for good or ill. You can use it not to educate but to corrupt. Not to increase your ideal heritage, but to squander

it. Not to make people wiser and noble, but to make them more ignorant and vulgar. Freedom can also be wasted. You can waste it to the point of making it look useless, an unnecessary asset. Indeed, harmful. And by dint of wasting it, one day or another (Near? Far?) we will lose it.

They will take it away. We do not yet know who: whether those who we have let prosper to our right or those who are impetuously growing to our left. We still have the suspicion, fuelled by a continuous, severe lesson lasting half a century, that the difference will not be very large.[1]

This concern with the ways in which freedom can be squandered was echoed by Pasolini. In June 1968 Pasolini was living in Rome and working as a film director. After a clash between students and the police he wrote a poem. Here are a few verses:

*Now journalists from all over the world (including those of televisions)
they lick you / . . . / the ass. Not me, dear.*

*You are fearful, uncertain, desperate
/ . . . / but you also know how to be
bossy, blackmailers, confident and shameless
/ . . . /*

This, dear children, you know.

*And you apply it through two imperative feelings:
the Awareness of your Rights (you know, democracy takes only you into consideration),
and Greed for Power.*

*Yes, your horrible slogans always focus
on the seizure of power.
In your beards I read impotent ambitions,
In your pallors I read desperate snobbism.*[2]

Like Bobbio, Pasolini was concerned with the ways in which the '68 uprisings might instil a 'greed for power' that would, ultimately, make the revolutionary aspirations of the left indistinguishable from the political hierarchies associated with the right. As well as their shared background in the war, what ideas informed this opposition to the 1968 movement? We could formulate many different answers to this question, but one central point joining these figures was a shared commitment to the work of a figure who had fallen out of favour with their colleagues: Benedetto Croce. It was in Croce's ethical and political philosophy that both Bobbio and Pasolini found an idea of individual freedom that had to be continually guarded in the face of the barbarism of both left and right. The '68 uprisings were, for them, the latest upsurge of this barbarism, the latest threat to hard-won freedoms in need of protection rather than violation. This was a deeply unfashionable view at the time. However, further reflection upon why Croce had lost favour amongst the Italian intelligentsia can help us understand not just Bobbio and Pasolini's position but also why the ideas formulated around '68 in Italy have shaped, in the end, the rise of right-wing populism, fifty years later.

Croce was one of the most influential and engaged public intellectuals of the twentieth century in Italy. He was admired by and had conversed with some of the world's most notable figures, from Dewey to Mann to Einstein. Antonio Gramsci, whose reception in the second half of the century was much happier, repeatedly recognised the importance of Croce in *The Prison Notebooks* and, indeed, said that for him Croce was the greatest twentieth-century philosopher in the world. In Gramsci's *Notebooks*, Croce's is by far the most cited name.[3] Croce, however, was not only a philosopher, but had become an important politician. In both the English-speaking world and in Italy he was considered one of the most important and influential Italian anti-fascists, and from 1943 to 1945 he became a crucial mediator between the British Foreign Office minister Anthony Eden, the American general Mark W. Clark, the prime ministers of the Kingdom of Italy Badoglio and Bonomi, the head of the largest anti-fascist political party (Democrazia Cristiana) and minister of the Kingdom Alcide De Gasperi, Crown Prince Umberto di Savoia and the King of Italy Vittorio Emanuele III.[4]

Croce's anti-fascism had three key characteristics: he was a liberal, he was an intellectual and he was without a political party of his own. While these gave a distinctive ideological perspective to Croce's anti-fascism, they also set him against other figures emerging from the wartime resistance. Indeed, it was these three characteristics that proved decisive for the Stalinist Palmiro Togliatti, head of the Italian Communist Party, who launched continuous personal and political attacks against Croce after April 1944.[5] Curiously, Togliatti was, in many respects, a follower of Croce's epistemology and ethics, and confessed to having formed his personality by reading and meditating upon Croce's *The Philosophy of Practice*. Togliatti adhered on the epistemological level to Croce's anti-positivism and, on the ethical level, to Croce's anti-existentialism. Furthermore, at the peak of his power in the 1950s he harshly attacked those Italian intellectuals who adhered to existentialism and neo-positivism, such as Antonio Banfi and Ludovico Geymonat respectively.[6] Nonetheless, immediately after the end of the war Togliatti orchestrated a cultural campaign to criticise and, he hoped, ultimately eliminate Croce's influence on Italy's left-liberal intelligentsia (the right-wing Catholics and

Fascists had already—for the most part—distanced themselves from Croce's liberal politics). By the time Togliatti died in 1964 he had succeeded in seriously diminishing respect for Croce's oeuvre amongst emergent Italian intellectuals. In particular, he succeeded—even if it had not been his intention—in ensuring that Croce's ethical works (a deep synthesis of parts of Kantian moral philosophy with parts of Hegelian ethics) and his epistemology (which was above all a theory of the nature of historical knowledge) were no longer considered an essential part of intellectual debates or public conversations.

In large measure, because of the space created by Togliatti's erasure of Croce's ideas from the cultural and intellectual scene, it was in those years (the late 1950s and early 1960s) that the ideas coming from France and America began to dominate in Italy. In particular, forms of left-wing existentialism engendered and also captured the mood of uprising in ways that seemed to render Croce's liberal and idealist approaches irrelevant. Yet, as Bobbio and Pasolini's responses to '68 make clear, while Croce's liberal political philosophy did not frequently appear in the public debates he was, to borrow from Pushkin, the 'stone guest.' The shadow of Croce's ideas loomed large over the events of '68 in Italy, with his attempted elimination from the intellectual scene leaving a trace that Bobbio and Pasolini picked up. Acknowledging this allows for a certain insight into the ideas that shaped Italy's '68 uprisings and creates a particular perspective on how we may understand the legacies of this moment up to the present day. On the one hand, we can see that the ground was prepared in the anti-Croce campaign for a form of Marxism peculiar to the 1968 movement in Italy: Romantic Marxism. On the other hand, we shall see how the promise of this Romantic Marxism was unfulfilled for the reasons Croce, Bobbio and Pasolini understood so clearly: the fight for freedom is often a cover for the fight for power.

ROMANTIC MARXISM

This brief history of twentieth century Italian ideas helps explain the rise of a particular version of Romantic Marxism in the lead up to the events of '68. Whereas Croce (and subsequently Bobbio and Pasolini) sought to hold on to the idea that freedom was hard won and had to be continually guarded, the erasure of this idea and the arrival of a left-wing existentialism with its tendencies toward the justification of spontaneous expressions of authenticity, mixed with the Marxist legacies of the anti-Croce campaign, seeded the intellectual atmosphere with a potent mix of Romanticism and Marxism. It is a set of ideas worthy of the name 'Romantic' because of the value given to notions of youth, beauty, Eros, imagination, Oriental gurus, and immediacy, to the praise of the passions over the intellect, and to the psychotropic 'trips' supposed to produce a sense of oneness with the cosmos. In all these respects, the ideas animating '68 were remarkably distant from traditional Marxism, so focused on economy, labour, class struggle, intellectual theories, planning, aesthetic realism and ascetic 'Calvinism' in ethics. Nonetheless, these ideas were mixed with forms of Marxism in Italy because of Togliatti's role in the anti-Croce campaign, and as a form of the communist appropriation of all this youthful energy. The result was, in short, a Romantic version of Marxism. Having outlined this, I will argue that the unfulfilled promises of the Italian '68 were, to a large extent, an expression of the failed synthesis of Romanticism and Marxism, one which ultimately created the conditions for the current rise of the populist right. There is much that could be said about the philosophical Romanticism underpinning this 1968 version of Marxism: in Italy, it was neither positivist à la Plekhanov-Bucharin-Loria, nor historicist à la Lukács-Gramsci. It would be interesting to explore, for example, the contrast between the rationalist foundations of both positivism and historicism in the broader Marxist tradition and the strongly irrationalist bases of the Italian Marxism that shaped 1968. However, this would require a different discussion. For now, we can sketch out the shape of this Romantic Marxism with a brief account of the materialism and Machiavellianism at its core.

Given the Romantic and, in some sense, idealist visions of spontaneous forms of authentic existence that shaped this set of ideas, it is interesting to note that there was a naïve form of materialism that emerged as these ideas blended with Marxism. Famously, albeit not without a wealth of subsequent debates and conflicting interpretations, Marx distinguished the base (economic facts, production, work relationships, market) from the superstructure (politics, religion, art). As suggested by Marx's metaphor, how the base is organised is fundamental to the workings of history. The superstructure tends to reflect these class relationships, often seeking to cover over the class antagonism structuring the base. For example, the industrial exploitation of workers in nineteenth-century Great Britain was sustained by a veneer of liberal institutions, liberal philosophy, and liberal education. There is no doubt that the activists of '68 were inspired by these ideas to support the factory workers' struggles. However, there was a tendency to idealise the so-called working class and their economic demands. Whereas Marx's analyses required a view of historical development based on class antagonism, many of the activists of '68 in Italy tended to downplay this aspect in favour of an ahistorical idealisation of the working class. The appeal to authentic forms of existence marked a break from history and, when mixed with a Marxist appeal to the revolutionary role of the working class, led to a naïve materialist and Romantic vision of the working-class hero. The intellectual space created by the anti-Croce campaign was filled from two, apparently contradictory, sides. Croce's sense of freedom as a value to be guarded was replaced by the idea that freedom was an experience to be won through struggle, and his sense that freedom was constituted in the relationship between civilisation and the individual was replaced by a sense of the working class as *the* bearers of revolutionary freedom.

One subtle but strong idea animating the Italian version of this blend of Romanticism and Marxism is Machiavellianism. While we can read Machiavelli in many ways—and, of course, Marx, Lenin and Gramsci all drew from his work in important respects—he is often associated with the famous statement that 'the ends justify the means.' This was a sentiment that found expression in the Italian '68. As we have already noted with respect to Bobbio and Pasolini's Croce-inspired response to these events, the public declarations of the movement to transform Italian society often hid the fact that the movement sought to achieve its aims through the hierarchical social formations that it sought to abolish. In pursuit of a revolutionary politics of spontaneous expression, activists often used illegitimate means such as nepotism and cronyism. In this sense they were embodying Machiavelli's idea in *The Prince* that politics must be independent from morality. It is intriguing that this separation of the means from the ends, and of politics from morality, was captured most directly by the undisputed intellectual guru of the Italian 1968: a priest, don Lorenzo Milani, the celebrated author of the cult book *Lettera a una professoressa*.[7] Later, he wrote to his friend Gian Paolo Meucci (a judge living in Florence):

> But tomorrow, when the farmers hold the pitchfork and submerge in blood along with so much evil also great values of good accumulated by the university families in their minds and in their specializations, remember that day not to do injustice in the historical evaluation of those events. Remember not to mourn the damage of the Church and science, thought or art for the destruction of so many heads of thinkers and scientists and poets and priests.[8]

In this passage we can see both the naïve materialism mentioned above and the expression of a Machiavellian attitude with respect to politics and morality. Despite Togliatti's respect for Croce's ethics, the anti-Croce campaign helped establish a space where it was possible for this renewed Machiavellianism to take root.

As the space left behind by the anti-Croce campaign was filled with both a naïve materialism without strong ethical basis and a call to liberate one's own authenticity, the ethical domain was stripped of its authority, of its moderating role and of its ability to connect people to each other. Romantic Marxism emerged to claim this space, and in so doing engendered a form of narcissistic activism where one's own feelings became the touchstone for radical change. This space was created by evacuating Croce from the intellectual scene; at the same time, however, the presence of this 'stone guest' also allows us to see how alternative tendencies were held together in this space by a strange blend of Romanticism and Marxism. Moreover, it helps us understand the legacies of this moment, and the legacies of Romantic Marxism in Italy.

UNFULFILLED PROMISES

More than fifty years have passed since '68, and today many of the movement's young leaders sit on the top rung of Italian politics, the economy and academia: 'if you dig into the biographies of important entrepreneurs or managers, if they are in the relevant age group, you will find that almost all of them have a past as 1968 militants / leaders.'[9] Having achieved the power they sought, these former 1968 radicals could have at least partially realised their ideals: reduced authoritarianism, greater individual freedom and forms of anti-fascism deeply woven into Italian political life. But, as we will see in three key respects, the opposite has happened, not just because Romantic Marxism was doomed to failure but because it seeded the ideas that would grow into its own inability to deliver the promised blend of spontaneous authenticity and working-class liberation.

1. The protests began in the university environment against so-called academic barons (corrupt and nepotistic professors, often involved in politics), and yet today such malpractices have markedly increased in Italian academia. The decline of Italy's universities, none of which currently appear in the world's top two hundred, is a constant source of frustration among the country's chattering classes. But the reason for this sorry state is laid bare by new research, which shows the extent of nepotism in higher education.

    In 2010 the investigative magazine *L'Espresso* revealed the astonishing degree to which lecturing jobs in Italy are a family business. In Rome's La Sapienza University, for example, a third of teaching staff have fellow lecturers as close family members. Overall, the country's higher institutions are ten times more likely than other places of work to employ two or more members of the same family.[10]

2. The movement wanted to free youths from the oppression of the family, but, while at that time young people would start working and live on their own in their mid-twenties, today half of them are unemployed and live with their parents, often well into their thirties. In 1968 the average age at

which young Italians left their parents' home was twenty-five. In 2016, the average age at which young people left their parents' home in Italy was 30.1, the fourth highest in Europe after Malta, Croatia and Slovakia. Relatedly, in Denmark the proportion of people between eighteen and twenty-five living with their parents is 23 percent, while in Italy it is 79 percent.
3. The movement was strongly anti-fascist, and today a neo-fascist party is forming the new Italian government. In 1968 students said they were the heirs to the Resistance partisans: they declared themselves anti-fascists and labelled their teachers and parents, the police, judges and all the political parties apart from the communists as 'fascist.' They failed to acknowledge that authentic, historically documented anti-fascism was carried out by very few people in Italy during the fascist period and during the war. Recently, in 2018–2019, the Deputy Premier was Matteo Salvini (who, when young, was a communist)—he wears a black shirt and has threatened to march on Rome. He has furthermore announced that the police should be ruthless in maintaining order and he has sympathised with explicitly fascist youth groups (Forza Nuova, Casa Pound) that openly praise Mussolini.[111]

CONCLUSION

In Italy, in 2018, the fiftieth anniversary of the 1968 protests, the celebrations by the 'intelligentsia' and the middle classes were very few, far fewer than the celebrations for the fortieth anniversary. It might appear that the left is in retreat and the right is on the rise. The reflections on the state of Italian intellectual life advanced in this chapter, however, suggest a more nuanced story. The left, with its Romantic Marxism, did succeed in their search for power, and yet one of the results of this has been the rise of the far right able to exploit many of the same features of this Romantic Marxism in the name of new forms of fascism. On the one hand, the activists of '68 have established themselves within universities, publishing houses, the media, municipalities, charities, political bodies at all levels, services and social assistance, and schools and educational institutions. Here the power of the former 1968 militants is stronger than ever, and their grip on Italian society more present. Equally, though, the intellectual space created by the Romantic Marxism that shaped their militancy has enabled the growth of right-wing populism. A revolutionary spirit based on naïve materialism, notions of spontaneous authenticity and a Machiavellian sense of politics devoid of purpose, and fed by moral narcissism, cannot challenge these forces when they arrive, albeit in different clothes, from the far right.

As this journey through twentieth-century Italian ideas has shown, it was the erasure of Croce's political ideas which made possible the arrival onto the scene of a Romantic Marxism that promised transformation but failed to deliver. More worryingly, in the wake of Romantic Marxism the scene was set for forms of right-wing populism that look very much like the fascism the Romantic Marxists were hoping to destroy. In addition, this reminds us that Croce's work brings to light the delicate relations between past and present, the individual and the collective, the ideal and the material, and the practical and moral, and that they all need to be considered more fully and more expansively than any position that simply glorifies one side over the other. More importantly, Croce's analysis reminds us of something that George Orwell put so well:

> O'Brien had pushed the lever of the dial up to thirty-five. 'That was stupid, Winston, stupid!' he said. 'You should know better than to say a thing like that.' He pulled the lever back and continued: 'Now I will tell you the answer to my question. It is this. The Party seeks power entirely for its own sake. We are not interested in the good of others; we are interested solely in power. Not wealth or luxury or long life or happiness: only power, pure power.'[12]

What is the legacy of the Italian '68 today? Despite the unfulfilled promises, there were many senses in which the aspirations of '68 were driven by good intentions. If the anti-Croce campaign by Togliatti had not been quite so effective, despite Bobbio and Pasolini's efforts to bring the stone guest back to life, there might have been room for greater dialogue about Italy's past, present and future. For this to be the case, though, it is necessary to learn, with Croce, that the blind pursuit of power will always corrupt.

NOTES

1. Norberto Bobbio, 'Arduo il dialogo con gli studenti,' *Resistenza*, no. 6 (June 1968): 5–9; even harsher criticisms followed in *Resistenza*, in April and May 1969.
2. Pierpaolo Pasolini, 'il PCI ai Giovani!,' *L'Espresso*, 16 June 1968.
3. Franco Manni, 'Antonio Gramsci e il Liberalismo,' in *Teoria politica e società industriale*, ed. Franco Sbarberi (Torino: Bollati Boringhieri, 1988), 128–45, 130.
4. Benedetto Croce, *Taccuini di Guerra (1943–1945)* (Milano: Adelphi, 2004).
5. See *Index ad nomen* 'Togliatti' in Croce, *Taccuini di Guerra*.
6. Fabio Minazzi, 'Il razionalismo critico neoilluminista italiano (la scuola di Milano, da Antonio Banfi a Giulio Preti),' *Protagora* 25/26, nos. 1–2 (2016): 9–42, 36–40.
7. Lorenzo Milani, *Lettera a una professoressa* (Firenze: LEF, 1967).

8. Lorenzo Milani, *Lettere di don Lorenzo Milani priore di Barbiana* (Milano: Mondadori, 1970), 65.

9. Massimo Fini, 'Altro che balle, io che c'ero vi dico che i leader erano solo borghesi in carriera', *Millennium*, October 2017, http://www.massimofini.it/articoli-recenti/1688-altro-che-balle-io-che-cero-vi-dico-che-ileader-erano-solo-borghesi-in-carriera.

10. Davide Carlucci and Giuliano Foschini, 'Ecco parentopoli dei prof. le grandi dinastie degli atenei,' *La Repubblica*, 24 Settembre 2010 (reported by Michael Day, 'Family Fiefdoms Blamed for Tainting Italian Universities,' *The Independent*, 25 September 2020).

11. David Broder, 'The Fascist Movement at the Centre of Italy's Culture War,' *The New Statesman* (UK edition), 13 June 2012, https://www.newstatesman.com/world/2012/06/fascist-movement-centre-italy-s-culture-war.

12. George Orwell, *1984* (London: Secker & Warburg), 1949.

Part II

FREEDOM AND RIGHTS

Chapter Five

On Ludic Servitude

Natasha Lushetich

In the eponymous study on voluntary servitude, Estienne de La Boétie suggests that freely accepted servitude is based on three factors: habit or acclimatisation to modes of exploitation and denigration; reverence for rites and rituals that sustain the existing tyranny; and fear.[1] In a prescient discussion of power—reminiscent of Michel Foucault's interaction-dependent notion of power, which departs from monolithic top-down oppression and where every move changes, or, at least, has the potential to change the existing constellation of relations[2]—La Boétie suggests non-cooperation as an exit route from voluntary servitude. In *Logics of Failed Revolt*, however, and, more specifically, in his analysis of the double bind of 1968, Peter Starr argues that attempts to challenge entrenched power by oblique, non-direct methods, such as non-cooperation or the refusal to take power, invariably end up reproducing power's mechanisms. For Starr, the double bind is based on the twin principles of 'specular doubling' and 'structural repetition,' which begin 'with the uncovering of a pseudo-opposition between the principles or structures of the established social order and an oppositional force whose action is found to be deeply complicitous with those principles or structures,' in the sense of repeating them, or 'being recuperated by them.'[3] Commenting on the events of '68, the role of such groups as the Situationist International (SI), students and workers, Starr suggests that their 'third way,' which sought to circumvent both the Gaullist establishment and its communist rivals, proposed—yet did not live up to—a new form of oppositional intelligence that would leave behind the old mechanisms of the state, the party and the union to assume a novel and authentic counter-institutional form, embodied in a series of ludic and poetic gestures. Starr's point is that the very refusal to organise, coordinate and negotiate created a fatal impasse. In his view, if change is to be initiated, some level of engagement or compromise with the ruling powers has to be accepted. But is this really so? Is engagement with the existing powers, on their terms, a sign that there is no alternative, as the subtitle of Mark Fisher's 2009 book, a reflection on Margaret Thatcher's infamous phrase—*Capitalist Realism: Is There No Alternative?*—suggests?[4] Or is this gradualist (as opposed to subitist) mode of thought,[5] which does *not* allow for sudden reversals, itself based on a supposedly 'realistic,' but in fact hegemonic conception of time and change, as entrenched in the progressivist paradigm exemplified by Walter Benjamin's notion of 'homogeneous and empty' time[6]—a sequence of identical moments marching indomitably towards a pre-ordained future? Are the oblique, ludic tactics practised by the SI and many culture-jamming groups after them—such as The Yes Men, the glitch and Dirty New Media movement—outdated, inefficient or simply useless?

It is undeniable that by the late 1960s the violence inherent in capitalism was steadily becoming both more invisible and more structural. The post-WWII productivist-consumerist society had reduced individuals to two kinds of heteronomy—both of which instituted a brand of covert violence embedded in routines and assignments of energy, a violence that appeared 'as natural as the air around us.'[7] While the heteronomy of work deprived individuals of voluntary social integration and forced them into systemic integration, the heteronomy of private consumption ensured the consumption of mass-produced commodities that were seen as the (sole) antidote to the strictures imposed by the productivist regime. The neo-avant-garde's response to the violence of the ideological-economic system that had, by the 1960s, mastered the 'high art of integrating, diffusing and marketing the most serious challenges'[8] in Europe and the US alike was a vehement contestation of the alienation of desire, chronarchy and the commodification of experience. The SI, and the neo-avant-garde more generally, faced a much bigger challenge than did the early twentieth-century avant-garde—like Dada and Futurism—during whose time capitalism had not yet entered the mercurial, ubiquitous and highly ambivalent stage of *enslavement through liberation*. This is precisely why oblique practices that were often also interactive—practicable by all, regardless of profession, education, class, gender, age or colour—were a necessary form of practical critique of the productivist-consumerist regime and its many forms of invisible violence. In what follows, I examine the relationship of ludicity to the increasingly invisible yet ever-more efficacious techniques of capitalist appropriation, via the logic of oblique contestation, pre-corporation and associated tactics—such as simulacric ludicity and obfuscation—and finally the oxymoron 'ludic servitude.'

LUDICITY AND CONTESTATION

Ludicity may not be the first thing that comes to mind when one thinks of social and political contestation. However, this is not to say that its role in contestation is nonexistent or insignificant. Comprising, on the one hand, play—an improvisational and 'enchanting' activity that 'lies outside the antithesis of wisdom and folly,' 'truth and falsehood'[9]—and, on the other, games—rule-based temporal structures—ludicity is usually associated with freedom, abandonment and *jouissance*. For Roger Caillois, both play and games lead to '*l'extase illuminante*' (illuminated ecstasy), a joyful identification with the 'totality of material and immaterial contents of the world.'[10] Etymologically, the word 'game' derives from the old English *gamen*—which means joy, entertainment and fun—as well as from the Gothic *gaman* where *ga* and *mann* mean 'people together.'[11] In Anatoly Liberman's, as in Caillois's account, 'people together' refers to a spontaneous or 'vertical' structuring of social relations, which, unlike its horizontal variant—social categories such as age, profession, class and ethnicity—forms fleeting communitas. Unlike (pre-formed, heteronomic) community, or even commonality, communitas is a mode of free 'coactivity' opposed to stable, horizontal social structures, to 'obligation' and to 'jurality.'[12]

Drawing on Karl Marx and the Indo-European etymology of the word 'freedom'—to be among friends—Byung-Chul Han anchors freedom in convivial, non-commodified, playful human relations, claiming, like Marx, that *individual* freedom is an illusion.[13] However, Giorgio Agamben is perhaps the most precise in elaborating the relationship between ludicity and contestation through the logic of profanation, where both play and games are a subversion of god's sovereignty:

> Most of the games with which we are familiar derive from ancient sacred ceremonies, from divinatory practices and rituals that once belonged, broadly speaking, to the religious sphere. The girotondo was originally a marriage rite; playing with a ball reproduces the struggle of the gods for possession of the sun; games of chance derive from oracular practices; the spinning top and the chessboard were instruments of divination.[14]

Ludic re-purposing of objects and activities defuses the sovereign power by dissolving the unity of the myth (which tells the story) and the rite (which stages it).[15] In other words, power is undone through a ludic re-arrangement and re-purposing of power's tools, goals and procedures. By re-arranging the rules of the game—and, in so doing, re-defining its goals—ludicity is simultaneously a disruptive and a restorative force. The SI formulated a disruptive-restorative revolutionary programme in the sphere of culture to subvert capitalist modes of existence, increasingly entrenched in all segments of daily life. *Détournement* (which means both diversion and reversal) was used to subvert signifying processes that make up advertising and televisual communication. This technique, often employed in *Internationale Situationiste*—a journal the SI edited from 1958 to 1969 where comics characters were given new balloons and made to discuss alienation and the spectacularisation of society—derives its efficacy from the ludic 'negation of the value of the previous organisation of expression'[16]—and, I would add, from *spieltrieb*. For Friedrich Schiller, spieltrieb is simultaneously ludic and a drive; it brings together ethical urgency and the jouissance of play.[17] Ethical urgency was also evident in the SI practice of 'symbolic urbanism,' a détournement of urban planning, consisting in the falsification of information about train departures at train stations,[18] the placement of museum exhibits in bars where contagious 'high spirits' had revolutionary potential,[19] and demands for 'free access to the prisons for everyone' without 'discrimination between visitors and prisoners.'[20] The quest for spontaneity *as* freedom also manifested in *la dérive* (the drift): 'a technique of transient passage through varied ambiances,'[21] a form of performative aesthetisation and a re-writing of space. La dérive had 'psychogeographical effects';[22] it erased ingrained psychophysical maps acquired through repetitive everyday movements performed in prefabricated environments, opening the 'drifters' up to chance, play and inspiration: night visits to 'houses undergoing demolition,' hitchhiking 'through Paris during a transportation strike in the name of adding to the confusion,' or 'wandering in subterranean catacombs forbidden to the public.'[23] Calling forth a renewed attentiveness and visceral empathy with place, the drift disrupted regimes of bodily control that had blunted the human ability to perceive, and that had contributed, through habituation, to the acceptance of invisible subjugation (*La Boétie*). The drift also opposed chronarchy through the creation of festive instants, which though 'minimal in the passing of time,' were nevertheless 'extremely important in terms of their plenitude,'[24] and which, like Callois's illuminated ecstasy, brought back 'the mysterious and the intense.'[25]

The contestation of invisible violence through ludicity, combined with the ability to include, in their ranks, diverse groups of people (students and workers), was the reason for the SI's structural involvement in the uprisings of 1968. Like the above interventions, their socio-politically revolutionary work had an aura of secrecy until they unexpectedly came to widespread attention during the 1966 Strasbourg scandal, which revealed that the SI had used funds of the local section of the student union, UNEF, to print a critical pamphlet. Titled 'On the Poverty of Student Life: Considered in Its Economic, Political, Psychological, Sexual, and Particularly Intellectual Aspects, and a Modest Proposal for Its Remedy,' the pamphlet subjected the university to unflattering scrutiny while offering a Situationist analysis of the productivist-consumerist regime, elaborated by Guy Debord in his 1967 *Society of the Spectacle* and by Raoul Vaneigem in *The Revolution of Everyday Life*.[26] The rest of the events were precipitous: a group of *Enragés* formed at the University of Nanterre in early 1968; on 13 May, after a demonstration attended by one million people, an open Sorbonne was converted into a stage for assembly democracy. In keeping with the SI's oblique tactics, the students and workers involved in the movement refused to take power, which arguably led to a stalemate and a re-election of the Gaullist government in June 1968.

In the aftermath of '68, the insistence on remaining 'outside' the existing power relations and their rule structures led to an expulsion of the spirit of 'gaman' (as illuminated ecstasy and vertical communitas) to the more traditional artistic forms—the novel, the poem and the film—as well as to the work of theory, all of which were seen, as Starr suggests, as a continuation of the 'third way of spreading the revolutionary spirit . . . in different guise.'[27] The idea here was that the revolution would begin not with a *collective* experience of freedom, as had previously been thought, but with a single 'dissident' subject. It was the single 'dissident' subject who would, as Julia Kristeva claimed, 'give voice to the singularity of unconsciousness, desires, needs,' and simultaneously become 'the analyst of the impossibility of social cohesion.'[28] For Kristeva, humans were most at risk of succumbing to *voluntary servitude* when engaging in small-group or collective forms of action, or structured interaction. As Starr rightly notes, the revolutionary impasse—or double bind—and the relegation of freedom to the virtual realm of the individual had the effect of 'displacing the political field' towards particularly 'transgressive forms.'[29] Unsurprisingly, these transgressive (artistic and cultural) forms communicated with a small part of the population, mostly art cognescenti. For example, Roland Barthes's call to arms: 'to write can no longer designate an operation . . . of representing' implied that the unbridled ludicity of the signifier, 'unimpoverished by any constraint of representation,' will model a new, non-instrumentalising consciousness.[30] Jean-François Lyotard opined that linguistic communication as such had become a battlefield where 'opponents' engaged in strategic 'moves' and 'countermoves' to advance their position.[31] In the years that followed, the spirit of militant individual experimentation created a *virtual playing field* demarcated by the artist or cultural worker. Alongside the work of Gina Paine, Orlan, Valie Export, Kiki Smith, Adrian Piper and many others, which foregrounded women's rights, sexism, racism, speciesism and the productivist-consumerist denial of embodied existence,[32] the 1970s and 1980s were characterised by two different tendencies. At one end of the spectrum there was radical abject art, executed by the individual artist—for example, Paul McCarthy's regressive-scatological orgies with urine, blood, ketchup and mayonnaise—wallowing in his own excrement in the 1974 *Shit Face Painting*, or urinating on food and walking on broken glass in the 1975 *Sailor's Meat*. Portrayed by Hal Foster as a regressive art that employs 'infantilism' in a 'paradoxical defense of the already damaged, defeated, or dead,'[33] abject art was a form of public outrage at the steadily growing yet invisible structural violence. At the other end of the spectrum, and increasingly throughout the 1980s and into the 1990s, the spirit of ludic contestation had given way to straightforwardly ameliorative practices like those of the Viennese group WochenKlausur. WochenKlausur have, since the early 1990s, performed interventions into designated communities or spaces. The titles of their works explain the context, leaving nothing to poetic or ludic interpretation, as their 1992 *Intervention to Provide Healthcare to Homeless People*, or the 1995 *Intervention in a School*, and *Intervention in Immigrant Labour Issues*, readily show. For WochenKlausur, political activism and by implication, political change, is aligned with a history of art that has sought to change its surrounding conditions through interaction—not with a group of art cognoscenti, but with the wider population through a transference of artistic skills. Artistic competence in finding creative solutions, traditionally utilised in shaping concepts, materials and environments, is—in the tradition of Joseph Beuys's social sculpture[34]—in WochenKlausur's work, applied to all spheres of society: ecology, health, education, immigration and urban planning. However, the entrenched opposition between radical, transgressive gestures and the 'down to earth,' ameliorative approaches was, on the cusp of globalisation, 'détourned' by capitalist pre-corporation. Facilitated by hyperreality, which, as Jean Baudrillard has argued, has implications of 'too much reality' (everything is on the surface, overexposed), 'para-reality' (reality with an extra layer laid over or in the place of reality), and the simulacric circulation of incestuous signs,[35] pre-corporation superseded in-corporation (or appropriation), considerably diminishing the possibilities of détournement.

LUDICITY AND PRE-CORPORATION

For Fisher, pre-corporation is the 'pre-emptive formatting' of 'desires, aspirations and hopes' in which '[a]lternative' and 'independent' do not refer to 'something outside mainstream consumerism' but are, on the contrary, 'the dominant styles within the mainstream culture.'[36] As the ultimate subsumption of the non-standardised, unusual or simply unpredictable, pre-corporation differs radically from in-corporation, which uses appropriation in such a way as *not* to preclude friction or ambivalence. An example of pre-corporation is the work of photographer Oliviero Toscanini who, in the early 1990s, pioneered the use of radical performance art gestures to create transgressive, and for this reason efficacious advertising strategies for Benetton's thoroughly middle-market, mediocre garments. Examples range from the close-up of three human hearts with the label 'white, yellow, black' to the use of a real, blood-stained uniform of a deceased Croatian soldier during the war in ex-Yugoslavia. McCarthy, too, is an example of pre-corporation. For almost two decades he has systematically used his formerly radical abject art in works such as the 2014 *Chocolate Factory*, a real factory set up at La Monnaie, Paris, producing miniature chocolate (edible) butt-plug-holding Santa Claus figures—a cutified, minaturised (and financially lucrative) reference to his extensive performance and installation variations on excretion, anality and over-consumption.[37] In broader terms, pre-corporation is found in the subsumption of potential negativity—or merely otherness—by positivity and sameness: coffee without caffeine, beer without alcohol, sex without sex (virtual sex), war without warfare (drone warfare).[38] Despite this increasingly claustrophobic semantic universe, artists-activists such as The Yes Men managed to 'detourn' the course of political summits and global legal disputes by placing ludic disruption firmly within hypperreality and pre-corporation, through the creation of fake websites and the impersonation of corporate culprits, commonly referred to as 'identity correction.'

For example, in November 1999, the World Trade Organisation found that their website had been directed to www.gatt.org, where individuals posing as WTO officials enumerated instances of the WTO's abuse of corporate power. The 'impostors' were Jacques Servin and Igor Vamos, the culture-jamming (h)activist duo with the legal status of a corporation, which significantly facilitated simulacric operations, given that, under American law, individuals who own or work for a corporation are not legally personally liable for its 'malfunctions.' When the WTO found out about the fake website, they issued a press release in an attempt to denounce the impostors. However, timing was not on their side. Thirty thousand people were heading to Seattle where an anti-globalisation protest was taking place at the WTO ministerial conference. The increased web traffic resulted in many search engines picking up the fake website, which, in turn, resulted in misdirected conference invitations, intended for the real WTO, but which Servin and Vamos gladly accepted, making landmark appearances in Salzburg, Sydney, Tampere and Philadelphia. In Salzburg, in October 2000, Servin (aka Dr. Bichlbaum) gave a speech on the need to privatise democracy. He explained how easily this could be done: 'by allowing corporations to bid on votes directly—to pay citizens to vote directly for candidates they wanted rather than go through campaign finance mechanisms,'[39] a prescient take on twenty-first-century targeted candidate profiling. At a Wharton Business School conference on business in Africa, held in Philadelphia in November 2006, Hanniford Schmidt (aka Servin) announced the WTO initiative for full private stewardry of labour. Pointing out how privatisation had been successfully applied to transport, energy, water, even to the human genome, the WTO proposed to 'extend these successes to the (re)privatisation of "humans themselves."'[40] Although the programme of full untrammelled stewardry was similar to slavery, Schmidt explained that 'just as "compassionate conservatism" had polished the rough edges on labor relations in industrialized countries, full stewardry, or "compassionate slavery", could be a similar boon to developing ones.'[41] For The Yes Men, the purpose of such ludic interventionist work is to disrupt 'flows of capital and power':[42] and effectuate real-world change. Their 2007 impersonation of Dow Chemical executives is perhaps the most notable of such real-world effects. In a CNN appearance, The Yes Men promised significant financial compensation to all those who had suffered irreparable damage in the Bhopal gas leak tragedy, which occurred in 1984 at the pesticide plant in Bhopal, Madya Pradesh, India. The fateful leak exposed more than 500,000 people to methyl isocyanate, a highly toxic substance causing death and/or permanent injury, but for which Dow Chemical had not taken responsibility. The media hype that issued from The Yes Men's CNN appearance, the thousands of emails and phone calls addressed to Dow Chemical, did make the company take financial responsibility, albeit belatedly. A similar style of détournement can be found in the work of the glitch artists-activists, who use programming, data and circuit bending to subvert proprietary software production. Significant in this respect is also the 'obfuscation movement,' which camouflages data from corporations and the government, through programmes and plugins. For Helen Nissenbaum and Finn Brunton, authors of *Obfuscation: A User's Guide for Privacy and Protest*, and co-designers (with Vincent Toubiana) of the browser extension TrackMeNot (which sends randomly generated queries to search engines overwhelming them with huge amounts of information, creating in this way a productive confusion between sender and receiver, intended and accidental): '[c]amouflage, whether seeking the complete invisibility of mimicry or the temporary solution of hiding a shape in a mess of other, ambiguous, obfuscating possible shapes, was always a reflection of the capabilities of the technology against which it was developed.'[43]

Yet although the jouissance of subversion is clearly present in The Yes Men's simulacric détournements, the obfuscation movement has more in common with the frantic efforts of prey to escape its predator than it does with jouissance. Both the SI's and the post-'68 'dissident' individualist's notion of freedom may have been utopistic, in both conceptual terms and performative dimensions. However, we cannot help but wonder what concept of freedom such initiatives as the obfuscation movement operate with—freedom from tracking, surveillance (or dataveillance), harassment and denigration? Which, as is plain to see, inscribes the freedom to play, communicate, engage in convivial social relations (on one's own terms) within the diffuse and invisible corporate, governmental or generally capitalist violence. In the last two decades, with the (digitally accelerated) spread of pre-corporation in many spheres of life, it is not an exaggeration to say that much of what was formerly expressive of freedom has come to be exploited through pre-corporation. Pre-corporation is, of course, inscribed in a long history of appropriation and amassment of signs, goods and territories, a strategy of self-insertion into the social sphere that began with the bourgeoisie, continued with the industrial entrepreneurs (and the myth of the 'self-made man'), and was further perfected by the early twentieth-century magnates, the late-twentieth-century financial engineers and yuppies, and the twenty-first-century netocrats—masters of the digital networks.[44]

Much like Callois claims that the ludic spirit is intrinsic to human beings, for Han, the 'human being is a creature of luxury.'[45] However, Han's notion of luxury has nothing to do with consumption; it is a mode of living that is free of necessity. In fact, luxury is, in Han's interpretation, luxuriance—the freedom to luxuriate in time, and in aesthetically pleasing, non-teleological, so-called useless activities.[46] In order to separate the concept of luxury from compulsive consumption, Han compares it to asceticism. He also compares play to idiocy. Commenting on the present-day invisible structural violence, which consists of permissive strictures, information overload and the never-ending tyranny of participation, among other elements, Han suggests that 'the idiot,' by nature, is 'un-networked and uninformed. The idiot inhabits the immemorial outside, which escapes communication and networking altogether, spinning about like a plucked rose in the whirling river of single-minded people.'[47] Etymologically, idiocy refers both to a specific mixture of bodily humours and to a person's particular perception of the world based on this mixture of humours.[48] While intelligence signifies choices confined to the already-existing system (inter-legere means to 'read between'), idiocy is willful and obstinate. But what does the placement of luxury and play in the field of asceticism and idiocy—which suggests abandoning ties to things and people, willful or not—mean for the concept of freedom? Can Han's asceticism and idiocy be seen as a détournement of the 'détourned' notions of the 'freedom from' and 'freedom to,' which, in historical and political terms, are very different from the above-mentioned evasion of predatory dataveillance practices and machinic subjugation[49] as contemporary examples of invisible violence?

LUDICITY AS A LIBERTARIAN PROSTHESIS

Originally stemming from the tradition of Thomas Hobbes, Jeremy Bentham and Isaiah Berlin, freedom from—or negative freedom—advocates the removal of obstacles and the throwing off of restraints. To be free is to have choices, and to have choices is to feel empowered. The freedom to, on the other hand—or positive freedom—which stems from the tradition of T. H. Green and Erich Fromm, foregrounds the preexisting conditions, rules and actors. Given that we are born into a world *not* of our own choosing, what matters is not whether we *feel* free, but whether the social conditions of our existence allow us to be free. For the proponents of positive freedom, human beings are neither 'naturally' free nor are they sufficiently rational to do what is right of their own accord. Instead, they need to be shown the path to freedom—a training ground where responsibilities are exercised, not a utopian paradise where one does as one pleases, regardless of consequences. Pointing to the dialectical relation between the two kinds of freedom, more recent commentators, such as Maria Dimova-Cookson, have queried the polarity of the configuration. Given that positive freedom is rooted in self-disinterest, and a consideration for the 'moral good' of others (because it acknowledges the positions of all actors), and that negative freedom is rooted in self-interest and the 'ordinary good of the agent' (because it is based on the so-called rational agent's pursuit of self-interest as the best way of regulating society's interests), '[o]ne's moral good translates as another's ordinary good. Referring to the (dated) dichotomy of the "lower" and "higher" self—as concerned with corporeal needs and psychological wellbeing, respectively—the "moral" action of the agent will result in the ordinary "good" of the recipient.'[50] The obvious problem, however, is that the reverse is not true: the self-interest of the agent does not translate into the recipient's good because there is no (immediate) recipient, even if, at a more abstract level, the self-organisation of particular agents may result in the self-organisation of society. Alongside new digital prostheses, the digital revolution—and in particular, the advent of mobile computing—has 'détourned' play. In the decades following the initial hope (still in evidence in the mid-1990s) that the internet and, more generally, the digital, will be the space of freedom from real-world oppression, ludicity has become a *libertarian prosthesis*: a stand-in for positive freedom in the corporeal, emotional and social sense of the word. At first glance, we may not think that there is anything wrong with supplementing negative freedom with a stand-in for positive freedom if the end-result is enjoyment, spontaneity, effervescence and insouciance—emotions usually associated with play. After all, the digital media are communicational prostheses that bring the far and the plural into the near and the singular. The same could be said of digitally mediated play. No longer confined to a single magic circle, which, according to Huizinga, is a spatio-temporal frame segregated from the rest of life by a set of ludic rules,[51] digitally mediated play permeates all spheres of daily life, both in the form of fixed structures—games and gamified labour, and looser performative constructs—such as the stalking service provided by Spy Games where customers pay to be stalked. On closer inspection, however, much of digitally mediated play appears to be a disciplinary mechanism that leads to ludic servitude via the detour of excess performance. Not only does such play not offer a much-needed respite from the goal-driven technocratics of economic Darwinism, instead, it provides a polygon for this very system in psychophysical and interactional terms.

Already in Foucault, discipline is a subtle form of power concerned with the subject's productive capacities. It works the body at a mechanistic level in order to control its movements, gestures, attitudes and moods. A disciplined body is a body trained for the production of specific corporeal operations; it is docile, not because it is passive, but because its life energies have been channelled in such a way as to increase economic utility and decrease non-regulated assignments of energy. The carefully constructed disciplinary rituals of observation, examination, isolation and subjection operate in the disciplinary institutions analysed by Foucault to instigate and monitor performance.[52] In networked digital society, performance is a multifaceted matrix comprising socioeconomic efficacy, techno-organisational efficiency and excess. For Jon McKenzie, new subjects of knowledge are produced through oppressive-excessive performance; they are constructed as 'fragmented,' 'decentered' through 'performative objects, themselves produced through a variety of sociotechnical systems, overcoded by many discourses, and situated in numerous sites of practice.'[53] Already in Herbert Marcuse, the 'performance principle' is an obliquely yet highly disciplinarian strategy, albeit different from Foucault's; it is a stratifying social force that divides society according to the competitive economic performance of its members who perform pre-established functions.[54] The acceptance of these preestablished functions comes from alienation—from Marcuse's reading of Marx through Sigmund Freud, and his theory of repression. The result is that alienated individuals not only tolerate performative alienation, they even take pleasure in it. Affect, pleasure and desire are displaced to the realm of market-related performance accompanied by the 'heroic' quest to attain preestablished goals, corresponding to the performative grid organised according to the principle of maximum productivity. However, the performance principle is also the ability to invest such skills profitably, not only on the labour market but also on the libidinal market, and this is what generates enjoyment. Already in the last decade of the twentieth century, 'the performative subject is constructed as fragmented rather than unified, as decentered rather than centered, as virtual as well as actual'; performative desire is not a repressive desire; it is instead 'excessive,' intermittently modulated and pushed across the thresholds of various limits by overlapping and sometimes competing systems.'[55] While repression was a negative relation of the subject to itself, it was related to the Other. Excess, by contrast, is an over-positive relation of the subject to itself and its environment. As if in response to McKenzie, game designer and theorist Jane McGonigal proposes that reality is broken, fragmented, dispersed and disordered. Amidst this deeply dissatisfying chaos, as McGonigal portrays it, games are the new order.[56] Partaking of the logic of the once corporate, but now ubiquitous performance reviews and evaluations, which rank individuals, services, gadgets and organisations according to the logic of efficiency, quantifiability and predictability, games are the link between two seemingly opposed poles: excessive performance and discipline. This is due to two factors: the advent of the experience economy, and the colonisation of reality by the gamespace. As B. Joseph Pine and James H. Gilmore argue, the experience economy 'ings the thing,' or 'experientializes the goods.'[57] By experientialising a service, or a gadget, and engaging the prospective buyer in multisensorial interaction, a fictitious world consisting of entertainment, aesthetics, escapism and learning is created.[58] 'Inging the thing' thus introduces a multifaceted performance principle into services, people and situations, eliciting a very particular form of engagement and creating bio-social and emotional bonds through interaction. The gamespace, as Kenneth McKenzie Wark contends, is not only 'colonised reality,' it is also 'the sole remaining ideal' because it provides a 'level playing field upon which all men [sic] are equal.'[59]

In other words, amidst the reign of (the neoliberal brand of) negative freedom, games alone hold forth the promise of fairness and redistribution. The only problem, as Richard Giulianotti has argued in relation to sport, is that they further reinforce the very same values: goal-orientated action, the pairing of achieved results with success, and of success with virtue.[60] This is even more problematic in the sphere of digital games, which are already based on the principle of extreme engagement, and, in addition to goal and rule architectures, have a very tight feedback system. They go much further in harnessing the McKenzian excess of performance: the joy, the effervescence and euphoria. Their bounded nature implies that the rest of reality is unbounded—an unchartered, non-rule-striated territory where one does as one pleases. Temporary participation in a bounded universe thus *reinstates* the appeal of negative freedom. The finite, rule-governed universe of the game resembles positive freedom but retains one important difference: the player is free to leave whenever s/he likes, which, too, reinforces the notion of negative freedom. Positive freedom is thus equated with the ludic universe: by entering the game the player is reassured that the game is stable, that the rules are clear and that the meta rule of most (if not all) games—fair play—is firmly in place. This is particularly important in the current neoliberal absence of a clearly delineated symbolic order—which was formerly god, humanity or the state—against whose firm and sublational rules a particular action was good or bad, beneficial or harmful.

Within the microcosmos of a game, goals are attention-chanelling dramaturgical devices that focus the players' attention and continually direct their participation, providing them with a clear (and minutely textured) sense of purpose. In Blizzard's *World of Warcraft* (WoW),[61] for example, the primary goal is self-improvement, a ludological echo of Max Weber's—and Guilianotti's—Protestant-capitalist paradigm, in which the work ethic is equated with virtue, and virtue with the amassment of (actual or virtual) attributes.[62] Players go on quests in order to make their avatar better and stronger in as many ways as possible, acquiring more experience, more abilities, stronger armour and a greater reputation. Game rules further create micro-dramaturgies within the striated field of attention. They mobilise the different species of time—physical time, psychological time (the highly flexible time shaped by expectations), thick time (characteristic of immersive environments) and vertical, trance-like time, characteristic of rituals and digital pursuits. They also provide an existential amplification—a heightened sense of existence—found in in all forms of performance. But this heightened sense of being is not a free-floating surplus. It is viscerally linked to a hierarchical value grid given that the WoW player's quests, such as exploring the landscape, fighting monsters and gathering resources, if successfully performed, allow the player to gain access to new abilities. The psychophysical conditioning that occurs in the game thus affirms the 'efficiency, quantifiability, predictability' paradigm; progress is equated with the most achievement within the given time unit and with clearly quantified levels.

One of the main ideas behind the expanding field of alternate reality (AR) games, which are pervasive and durational, and which, unlike WoW, do not take place in a fictional world but are anchored in a real-life activity—which also commodifies or 'ings the thing'—is that they re-introduce the lost Gramscian link with work as a corporeal-social nexus. For Antonio Gramsci, praxis is a permanent flux of mutual configuration of subject, object and environment, one which makes human beings simultaneously 'a process,' and the result 'of [their] own activities.'[63] It is this inherently fulfilling process, undermined by the managerial politics of the McKenzian 'perform or else' type, that AR games and apps seek to reclaim. For example, Nike+ is designed as a motivational tool for running. Apart from the obvious health advantages, running is a meditation in movement, the key component being the will to run, regardless of the climatic or body weather.[64] Nike+ takes the motivational struggle out of the runner's hands and places it in the hands of the prosthesis incarnated in the 'little running partner' which appears on your mobile phone and which most people customise to look just like them. If you miss a few days, the little running partner starts sulking, or even throwing tantrums. This is, of course, humorous, but it has another dimension: the transference of the little self—the ego and the id—to the realm of an unquestioningly accepted order under the pretext that such things are not meant to be taken seriously. It decouples the corporeal process of progressing from lassitude to determination from intrinsic rewards and externalises as well as iconises this process. But one is amply rewarded in return. Based on the data the Nike+ sensor collects, the runner earns personal online trophies for best times and longest runs, even a congratulatory message from Ussein Bolt. One can also invest this excess of performance in social capital by immediately advertising one's achievements on Facebook and Twitter and, in this way, turning instant gratification into instant gain. What Nike+ effectively does is overwrite the previously individually shaped corporeal-emotional-social landscape with a goal-rule-feeback grid which turns the act of running into a standardised and quantifiable activity, not to mention the infantilisingly tight feedback loop, which nurtures the diffident individual, in constant need of attention and approval. Despite the fact that such an activity is as far removed as can be from the Gramscian work-life nexus, it sets the activity of running to a liberatory score by adding pseudo-Marxist and Gramscian overtones to the Weberian paradigm: you, the worker, here reap the fruit of your labour, while utilising your own means of production, all embodied in the tiny icon, which is—you: ego, id, superego; visibly self-improving all the time.

Similar inspirational and instigational AR games exist in the field of cooking, recovering from a cold, going through airport security and aging. But perhaps the most interesting, as well as potentially the most disturbing, is the Quest to Learn, an experimental response to the current predicament of attention deficit in children. Non-adrenalised activities, such as school, are so boring that children used to the 'engaged life' cannot bear it.[65] The reform implemented at the Quest to Learn in New York City is therefore entirely game-based, which does of course have many positive features; however, every course, every activity, every assignment, every moment of instruction utilises the participation strategies borrowed from the most addictive multi-player games. Assignments are quests which combine physical and digital locations with a series of clearly defined goals, full of levelling-up activities, which makes it possible for the pupil to earn points for making the minutest progress. The problem here is not only that the entire learning process is overwritten and placed in a standardised, quantified grid which links neuronal circuits to response mechanisms, the way the old overt disciplinary systems (the school, the army, the prison) did—only this time in adrenaline-stimulating, rather than pain-inflicting ways. Far more worrying is the linking of technological and organisational challenging to ludological impulses and the sphere of disinterested play,[66] as this destroys the minutest possibility of what Heidegger has called '*Gelassenheit*'—an aesthetic-ethical form of letting be formerly found in art and play.[67] The question here is not: How many uncolonised sites of existential amplification, which link neuronal, cardio-vascular, respiratory and kinaesthetic activity and the excess of performance to prosthetic libertarianism, are there? According to McKenzie Wark, there are none: '[h]istory, politics, culture—gamespace dynamites everything which is not in the game. . . . Everything is evacuated from an empty space and time which now appears natural, neutral. . . . The lines are clearly marked. Every action is just a means to an end. All that counts is the score.'[68]

Objective Logistics have created a gamified system for motivating workers in the catering industry. The waiters' performance, based on speed, dexterity, tip revenue and customer satisfaction is continually monitored. Individual results are displayed in staff-only parts of the restaurant, such as the kitchen. Based on Mihaly Csikszentmihaly's theory of intrinsic motivation,[69] the developers claim that continuous feedback improves performance and promotes greater concentration in staff. As 'the process of total merging of cultural values with the methods, metaphors and attributes of games,'[70] gamification and playbour (ludified labour) shape behaviour with the aid of feedback, nudging and status. New, increasingly difficult content with rewards is repeatedly introduced (nudging), so that participants will want to tackle new tasks in order to be recognised as the strongest of all (status). However, while the autonomy granted to the player is linked to agency and decision-making, all gamification by necessity utilises persuasive design.[71] Persuasive design, combined with the grinding dynamics,[72] translates into bio-political libertarian paternalism. According to Richard H. Thaler and Cass R. Sunstein, libertarian paternalism sets out to openly 'influence the choices of affected parties in a way that will make those parties better off';[73] however, such choice paths invariably benefit the producers of these very choice paths. AR games, ludic apps and playbour overwrite entire segments of daily life with the neoliberal goals-rules-feedback grid. It is highly ironic that positive freedom was initially defined by Berlin as 'patronising' and 'bullying,'[74] because it depicted the social world as a non-level playing field with very few possible moves and because it openly sought to guide. AR games, ludic apps and playbour 'negativise' positive freedom. In reinstating the absolute dominance of *feeling* over *being* free, they obliterate the difference. Ludic servitude would, indeed, be that state in which all 'bullying' is turned into (a feeling of) freedom via the detour of extreme engagement, existential amplification, excess performance and spieltrieb, seen *not* as ethical urgency but, rather, as compulsion. In this sense, ludic servitude also represents a crystallisation of a historical trajectory, from (the possibility of) open opposition, subversion through re-appropriation, détournement, or obfuscation, to ludified internalised oppression, which mirrors the 'closure' of what Shoshana Zuboff has called the 'instrumentarianism' of communicational networks,[75] reinforced by machinic operations that make generalisations as well as predictions on the basis of limited data, thus acting as a 'determinist trap' where what is possible necessarily becomes what is probable.[76]

NOTES

1. Estienne de la Boétie, *Discourse on Voluntary Servitude*, trans. J. B. Atkinson and David Sices (Indianapolis: Hackett Publishing Company, 2012 [1576]).
2. Michel Foucault, *Discipline and Punish: The Birth of the Prison*, trans. Alan Sheridan (Harmondsworth: Penguin, 1979).
3. Peter Starr, *Logics of Failed Revolt: French Theory after '68* (Stanford: Stanford University Press, 1995), 114.
4. Mark Fisher, *Capitalist Realism: Is There No Alternative?* (Winchester: O Books, 2009).
5. Bernard Faure, *The Rhetoric of Immediacy* (Princeton: Princeton University Press, 1991), 33.
6. Walter Benjamin, 'Theses on the Philosophy of History,' in *Illuminations*, trans. Harry Zorn (New York: Shocken, 1999), 263.
7. Johan Galtung, 'Violence, Peace and Peace Research,' *Journal of Peace Research* (1969): 173.
8. Andreas Huyssen, cited in Mike Sell, *Avant-Garde and the Limits of Criticism* (Ann Arbor: University of Michigan Press, 2008), 178.
9. Johan Huizinga, *Homo Ludens: A Study of the Play-Element in Culture* (Boston: Routledge and Kegan Paul, 1955), 1–2.
10. Roger Caillois, 'Les Jeunes gens de Reims,' *Europe*, no. 782 (1994): 121.
11. Anatoly Liberman, *An Analytic Dictionary of English Etymology: An Introduction* (Minneapolis: University of Minnesota Press, 2008), 15.
12. Victor Turner, cited in Richard Schechner, *Performance Theory* (London and New York: Routledge, 1978), 113.
13. Byung-Chul Han, *Psychopolitics: Neoliberalism and New Technologies of Power*, trans. Erik Butler (London and New York: Verso, 2017), 2–3.
14. Giorgio Agamben, *Profanations*, trans. Jeff Fort (New York: Zone Books, 2007), 75.
15. Agamben, *Profanations*, 75.

16. Asger Jorn cited in Anon. in Ken Knabb, *Situationist International Anthology*, trans. Ken Knabb (Berkeley, CA: The Bureau of Public Secrets), 55.

17. Friedrich Schiller, *On the Aesthetic Education of Man*, ed. and trans. Elizabeth M. Wilkinson and L. A. Willoughby (Oxford: Oxford University Press 1987), 25.

18. Anonymous, cited in Tom McDonough, *Guy Debord and the Situationists International* (Cambridge, MA, and London: MIT Press, 2009), 69.

19. Anonymous, cited in McDonough, *Guy Debord and the Situationists International*, 70.

20. Anonymous, cited in McDonough, *Guy Debord and the Situationists International*, n.p.

21. Guy Debord, 'Theory of the Dérive,' in *Situationist International Anthology*, ed. and trans. Ken Knabb (Berkeley, CA: The Bureau of Public Secrets, 1981), 50.

22. Debord, 'Theory of the Dérive,' 50.

23. Debord, 'Theory of the Dérive,' 53.

24. Henri Lefevbre, *Critique of Everyday Life I*, trans. John Moore (London: Verso, 1991), 118.

25. Lefevbre, *Critique of Everyday Life*, 118.

26. The original title of which was *Traité de savoir-vivre à l'usage des jeunes generations*.

27. Starr, *Logics of Failed Revolt: French Theory after '68*, 115.

28. Kristeva cited in Starr, *Logics of Failed Revolt: French Theory after '68*, 163.

29. Starr, *Logics of Failed Revolt: French Theory after '68*, 114.

30. Barthes cited in Starr, *Logics of Failed Revolt: French Theory after '68*, 121.

31. Jean-François Lyotard, *The Postmodern Condition: A Report on Knowledge*, trans. Geoff Bennington and Brian Massumi (Minneapolis: University of Minnesota Press, 1984), 17.

32. For more information, see Natasha Lushetich, *Interdisciplinary Performance Reformatting Reality* (Basingstoke and New York: Palgrave, 2016).

33. Hal Foster, *The Return of the Real* (Cambridge, MA: MIT Press, 1996), 124.

34. See Lushetich, *Interdisciplinary Performance Reformatting Reality*, 2016.

35. Jean Baudrillard, *Simulacra and Simulation*, trans. Sheila Faria Glaser (Ann Arbor: University of Michigan Press, 1994), 3.

36. Fisher, *Capitalist Realism*, 9, emphasis in the original.

37. For more information on Paul McCarthy's work, see Natasha Lushetich, 'A Santa with a Butt Plug: Paul McCarthy and the Obliterating Violence of Positivity,' *Body, Space and Technology* 19, no. 1 (2020): 203–23, DOI: http://doi.org/10.16995/bst.340.

38. Slavoj Žižek, *La Subjectivité à Venir* (Editions Climats: Castelnau-leNez, 2004).

39. Bilchbaum, cited in William Smith, 'Corporate Aesthetics: The Yes Men Revolt,' *Art in America*, 22 April 2014, http://www.artinamericamagazine.com/news-features/interviews/corporate-aesthetics-the-yes-men-revolt/.

40. The Yes Men, 'WTO Proposes Slavery for Africa,' 2006, http://theyesmen.org/hijinks/wharton, n.p.

41. The Yes Men, 'WTO Proposes Slavery for Africa.'

42. Servin and Vamos, cited in Nato Thompson and Gregory Scholette, *The Interventionists: User's Manual for the Creative Disruption of Everyday Life* (Cambridge, MA, and London: MIT Press, 2006), 106.

43. Finn Brunton and Helen Nissenbaum, *Obfuscation: A User's Guide for Privacy and Protest* (Cambridge, MA: MIT Press, 2015), 46–48.

44. Alexander Bard and Jan Söderqvist, *Netocracy* (Harlow: Pearson Education Ltd., 2002).

45. Han, *Psychopolitics*, 52.

46. Han, *Psychopolitics*, 53.

47. Han, *Psychopolitics*, 83.

48. Han, *Psychopolitics*, 82.

49. Maurizio Lazarrato, *Signs and Machines: Capitalism and the Production of Subjectivity*, trans. J. D. Jordan (Cambridge, MA: MIT Press, 2014).

50. Maria Dimova-Cookson, 'A New Scheme of Positive and Negative Freedom: Reconstructing T. H. Green on Freedom,' *Political Theory* 31, no. 4 (2003): 516.

51. Huizinga, *Homo Ludens*, 6.

52. Foucault, *Discipline and Punish*, 1979.

53. Jon Mckenzie, *Perform or Else: From Discipline to Performance* (London: Routledge, 2001), 18.

54. Herbert Marcuse, *Eros and Civilization: A Philosophical Inquiry into Freud* (New York: Routledge, 1987).

55. McKenzie, *Perform or Else*, 18–19.

56. Jane McGonigal, *Reality Is Broken: Why Games Make us Better and How They Can Change the World* (New York: Penguin Press, 2011).

57. B. Joseph Pine II and James H. Gilmore, *The Experience Economy: Work I Theatre and Every Business Is a Stage* (Boston: Harvard Business School Press, 1999), 23–24.

58. Pine and Gilmore, *The Experience Economy*, 35–37.

59. Ken McKenzie Wark, *Gamer Theory* (New York: Institute for the Future of the Book, 2007), n.p.

60. Richard Giulianotti, *A Critical Sociology* (Cambridge: Polity Press, 2005), 4.

61. See https://worldofwarcraft.com; other examples would be *Dragon Age* (BioWare, 2009–2015) or numerous *Star Wars* games, such as *Star Wars: Knights of the Old Republic* (BioWare, Obsidian Entertainment 2003–), among many more.

62. Max Weber, *The Protestant Ethic and the Spirit of Capitalism*, trans. Stephen Kalberg (Oxford: Oxford University Press, 2010).

63. Antonio Gramsci, *The Open Marxism of Antonio Gramsci*, trans. Carl Marzani (New York: Cameron Associates, Inc., 1957), 45.

64. Body weather is a phrase used in butoh training. Butoh is a Japanese dance form. For more information see https://www.astarti-athanasiadou.com/body-weather.

65. Marc Prensky, *Teaching Digital Natives: Partnering for Real Learning* (New York: Corwin, 2010).

66. For Huizinga, play is essentially freedom from restraint and/or preexisting plan, Huzinga, *Homo Ludens*, 197–98.

'Gelassenheit' is usually translated as 'realeasement,' 'letting go' or 'letting be.' Se67. e Martin Heidegger, *Country Path Conversations* (Bloomington: Indiana University Press).

68. McKenzie Wark, *Gamer Theory*, n.p.

69. Mihalyi Csikszentmihalyi, *Beyond Boredom and Anxiety: Experiencing Flow in Work and Play* (San Francisco, CA: Jossey-Bass, 2000).

70. Fuchs Mathias, 'Predigital Precursors of Gamification,' in *Rethinking Gamification*, ed. Mathias Fuchs et al. (Lüneburg: Meson Press, 2014), 119–20.

71. B. J. Fogg, *Persuasive Technology: Using Computers to Change What We Think and Do* (Amsterdam: Morgan Kaufmann Publishers, 2003). For more information on persuasive design, see also Iain Bogost, *Persuasive Games: The Expressive Power of Video Games* (Cambridge: MIT Press, 2010).

72. Scott Nicholson, 'Exploring the Endgame of Gamification,' in *Rethinking Gamification*, 289–303.

73. Richard H. Thaler and Cass R. Sunstein, 'Libertarian Paternalism,' *The American Economic Review* 93, no. 2 (2003): 175.

74. Isaiah Berlin, *Four Essays on Liberty* (Oxford: Oxford University Press, 1969), lviii.

75. In *The Age of Surveillance Capitalism* Shoshana Zuboff argues that the totalising system of dataveillance, produced by the contemporary mode of data extraction, turns human beings into raw material for capital accumulation, while also turning knowledge of present behaviour into an authoritarian project for total certitude. See Shoshana Zuboff, *The Age of Surveillance Capitalism: The Fight for a Human Future at the New Frontier of Power* (London: Profile Books, 2019).

76. Franco 'Bifo' Berardi, 'Simulated Replicants Forever: Big Data, Engendered Determinism, and the End of Prophecy' in *Big Data: A New Medium?*, ed. Natasha Lushetich (New York: Routledge, 2020), 32–45.

Chapter Six

Contrasting Legacies of '68
Deleuze and Human Rights
Christos Marneros

More than fifty years after the events of 1968, their legacy remains a matter of multiple debates.[1] During the events of 1968, a multiplicity of heterogeneous groups of people from all around the globe (from students to workers, intellectuals, leftists of any kind to anarchists and so forth)[2] imagined a different world—a world that, however, was not to be the outcome or endpoint of the particular programme of a political party, but rather a celebration of insurrectionary spontaneity and heterogeneity. More than half a century later, we witness not only their failure to actualise radical change but we are also at a point where the triumph of the conservative, right-wing forces of reaction—'the (Neo)Liberal forces of counter-revolution,'[3] as pertinently called by Gilles Châtelet—seems to be the unquestionable outcome of the events of '68.

Indeed, the neoliberal, nihilistic politics of the capitalist market not only dominate and capture every aspect of life, but they have also become a part of our very own fabric and our modes of being and thinking—forming a powerful 'consensus'[4] that suggests *there is no alternative*, making even the speculation of living and thinking *otherwise* an impossibility. Are, then, the recent fifty-year commemorations of May '68 a depressing or pessimistic practice that on the one hand, celebrates the total victory of counterrevolutionaries and on the other, serves to remind revolutionaries that they are the 'romantic remnants' of an older era? The short answer is 'no.' Alain Badiou is right to counter this pessimistic view of the event of '68 with the existence of a radically optimistic potentiality.[5] Irrespective of the outcome, the optimism of '68 lies in the events' demonstration that another world is possible. The commemoration of the events is therefore the celebration of 'a fundamental sense of possibility,'[6] a possibility never exhausted in the actualisation of a certain state of affairs. It is in this sense that we can refer to May '68 as a peculiar *double bind*. The double bind lies in the fact that we understand the events of '68 as something which led to *contrasting legacies* (pessimistic and optimistic) with one negating the other. While the pessimistic outcome of May with the triumph of the forces of reaction seems to prevail, this does not and *should not* negate May's insurrectionary potentiality.

In this chapter, I examine this phenomenon of the double bind by discussing the two contrasting legacies of May '68 through the lens of Gilles Deleuze's ferocious, albeit brief, critique of human rights. As I argue, human rights—as a mode of being, thinking and doing politics—are a fundamental manifestation of the pessimistic outcome of the events of '68, because they form a new sort of transcendent morality, a 'secular theology'[7] that thinks in terms of foundational principles that are distinctively dogmatic.[8] This human-rights mode of being 'blocks' every form of creative resistance, presenting itself as a universal, all-inclusive discourse. To that extent, this mode of being manages to form a consensus regarding rights' supposedly emancipatory promise. Human rights are not only unable to protect against the state's brutality (with the state being broadly understood here) but they further strengthen the view that there is no alternative to the neoliberal politics of the market. Deleuze, in contrast to many human rights critics, even the harshest of them, does not aim to 'salvage' any emancipatory promise of rights' discourse that was supposedly 'hijacked' by neoliberal narratives.[9] Instead, he dismisses human rights as a philosophico-politically decadent (and as such dangerous) mode of being. To that extent, Deleuze's powerful critique of rights exposes their pseudo-benevolent stature and questions their so-called foundational moral(ising) values. At the same time, and more importantly, his critique points towards an alternative mode of being and thinking, an *ethos* which is distinctively immanent and thus non-dogmatic. Such an *ethos*, as I argue, belongs to the very heart of the optimism of '68 and its radical potential for a new politics.

HUMAN RIGHTS AS A PATHOLOGICAL ATTACHMENT

Recent historiographies of human rights have shifted their emphasis from human rights as a mere development and re-introduction of the nineteenth century's 'natural' rights, onto human rights and their 'breakthrough' as a product of the 1970s.[10] This view is well justified by several largely interconnected events. First, both citizens and, in particular, activist groups in the East and the West were exhausted by the polarisation between Western liberal democracies and the Soviet bloc. As such, they started seeking alternative ways of governing (or nongoverning). Second, the events of the Prague Spring and the Soviet invasion of Czechoslovakia led many Eastern dissidents to oppose their regimes and to demand more political rights in the East, while Western leftists started to become disillusioned with the Soviet model.[11] Third, the events of 1968, as mentioned earlier, did not lead to a radical change and, thus, many participants in the events felt that a radical change was not going to happen in the political or social sphere but rather in the form of 'a new global morality.'[12] Thus, all of the above left a vacuum, which human rights seemed ideally poised to fill. Human rights also played to a sense of hope for a more 'rational,' 'mature' world, in the name of a new universal morality that would act as 'a measure for action' for all times to come.[13] This is not surprising if we pay attention to one of the fundamental ways that human rights are presented by their supporters in a post-ideological or *a*political manner,[14] that is their promise to defend and protect every human being against all sorts of barbarism, simply by virtue of his or her humanity (whatever the notion of 'humanity' entails). In that sense, human rights are often seen as 'a common ground' or a form of 'common language' shared by the totality of humanity.

For example, within the French milieu and in the aftermath of the French May, this homogenising language of human rights flourished with the emergence of a new movement of self-proclaimed intellectuals, that of the 'New Philosophers' [*Nouveaux Philosophes*].[15] While the individual members of this group cannot be defined by a shared characteristic that identifies them as belonging to a particular school of thought, or as having clear-cut ideological sympathies, they were united in their criticism of the leftist and anarchist tendencies that informed the movements of 1968.[16] As Châtelet humorously notes, their shared 'slogan' can be summed up as 'Marx Is Dead.'[17] A prominent member of the New Philosophers, Bernard-Henri Lévy, revisiting the origins of the group, sums up their purposes as follows:

> The New Philosophy . . . dismissed any idea of a final solution to misery, disorder, or the tragedy of mankind. It thought it was better to agree on Evil than on Good, and that once we've agreed on what is Evil, we can figure out how to lessen it. And it was the choice of a politics that, in place of the ancient concern to shape the world according to a moral ideal, thought we should make the world a bit more livable for the greatest number of people, and that we would not, therefore, make concessions on the little things: life, rights here and now, human rights; and a politics, above all, that would no longer slip into the easy rhetoric of the radicals or what was called, back in the days of Stalinism, the 'politics of the worst.'[18]

This decision on what constitutes Evil is the crucial point that shapes human rights' *modus operandi*. Here, the New Philosophers suggest that humanity needs to be united under a common language or, rather, against a common enemy—Evil. The immediate effect of this mission, that the New Philosophers call 'politics,' is in effect a total depoliticisation of politics in the name of a common, and rather abstract morality, namely human rights. As Badiou explains, this mode of thinking suggests that 'good is what intervenes visibly against an Evil that is identifiable *a priori*' and, as a consequence, 'law [*droit*] itself is first of all law "against" Evil.'[19] As such, a 'human rights culture'[20] is formed where law and rights become the common language that we speak, as so-called civilised beings, against Evil and barbarism.

The effectiveness of the universalist language of rights was soon to become evident. In the 1990s we witness, perhaps for the first time, the justification of massacres under the banner of 'humanitarian interventions.' This inauguration of 'human rights wars,' so called by Paul Virilio, was endorsed by many, including so-called progressives and intellectuals, as a just cause against Evil.[21] Thus, human rights language started to be directly utilised as part of neoliberal and neo-imperial policies, with unprecedented success. Unsurprisingly, these events led many to start becoming critical of human rights and of the ways rights' language was being utilised by neoliberals and neo-imperialists.[22] Ironically, however, it is these critical approaches that help us to understand how rights have come to be seen as the foundation of morality. This is because, and despite their many differences and approaches, the vast majority of these critics, from the most moderate to the most radical ones, refuse to let go or even think about the possibility of moving *beyond human rights as such*.

For example, one strand of radical critique of human rights coming from critical legal theorists such as Costas Douzinas is not ready to move beyond human rights thinking, insisting instead on the idea of (re)appropriating the emancipatory potential of rights. Douzinas's critique of the dominant understanding of human rights is, indeed, in many respects a powerful one. Especially so when he critiques the ways that human rights contributed to the expansion and justification of neo-imperial and neoliberal programmes and the further marginalisation of underprivileged groups of people. Nevertheless, his critique does not go 'all the way' by thinking a possible alternative to a human-rights framework. Douzinas identifies the problem with human rights as the fact that their language was 'hijacked' by the elites: 'Official thinking and action on human rights has been entrusted in the hands of triumphalist column writers, bored diplomats and rich international lawyers in New York and Geneva, people whose experience of human rights violations is confined to being served a bad bottle of wine.'[23]

His response to this problem is a call for an effort to try to restore the radical potential of rights. Douzinas's trust in an emancipatory potential of human rights, based on radical politics, manifests a certain element of belief in the potentiality of human rights to emancipate and to combat oppression *if* they are used in the 'right' or 'proper' way. Douzinas's response suggests that rights must be seen as a promise, 'a not yet,'[24] and thus, influenced by Derridean terms, the utopian element of human rights lies in that they are always *to come*. In other words, the engagement with human rights is a matter of an ongoing process, an agonistic aspiration, where through a form of an emancipatory, radical politics, people's 'indelible right to resistance' facilitates their move from right to right in order to gain 'recognition' of their singular characteristics, because as Douzinas suggests: 'rights are about recognition and distribution among individuals and communities.'[25] To that extent, for Douzinas, human rights entail 'a utopian promise' and their catastrophic end 'comes when they lose their utopian end.'[26] Ultimately, then, a definition of human rights for Douzinas is ever-changing. Nonetheless, this notion of 'change' remains bound to a particular starting point from which to change and perhaps through which to change, 'a ground' which takes for granted that human rights hide their radical, emancipatory potential.

The above example manifests a situation where human rights form a sort of pathological attachment that becomes part of our very own being. The understanding of the term 'attachment' here must be read in similar terms to the ones Michel Foucault uses when describing the term. According to Foucault, 'in this age we are concerned with, the aim of all these institutions—factories, schools, psychiatric hospitals, hospitals, prisons—is not to exclude but, rather, *to attach* individuals.'[27] Expanding on this line of thought, *The Invisible Committee* states that this is how modern democratic states operate: 'It goes without saying that the *attachment* of the French to the state [something which was, arguably, challenged by the events of May '68]—the guarantor of universal values, the last rampart against the disaster—is a *pathology* that is difficult to undo. It's above all a fiction that no longer knows how to carry on.'[28] Similarly, this 'human rights culture' forms a form of attachment—a form that, in most situations, stops any other effort to experiment with a different, creative way of *doing politics* or *resisting* oppression. Thus, human rights and their principles can act as a dogma. To that extent, borrowing the term from *The Invisible Committee*, this dominance of human rights in shaping and dictating our modes of being and thinking, becomes a *pathology*. It is at this dire point that the optimistic potential of May '68, as epitomised by Deleuze's critique of human rights, becomes a timely and refreshing voice of dissent.

EXPOSING RIGHTS' PESSIMISM: FIRST STEPS TOWARDS A DIFFERENT *ETHOS*

Deleuze's critique of human rights is, perhaps, one of the most underexamined areas of the philosopher's corpus. His comments on rights are dispersed over a handful of interviews and a few pages in *What Is Philosophy?*.[29] While the brevity and relative vagueness of his critique partially justifies the limited engagement with his critique of rights, its importance and relevance to the events that followed May '68, and especially its role in the emergence and subsequent triumph of human rights' morality, calls for closer attention.

In a series of interviews with Claire Parnet, Deleuze does not hide his contempt for human rights, seeing them as a fundamental manifestation of a decadent culture and the intellectually barren thought of 'imbeciles' [*débiles*].[30] As he notes:

> Listen, this respect for the 'rights of man'—this really makes me want to say, almost make some odious statements. It belongs so much to the weak thinking of the empty intellectual period that we discussed earlier [here he refers to his view that culture is in a state of decadence, as expressed in section *C as in Culture*]. It's purely abstract these 'rights of man.' What is it? It's purely abstract, completely empty.[31]

Deleuze specifies in another instance, when he speaks with Raymond Bellour and Francois Ewald, that the emptiness and abstraction of rights are the result of the very mode of being and thinking they are based on. As he explains, the emergence and triumph of this human rights mode of being and thinking leads back to a certain engagement with 'empty' questions that merely reflect on 'new forms of transcendence, new universals, [which] restore [the] reflective subject as the bearer of rights, or [they] set up communicative intersubjectivity.'[32] What Deleuze means by this is that human rights promote a certain mode of thinking—*an image of thought*—that thinks in terms of universal categories (the human, the citizen, the law, right, Evil, Good and so forth). In other words, human rights try to find a solution to *singular* issues and very *real* and *specific* predicaments of the world's marginalised by reducing these situations to abstract and supposedly higher categories of the 'One'—that is, a certain dogmatic understanding, that acts in a mode of judgement[33] that decides 'what life is' or who is to be considered a human or not, or even who is to be considered a human who is *worthy* of rights.

This *modus operandi* of rights has two consequences. First, because they act in the name of universal categories, rights are usually unable to adapt and respond to singular situations, or as Deleuze puts it, 'human rights declarations are never made as a function of the people who are directly concerned.'[34] In order to illustrate this view further, the philosopher gives the example of an Armenian population:

> There is an enclave, an Armenian enclave in another Soviet republic and there is an Armenian republic. So that's the first aspect of the situation. There is this

massacre by some sort of Turkic group. . . . This massacre of Armenians, in the enclave. So from the enclave, the Armenians retreat into their republic, I guess—please correct me if I am wrong—and then, there is an earthquake. You'd think you were in something written by the Marquis de Sade, these poor people go through the worst ordeals inflicted by men, and when they reach shelter, it's nature that gets involved. When people say 'the rights of man' it's just intellectual discourse, for odious intellectuals. For intellectuals who have no ideas.[35]

The example manifests the impotence of rights to protect their supposed subjects and how the fixation on moral(ising) values and 'eternal norms' renders them unable to adapt and respond to a situation. At the same time—and this is the second and more important consequence of their *modus operandi*—by professing themselves as the holders of a 'higher notion of truth,' of a transcendent, global morality, they cause a blockage or a 'fettering of thought' as a creative process.[36] This is because human rights' moral(ising) values are presented as a notion of a fundamental truth that transcends the singular in the name of the universal ground that shapes our mode(s) of being. Thus, instead of being interested in engaging in a creative method of thinking, human beings merely try to apply universals or to act in ways that are dictated by these supposedly eternal and higher values. This mode of thought and all notions of higher values are, according to Deleuze,

> not created by acting but by holding back from acting, not by affirming, but by beginning with denial. This is why they are called un-created, divine, transcendent, superior to life. But think of what these values hide, of their mode of creation. They hide an extraordinary hatred, a hatred for life, a hatred for all that is active and affirmative in life.[37]

This 'hatred for life,' hidden within rights' homogenising and universalist discourse, renders human beings in a state of inaction, reducing them to mere spectators that wait for rights' higher values to dictate their ways of existing and to save them and, as such, they end up being *spectators of their own lives*. At the same time, this alienated subject of rights, *Bloom*,[38] feels vulnerable due to its inability to create new, inventive ways of *resisting* and *existing*. Ultimately, not only are human rights unable to 'moralise nations, State and the market'[39] but their ability to form a pathological attachment and kill any potentiality of creativity and revolt, gives an unprecedented impetus to the neoliberal mantra, suggesting that *there is no alternative*.

ZONES OF AN IMMANENT LIFE: MAY'S RADICAL POTENTIALITY

Writing in 1972, in his preface to *Anti-Oedipus*, a book that carries May's radical potential at its very core,[40] Michel Foucault states: 'I would say that *Anti-Oedipus* (may its authors forgive me) is a book of ethics, the first book of ethics to be written in France in quite a long time.'[41] Foucault continues by adding that this ethical aspect of *Anti-Oedipus* speaks of an 'art of living counter to all forms of fascism.'[42] While Deleuze was not interested in producing a philosophy based on a system of ethics (at least, in a disciplinary sense)—hence, Foucault's asking for forgiveness—his whole philosophical corpus can be characterised as an *ethology*, that is a theory of being that opposes any form of dogma and moral(ising), higher values. An ethology, thus, does not rely on notions of Good or Evil that function as a ground (similar to the principles that shape human rights' mode of being and thinking) or as *a priori* that we must follow in order to achieve a supposed 'status' of moral or ethical beings. Deleuze's philosophical approach to ethology, instead, speaks of an *ethos* which is distinctively immanent, it speaks of the 'study' 'of the capacities for affecting and being affected that characterise each thing.'[43] In other words, it is an attentive process of creating and inventing new, non-dogmatic ways of living, and since it participates in all aspects of life, it is not the static subordinate of these higher values of morality. Such an *ethos* is interwoven with a demand for a radical politics and to that extent, it is, as I argue, a manifestation of the radical potentiality that May '68 gave rise to. In order to better illustrate this immanent *ethos* that 'disturbs' and 'disorients' the moral(ising) dogma of human rights, I focus on two short, albeit significant, essays by Deleuze: 'Immanence: A Life'[44] and 'Zones of Immanence.'

In 'Immanence: A Life,' Deleuze defines pure immanence as 'A LIFE and nothing else.'[45] This suggests that pure immanence exists at a point where there is not a point of reference, of origin or end, there is only *a life*, an indefinite life. The use of the indefinite article succeeds in articulating 'the fundamental character of Deleuzian immanence, that is, its "not referring to an object" and its "not belonging to a subject", in other words, its being immanent only to itself and, nevertheless, in movement.'[46] Here, we can see how pure immanence is not defined by anything which is external to life, being independent from rules coming 'from above' or independent of any categories of higher values (such as those dictating human rights' mode of thought) that try to define or to represent what life 'is.'

The meaning and the importance of the indefinite article can be exemplified better in the example given by Deleuze of a scene from Dickens's *Our Mutual Friend*, where the scoundrel Riderhood is almost dead. The scene is a great way to get a sense of the *how* of immanence. In this particular scene, the scoundrel who is hated by everyone

> is found as he lies dying. Suddenly those charged with his care display an urgent respect, and even love for the dying man's least sign of life. Everybody bustles about to save him, to the point where, in his deepest coma, the wicked man himself senses something soft and sweet penetrating him. But to the degree that he comes back to life, his saviours turn colder, and he becomes once again mean and crude.[47]

As a consequence, Deleuze suggests that this moment between life and death 'is a moment where *a* life [is] merely playing with death.'[48] At this point, as I explain below, we can grasp this moment as a manifestation of an ethical event. It seems that, for an instant, the 'definite' life of a particular individual is 'suspended,' in the sense that it is not judged by its qualities in terms of behaviour, characteristics or any other societal values and codes or norms. For that singular moment the dying person goes, arguably, 'beyond' the categories of 'Good and Evil.'

The encounter with the dying man makes the people around him *evaluate* the situation, rather than judge the person in front of them. This is because they do not rely on the scoundrel's previous life and habits in order to decide their actions but they instead assess the critical situation of the scoundrel and they act according to the singular 'demands' of this situation. At this particular point the scoundrel is a non-person, who nevertheless can be seen as possessing a 'spark of life'[49] within its manifestation as an 'impersonal singularity.' It is important to note that this 'spark of life' does not belong to the individual as such, but it is to be described as something between life and death or, as Giorgio Agamben, puts it, that moment is 'a kind of happy netherworld.'[50] Here we need to ponder further this suspension of individual identities and of previous qualities that defined the scoundrel (and to that extent every individual) before this 'moment between life and death.' At the moment between life and death, Riderhood can be understood as a manifestation of a *whatever being* or a *whatever singularity*.[51] Agamben explains:

> The Whatever in question here relates to singularity not in its indifference with respect to a common property (to a concept, for example: being red, being French, being Muslim), but only in its being *such as it is.* Singularity is thus freed from the false dilemma that obliges knowledge to choose between the ineffability of the individual and the intelligibility of the universal.[52]

The reaction of the people around Riderhood to his condition is not a negative indifference to his qualities as an individual human being, in the sense that they 'transcend' a mundane idea of an anthropological understanding but, instead, it is a limited, *ethical* moment when the singularity of the scoundrel escapes or suspends, in a positive manner, the fixed boundaries of his identity. The scoundrel and the people around him 'enter' into 'a zone of immanence' where, as Deleuze writes: 'Every entity is equally being, in the sense that each actualizes its powers in immediate vicinity with the first cause. The distant cause is no more: rocks, flowers, animals and humans equally celebrate the glory of God in a kind of sovereign an-archy.'[53] In other words, we witness a suspension of a life defined by certain universal(ising) and moral(ising) categories. To that extent, the importance of such a rare situation is that it opens up a multiplicity of possibilities for changing our mode of being and thinking (our *ethos*). Yet, it is a matter of being attentive to the singularity of the situation in order to be able to 'grasp' that in reality this singular mode of life is hidden in every moment. According to Deleuze, 'we shouldn't enclose life in a single moment when individual life confronts universal death. *A* life is everywhere, in all the moments that a given living subject goes through and that are measured by given lived objects.'[54] This situation, however, is a matter of a moment, 'a mere flash' and to that extent, it is fair to question whether such a moment can have a greater impact on the formation of an *ethos*. This is especially the case since as we have seen from the scene, the behaviour of the people and the scoundrel tends to revert to 'normality' once the latter comes back to his senses.

Subsequently, could it be argued that, in a similar manner, the events of May '68 were a mere 'spark' of an alternative way of living and a different politics that very quickly faded from view? Admittedly, as stated above, a dogmatic image of thought infused with the rules of the market and human rights' moral(ising) values prevailed, and it dictates our modes of being and thinking in a totalising manner. However, May '68 (like every event in history) is not only a matter of history, a historical sociopolitical event which is determined by sociopolitical causes, their effects or outcomes. 'May '68 is more of the order of a pure event, free of all normal, normative causality.'[55] In that sense and as a pure event, May '68 retains its radical potentiality for an *ethos* and a politics that question the authority of moral(ising) principles. In other words, as Deleuze notes in the 'Zones of Immanence' essay, despite the dominance of a universalist, transcendent understanding of the world, 'a whole other inspiration traverses this cosmos. Zones of immanence seemingly proliferate at the various stages or levels, even establishing connections between levels.'[56] In this proliferation of zones of immanence, argues Deleuze, 'there is something [that] tends to overtake the vertical world, to reverse it, as if the hierarchy bred a particular *anarchy*, and the love of God, an internal atheism proper to it.'[57] The events of May were, perhaps, such an ethical event where the dogmatism of a moral(ising) thought and politics of the *ancien régime* were overturned. During the events, immanence overtook transcendence. The people who were 'attentive' to the singularity of the events that unfolded in May encountered and became a *whatever singularity*—a singularity that is, radically, *an-archic* in the sense that it is not defined by any foundational principle (man, moral, good, evil, scoundrel). Thus, they were caught somewhere 'in the middle,' in the 'between-ness' of a singular situation. The middle, as Deleuze and Guattari have taught us, is the dissolution of a dogmatic, moral(ising) mode of being.[58] This 'between-ness' or the middle suggests that there are no fixed points, nor are there predetermined ends.[59] May's radical potentiality is to be found in this between-ness that suspends and questions any universalist and dogmatic discourses presenting themselves as 'coming from above.'

CONCLUSION

At a crucial moment when everything seems futile and the spirit of resistance and revolt seems pacified, when the over-reliance on (human) rights, laws and all sorts of abstract, pseudo-higher values won't save us, the commemoration of May '68's pessimistic outcome and optimistic potentiality becomes even more pertinent. However, such commemoration should not become either a source of despair because of the failure to form a different world, or a superfluous source of empty hopes and hollow, pseudo-revolutionary speeches. May '68 should be rather remembered as an *event* (in a philosophical manner) when a multiplicity of radical potentialities for living a life and doing politics in a non-dogmatic way did not seem as impossible as they seem today. Its ethical point of view calls for an identification or awareness of such moments when the encounter with a singular case or event calls for an evaluation, which escapes any higher norms, representations and fixed identities. At that moment an ethical, evaluative reversal took place. And this ethical reversal calls for a different mode of doing politics. Such a politics, as Foucault writes: 'Do not use thought to ground a political practice in Truth; nor political action to discredit, as mere speculation, a line of thought. [They] do not demand . . . [to] restore the "rights" of the individual, as philosophy has defined them.'[60] Finally, such politics 'do not become enamoured with power.'[61] They are, instead, a politics of pure potentiality and creativity that does not aim to pacify life in the name of any sort of higher or 'truer' values. In our current state of affairs, the radical potentiality of May '68 shall then function as a call or a demand to change, significantly, our modes of being rather than 'improve on' or 'progress beyond' them. Such a change ought to be a radical one because a mere 'detachment' that happens gradually and not totally runs the risk of falling again within the dogmatism of hierarchy or hierarchy disguised as 'progress'—be that in the form of human rights or any other form of moral(ising) rightness. Perhaps, some may protest that such a radical shift is, in fact, in itself dogmatic or some may say that this is an impossibility, a totally utopian proposal. I argue against these claims by stressing that the criticality of our times *demands* radical changes and presents an imminent necessity of thinking *otherwise*. To those suggesting that such a call is a utopian one, I respond by saying that a different ethical mode of 'doing politics' is one that is interested in the *how* of an encounter and our response(s) to such an encounter that would precisely not render something as a-topic, or u-topic (i.e. as a non-place, or without-a-place) in the first place. It is a matter of assessing and experimenting with a situation, rather than acting within a presupposed framework based on 'higher principles' that predetermine first the *topos*, or field of action of what can count as 'political' properness and property. Such a process of 'doing politics' is, thus, in a mode of constant *strife* and it operates within the categories of 'the interesting, the remarkable, or the important.'[62]

NOTES

1. Some of the ideas in this chapter have been previously published as Christos Marneros, 'Deleuze and Human Rights: The Optimism and Pessimism of '68,' *La Deleuziana: International Journal of Philosophy*, 8 La pensée dix-huit (Winter 2019): 39–52. Most of the sections in this chapter are new and the rest have been rewritten by adding, omitting or amending certain parts. I want to thank the editors of *La Deleuziana,* and especially the editor of the issue, Guillaume Collett, for giving me the permission to reproduce materials from the article.

2. The *Situationist International*, commenting on the events in France, wrote: 'The movement was a rediscovery of collective and individual history, an awakening to the possibility of intervening in history, an awareness of participating in an irreversible event. ("Nothing will ever be the same again").' Situationist International, 'The Beginning of an Era,' *Situationist International* 12 (1969), https://www.cddc.vt.edu/sionline/si/beginning.html (accessed 23 February 2021).

3. Gilles Châtelet, *To Live and Think Like Pigs: The Incitement of Envy and Boredom in Market Democracies*, trans. Robin Mackay (New York: Sequence Press, 2014), 3, 145.

4. Gilles Deleuze, *Negotiations*, trans. Martin Joughin (New York: Columbia University Press, 1995), 152–53.

5. Alain Badiou, *The Communist Hypothesis*, trans. David and Steve Corcoran (London and New York: Verso, 2015), 33–34.

A strong piece of evidence for the radical potential of May '68 is the fear and the effort of the Right to bury and make people forget about the events, e.g. Sarkozy's effort to 'put an end to May '68 once and for all.' See Alain Badiou, *The Meaning of Sarkozy*, trans. David Fernbach (London and New York: Verso, 2008), 36.

6. Julian Bourg, *From Revolution to Ethics: May 1968 and Contemporary French Thought* (Montreal and Kingston: McGill-Queen's University Press, 2017), xii.

7. Peter Fitzpatrick, 'Is Humanity Enough? The Secular Theology of Human Rights,' *Law Social Justice and Global Development* 1 (2007): 2–14.

8. For an understanding of foundation as a dogmatic, *archist* principle, see Reiner Schürmann, *Heidegger on Being and Acting: From Principles to Anarchy*, trans. C-M. Gros. (Indiana: Indiana University Press, 1987).

9. For a recent account of human rights' relationship to neoliberalism, but also for an account of the emancipatory potential of a 'properly politicised' understanding of human rights, see Jessica Whyte, *The Morals of the Market: Human Rights and the Rise of Neoliberalism* (London and New York: Verso, 2019).

10. The most prominent entry in these 'new human rights histories' is, perhaps, Samuel Moyn's book *The Last Utopia* (Cambridge, MA: Harvard University Press, 2010).

11. Benjamin Nathans, 'The Disenchantment of Socialism: Soviet Dissidents, Human Rights and the New Global Morality,' in *The Breakthrough: Human Rights in 1970s*, ed. Jan Eckel and Samuel Moyn (Philadelphia: University of Pennsylvania Press, 2014), 33–48.

12. Micheline R. Ishay, *The History of Human Rights: From Ancient Times to Globalization Era* (Oakland: University of California Press, 2008), 248–49.

13. Steward Motha and Thanos Zartaloudis, 'Law Ethics and the Utopian End of Human Rights,' *Social and Legal Studies* 12, no. 2 (January 2003): 243.

14. Costas Douzinas, *Human Rights and Empire: The Political Philosophy of Cosmopolitanism* (London: Routledge, 2007), 4.

15. Some of the most prominent of them are Bernard-Henri Lévy, André Glucksmann, Christian Jambert and Pascal Bruckner. According to Lévy, the term 'New Philosophers' was coined by him to signify the shift from 'the totalitarianism' of the left and the 'hegemonic position' that certain left intellectuals held within the circles of French intelligentsia of the time. See his book, *La Barbarie à Visage Humain* (Paris: Éditions Grasset & Fasquelle, 1977), Kindle Part V, chapter 4.

16. This is very much justified by the fact that they wanted to present themselves as 'post-ideological,' as is usually the case with movements towards a so-called democratic consensus of normality. Ironically but not surprisingly, both the extremity of far-right fascists and the 'the humanitarian interventions of the West' were and are often justified by individuals belonging to the group. The support of Bernard-Henri Lévy for NATO's intervention in Libya and his visit to the 'killing field' of Tarhuna where many children lost their lives, perhaps, stands out amongst the rest of the actions and ideas of these 'humanitarians.'

17. Châtelet, *To Live and Think Like Pigs*, 171. Of course, it was not just Karl Marx who was 'dead' but also many of the 'influences' of May's insurrectionists such as Friedrich Nietzsche, Jean-Paul Sartre, the Situationists and so forth.

18. Bernard-Henri Lévy, *Left in Dark Times: A Stand Against the New Barbarism*, trans. Benjamin Moser (New York: Random House, 2008), Kindle, chapter 3.

19. Alain Badiou, *Ethics: An Essay on the Understanding of Evil*, trans. Peter Hallward (London and New York: Verso, 2001), 9.

20. Badiou, *The Communist Hypothesis*, 2.

21. Paul Virilio, *Strategy of Deception*, trans. Chris Turner (London and New York: Verso, 2007), 49.

22. This is a central claim of Costas Douzinas's first book on human rights, *The End of Human Rights* (Oxford: Hart Publishing, 2000), as I explain below in the chapter.

23. Douzinas, *The End of Human Rights*, 7.

24. Douzinas, *The End of Human Rights*, 145.

25. Costas Douzinas, *The Radical Philosophy of Rights* (London: Routledge, 2019), 194.

26. Douzinas, *The End of Human Rights*, 380.

27. Michel Foucault, 'Truth and Judicial Forms,' in *Essential Works of Foucault 1954–1984, Vol. 3: Power*, ed. James D. Faubion and trans. Robert Hurley (London: Penguin, 2002), 78, emphasis mine.

28. The Invisible Committee, *The Coming Insurrection* (California: Semiotext(e), 2009), 12, emphasis mine.

29. Gilles Deleuze and Félix Guattari, *What Is Philosophy?*, trans. Hugh Tomlinson (London and New York: Verso, 1994), 107–8. It is important to note here that Deleuze in his *Empiricism and Subjectivity*, trans. Constantin V. Boundas (New York: Columbia University Press, 1991) critiques natural rights via Hume. Human rights, however, should be understood and approached as a different phenomenon that arises in the 1970s, as a direct outcome of the events of 1968.

30. Gilles Deleuze, 'What It Means to be on the Left,' in *From A to Z*, DVD (California: Semotext(e), 2004). Deleuze, most probably, indirectly attacks the movement of the New Philosophers. In another instance he directly criticises their thought as empty because it thinks in terms of universal or 'big concepts' (e.g. the law, human rights) and 'empty propositions' (e.g. in terms of a concrete, unified subject). See *Two Regimes of Madness*, trans. Ames Hodges and Mike Taormina (California: Semiotext(e), 2007), 13.

31. Deleuze, *Two Regimes of Madness*, 13.

32. Deleuze, *Negotiations*, 152.

33. Gilles Deleuze, *Essays Critical and Clinical*, trans. Daniel W. Smith and Michael A. Greco (London and New York: Verso, 1998), 126–35.

34. Deleuze, *From A to Z*.

35. Deleuze, *From A to Z*.

36. Deleuze, *Negotiations*, 122.

37. Gilles Deleuze, *Nietzsche and Philosophy*, trans. Hugh Tomlinson (New York: Columbia University Press, 2006), 107.

38. The subject of human rights is perhaps akin to what the French militant collective and magazine, *Tiqqun*, calls *Bloom*—that is, a human being in a state of total

alienation, which ends up being a mere passer-by or a 'tourist' in its own life. See their *Theory of Bloom*, trans. Robert Hurley (Berkeley, CA: Little Black Cart, 2012).
39. Deleuze and Guattari, *What Is Philosophy?*, 107.
40. See Ian Buchanan, 'Is *Anti-Oedipus* a May '68 Book?,' in *Deleuze and History*, ed. Jeffrey A. Bell and Claire Colebrook (Edinburgh: Edinburgh University Press, 2009), esp. 211–22. Buchanan explains that *Anti-Oedipus* is the outcome of a process of rethinking political concepts that has as its starting point May '68. As he states: 'Ultimately for Deleuze and Guattari, accounting for May '68 necessitated a complete rethinking of political concepts like power, power relations, groups, group identity, the event, and so on, and insofar as it takes up this challenge, *Anti-Oedipus* is appropriately described as a May '68 book' (222).
41. Michel Foucault, 'Preface,' in Gilles Deleuze and Félix Guattari, *Anti-Oedipus*, trans. Robert Hurley, Mark Seem and Helen R. Lane (Minneapolis: University of Minnesota Press, 1983), xii.
42. Foucault, 'Preface,' xii.
43. Gilles Deleuze, *Spinoza: Practical Philosophy*, trans. Robert Hurley (San Francisco, CA: City Lights Publishers, 2001), 125.
44. Gilles Deleuze, 'Immanence: A Life,' in *Pure Immanence: Essays on A Life*, trans. Anne Boyman (Princeton: Zone Books, 2001); Deleuze, *Two Regimes of Madness*.
45. Deleuze, *Pure Immanence*, 27.
46. Giorgio Agamben, 'Absolute Immanence,' in *Potentialities: Collected Essays in Philosophy*, trans. Daniel Heller-Roazen (Redwood City: Stanford University Press, 1999), 224.
47. Deleuze, *Pure Immanence*, 28.
48. Deleuze, *Pure Immanence*, 28.
49. Agamben, *Potentialities*, 229.
50. Agamben, *Potentialities*, 229.
51. Giorgio Agamben, *The Coming Community*, trans. Michael Hardt (Minneapolis: University of Minnesota Press, 1993), 1.
52. Agamben, *The Coming Community*.
53. Deleuze, *Two Regimes of Madness*, 261.
54. Deleuze, *Pure Immanence*, 29.
55. Deleuze, *Two Regimes of Madness*, 233.
56. Deleuze, *Two Regimes of Madness*, 261.
57. Deleuze, *Two Regimes of Madness*, 262.
58. Gilles Deleuze and Félix Guattari, *A Thousand Plateaus*, trans. Brian Massumi (London: Bloomsbury Revelations, 2015), especially 26.
59. Schürmann, *Heidegger on Being and Acting: From Principles to Anarchy*, 12.
60. Foucault, 'Preface,' xiii.
61. Foucault, 'Preface,' xiii.
62. Deleuze and Guattari, *What Is Philosophy?*, 82.

Chapter Seven

'68 and Sexuality

Disentangling the Double Bind

Blanche Plaquevent

In 1994, Michel Houellebecq published his first novel, *Extension du Domaine de la Lutte* (*Whatever*), about a disillusioned thirty-year-old executive struggling to find sex in a society obsessed by sex.[1] In the novel, Houellebecq introduces a theme that runs throughout his work: a critique of the sexual revolution. For Houellebecq, the sexual politics of the 1960s and 1970s in France and in the West led to a marketisation of sexuality and ultimately fuelled sexual misery. A few years later, in 1998, he reiterated this argument in *Les Particules Elementaires* (*Atomised*): 'It is interesting to note that the "sexual revolution" was sometimes portrayed as a communal utopia, whereas in fact it was simply another stage in the historical rise of individualism.'[2] Houellebecq described a double bind situation: even if activists of the sexual revolution aimed at building a communist and revolutionary society, they ultimately paved the way for a marketisation of sex and love and therefore fuelled the very capitalism they wanted to destroy.

Houellebecq is a topical public figure in France, often labelled reactionary, but the idea of the double bind of the sexual revolution is not unique to him, and it is not unique to France. In a variety of fields and academic disciplines, public figures, scholars and journalists across the political spectrum have introduced and perpetuated the idea that the sexual revolution of the 1960s has resulted in a double bind. As we will see, the suspicion of the sexual revolution generally comes from the view that the private and individual aspect of sex would make it particularly susceptible to being co-opted by capitalism. The double-bind narrative has been defined in different ways and used to support varying agendas. It has spread a critical narrative of the sexual revolution, now prevalent in the French public space and beyond.

Focusing on the French context, this chapter critiques the idea that the sexual revolution necessarily presents a double bind. The first half aims at understanding how the narrative of the double bind emerged. The second half constitutes a historical exploration of the sexual revolution. The chapter disentangles the 1960s discourses on the sexual revolution from their later interpretations. These two dimensions are too often problematically entangled in current critiques of the sexual revolution. I argue that going back to the history of radical sexual politics in 1950s and 1960s France enables us to challenge the dominant narrative of the double bind and to envision the revolutionary potential of sexual politics. The aim of this chapter is to challenge the fatalism of the double-bind narrative and to show that if the sexual revolution might always be at risk of recuperation by capitalism and individualism it is nonetheless not doomed to lead to a double bind. Recovering the history of the 1950s and 1960s may provide a glimmer of hope about the possibility of a sexual politics that would fuel a revolutionary strength and sense of agency.

NARRATIVES ON THE DOUBLE BIND

Several kinds of discourses on the double bind of the sexual revolution have emerged since the 1970s. Surprisingly, critiques of the sexual revolution did not necessarily emerge from conservative fringes, but also from the left. Houellebecq's statement, for instance, strikingly echoes the progressive sociologist Eva Illouz's position: 'While the early liberation movements had imagined a free sexuality as an essentially non-commercial, non-monetized aspect of the self, sexuality became both a remunerated and non-remunerated source of surplus value for a consequential number of industries controlled by men.'[3] The idea that something has gone wrong with the 1960s' sexual revolution is widespread. The ideal of sexual revolution which circulated in avant-garde intellectual circles from the 1950s and within the student movement in the second half of the 1960s is often described as either too naïve or too extreme, depending on where the critique comes from. We can distinguish four different types of narratives where the sexual revolution is ultimately described as a co-optation of liberalism. Each of them focuses on a different level of reality: societal, economic, individual and subjective.

The most obvious critique of the sexual revolution emerged from conservative circles. They argued that sexual permissiveness endangered the core structure of society. Right-wing political figures like Nicolas Sarkozy have blamed the heritage of '68 for threatening traditional values. The May '68 slogan 'Il est interdit d'interdire' (It is forbidden to forbid) has come to epitomise the excess of permissiveness.

The second analysis of the double bind of the sexual revolution relies on an economic critique from a societal point of view. This holds that the sexual revolution paved the way for a marketisation of sex. This critique has emerged from the radical left, which applied a critical Marxist analysis to sexuality. The commodification of sex, through advertisement, pornography, sex work, sex-shops and so on, was seen as a consequence (potentially unintended, but a consequence nonetheless) of the demands for sexual revolution. Furthermore, the marketisation of sex has been seen not only as a consequence but also as a cause of the sexual revolution. The historian Dagmar Herzog has suggested that liberalism paved the way for the so-called sexual revolution. She describes the discomfort of radical activists who wondered if, 'rather than being the path to revolution, maybe sex was an antidote to revolution.' Indeed, she argues that:

> The hopes that making love would also make revolution were rather quickly dashed. Perhaps pleasure, sex, and politics did not really belong together after all, since evidently encouragements to ever new sexual experimentation could coexist quite comfortably with support for militarism in Vietnam and a profit-oriented market economy.[4]

At a societal level, the sexual revolution is seen to have fostered liberalism.

A third strand of critique focuses on the personal dimension of the marketisation. In this view, economic and liberal logics are thought to have pervaded intimate lives and relationships. The ideal of sexual liberation is regarded as innately flawed because it would advocate a consumeristic freedom, as is suggested by the title of one of Illouz's subsections in *The End of Love*: 'Sexual Freedom as Consumer Freedom.'[5] Illouz has continuously argued that, since the 1960s, emotions and relationships have increasingly come to rely on capitalist logics.[6] More generally, for Illouz, as for Houellebecq's characters, claims to a free sexuality are seen as relying on individualist values. The double bind of the sexual revolution is therefore also seen to play out on an intimate level.

The fourth narrative focuses on how sexual freedom has been experienced subjectively. Several scholars have argued that sexual emancipation became a new imperative which created an emotional toll, borne mostly by women. This critique has emerged from sociology and gender studies and relies on a discussion of the very possibility of sexual liberation. In the 1970s, Michel Foucault invited his contemporaries to reflect on how well-intentioned, liberating discourses produced a variety of effects, and not only emancipation. He argued that notions of repression and liberation could not capture dynamics around sexuality because he did not consider power to be a simple top-down force: sex was never simply repressed by institutions.[7] Because there is no natural or authentic state of sexuality that is free from alienation, Foucault thinks we should speak about reconfigurations of norms rather than 'sexual liberation.'[8] Many sociologists have followed Foucault's insights since the 1970s. They have analysed the emerging discourse of sexual liberation as a new norm. An issue of the sociology journal *Mouvements*, in 2002, titled 'Sexe: sous la revolution, les normes' gave voice to that critique. As Michel Bozon explained:

> I am wary of the term of revolution to qualify changes that occurred in sexual practices since the sixties. The overuse of the expression of sexual revolution stems from an old-fashioned conception of sexuality. We do not consider, as Reich or Marcuse, that sexual conducts are hindered by social constraints we would just need to suppress to allow the full liberation of sexual impulses.[9]

Scholars have insisted on the new gendered injunctions created by the so-called sexual liberation. They argue that the radical sexual politics that emerged before second wave feminism, in the 1950s and 1960s, overlooked gender hierarchies. Focusing on the student sexual liberation, Judith Coffin argues that 'The role of sexual subjectivity in the student movement of 1968 was eye-catching. So were the glaring blind spots and sexism of that movement, and those did much to metabolize feminist anger.'[10] Lucile Rouault has written about the gendered double standards around free sexuality, and the anxiety resulting from a blurring of traditional sexual norms within a patriarchal society.[11] Eva Illouz has argued that the sexual revolution has generated uncertainty around the nature of relationships and sex, which has created an emotional double bind for women. In opposition to traditional systems of courtship and lifelong marriage, relationships since the 1970s have increasingly relied on freedom and have therefore become more fluid: their beginnings are often ambiguous, they do not last forever and so on. Illouz has analysed the burden of this new sexual freedom, which creates insecurities and ontological uncertainty, especially for women.[12] This critique was more widely circulated in France through the book by the feminist Malka Malkovitch, published by the famous editor Albin Michel and reviewed in many national newspapers.[13] While rooted in different approaches, critiques of '68 and of its sexual revolution are therefore widespread in France. Many of them describe the 1960s' radical sexual politics as leading to a double bind.

SEXUALITY AS DEPOLITICISATION?

The sexual revolution has also been challenged by historians who have tended to deny sexuality its political relevance in the context of May '68. On the occasion of the fortieth anniversary, historians wanted to repoliticise accounts of '68 to counter the media and popular culture's focus on the cultural consequences of '68.[14] By insisting on the political dimension of May '68, these historians were opposing the double-bind narrative: they wanted to show that May '68 was politically radical and that it could not be recuperated by liberalism. Historians considered sex as a cultural rather than political issue, and they therefore largely left sex out of their narrative. Talking about sex in relation to '68 came to be interpreted as a depoliticisation. Sexual politics, unlike the more straightforwardly revolutionary politics of the 1960s, could be coopted by liberalism. For example, in *May '68 and Its Afterlives*, Kristin Ross argued against the cultural interpretation of '68 and its focus on individual rights at the expense of collective action. She argued that '68 was first and foremost the greatest strike in recent French history, which united workers and students. It was not a mere 'cultural revolt of "youth".'[15] Michelle Zancarini-Fournel added to Ross's insights a few years later: she argued that a hedonistic and cultural reading of '68 had prevailed in the intervening decades and affirmed the need to repoliticise '68. In an article on 'The Mystery of May 1968,' the British historian Julian Jackson astutely described this historiographical debate. He distinguished between approaches that 'subsumed May 1968 into its alleged cultural consequences' and attempts to analyse '68 as a specific political social movement.[16]

On the occasion of the fiftieth anniversary, scholars were more open to discussing the sexual politics of '68, but they continued to disown the radicality of the sexual revolution. As the question of gender came to the forefront of the scholarship on May '68 in 2018, the sexual revolution was however predominantly described as a superficial and provocative sexualisation rather than a real challenge to gender hierarchies.[17]

Beyond discussions on the French '68, the political relevance of sexuality has been more generally debated among leftist scholars. The Marxist historian Eric Hobsbawm argued that calls for sexual liberation did not really bring about any revolutionary change: 'All it has obviously brought is a lot more public sex in an otherwise unchanged social order.'[18] He did not take seriously the idea of sexual revolution, which articulated sex with revolutionary politics. Hobsbawm associated sexuality with culture and argued that 'taken by themselves, cultural revolt and cultural dissidence are symptoms, not revolutionary forces.' He concluded: 'Politically they are not very important.'[19] The American historian and sociologist Christopher Lasch shared Hobsbawm's suspicion towards the political dimension of countercultural movements. His critique was initially rooted in a defence of revolutionary politics, even if he later embraced conservative positions. He argued that sexual politics could easily be recuperated by the capitalist system: 'a society organised around consumption can easily absorb movements demanding sexual freedom, enlisting them into the propaganda of commodities so as to surround consumption with an aura of libidinal gratification.' Lasch distinguished between serious, structural, economic revolutionary politics challenging capitalist structures on the one hand, and claims for the sexual revolution focusing on individual freedoms on the other.[20]

More recently, the sociologist Eva Illouz has revived and updated these critiques by relying less on a 1970s schematic Marxist understanding of politics. Illouz argues that 'capitalism has hijacked sexual freedom.'[21] Although Illouz acknowledges that capitalism is responsible for diverting sexual freedom from its original goals—'ideas and values, once institutionalised, have a trajectory that is not always the one intended by their proponents'[22]—she also dismisses the political dimension of the original sexual liberation of the 1960s. She states that this cultural revolution 'did not have its public demonstrations, Parliament bills and physical struggles' and describes sexual claims as only 'proto-political.'[23] Illouz therefore seems to deny that the sexual revolution was fully political or revolutionary. Her position is ambiguous. On the one hand, she does not seem to consider the ideals of sexual liberation to be innately problematic and observes that the problem lies rather in their recuperation. On the other hand, she resists taking the political dimension of these ideals seriously. Her scepticism arises from the fact that these ideals were too easily recuperated by capitalist logics to inspire her trust.

Critiques from the left often associate discussing sexuality with depoliticisation. The narrative of the double bind often relies on the idea that sexuality is not a fully political or revolutionary issue, because its private and individualistic dimension leaves it too susceptible to co-option by capitalism. While acknowledging internal tensions, the idea of the double bind tends to discredit sexual politics. It associates the 1960s' sexual politics with its instrumentalisations and later developments, through a simplistic and ahistorical narrative. I do not deny that some aspects of the 'sexual revolution' were appropriated by the capitalist and liberal system. In the last decades, many Western countries have certainly found themselves in a double-bind dilemma when faced with these questions. However, the ideal of sexual revolution that emerged in the 1960s is arguably not responsible for this double bind. The fact that the sexual revolution got recuperated by capitalism has more to do with capitalism than with discourses on the sexual revolution. We should refrain from teleologically looking for the origins of the double bind in the historical moment of the 1950s/1960s itself. The second part of this chapter aims to disprove this misrepresentation by looking back at postwar historical material. Exploring historical sources that defended sexual politics allows us to separate the ideal of sexual revolution from its unintended consequences, therefore disentangling arguments made in the past from their later interpretation and challenging the narrative of the double bind.

HISTORICISING AND REPOLITICISING THE SEXUAL REVOLUTION

In the 1950s and 1960s in France, intellectuals, activists and then students defended the idea that sexuality was revolutionary. The meaning of postwar revolutionary sexual claims has been saturated with later interpretations and we therefore need to go back to the original discourses to evaluate their potential for capitalist co-optation. Activists of the time were not entirely naïve: they were already aware of the tension between sexual liberation and individualism. The spectre of the double bind was already present in the original discourses, but activists and intellectuals actively tried to avert it by keeping revolutionary politics on the table when they wrote about sexuality.

After emerging in marginal anarchist circles in the nineteenth century and circulating in Europe, USSR and the United States in the 1920s and 1930s,[24] the idea of sexual revolution regained traction after the Second World War, especially in France. From the late 1940s, some French activists, writers and intellectuals took up the idea that the revolution should not only be about socioeconomic structures but also about sex. They came to constitute a network of people who all defended a new approach to revolutionary politics despite their different intellectual and political backgrounds. The first stirrings of this came from the periphery, initially including relatively marginal public figures such as the anarchist sexologist Daniel Guérin, the writer Françoise d'Eaubonne, and the philosophers Kostas Axelos and Edgar Morin. Radical sexual politics were gradually appropriated by students from the mid-1960s, surfacing through strikes in university accommodation, and then during May–June 1968 itself. Through sexual claims, students challenged what was expected of the youth at the time. They claimed their right to a fulfilling sexual life. These claims for sexual politics were then appropriated, criticised and reformulated by feminists and gay and lesbian activists from the early 1970s.

What did it mean to politicise sexuality in a revolutionary way before the 1970s? In a nutshell, it meant two things: addressing sexuality in revolutionary discussions and envisioning sex itself as a revolutionary practice. Even before the advent of the feminist idea that the personal is political, some intellectuals and activists between 1945 and the late 1960s were already rethinking the delineations between the public and the private, the collective and the intimate, and therefore redefining politics. Sex could be revolutionised at a structural and intimate level. On the contrary, the narrative of the double bind opposes the idea that the personal can be fully political: it suggests that making the personal political necessarily leads to individualism and therefore liberalism. But how did the actors of the time envision this tension?

First of all, these intellectuals of the 1950s and 1960s consciously tried to question the frontiers of politics: in the context of the Cold War, when Stalinism increasingly appeared as repressive, they wanted to rejuvenate Marxism by addressing issues previously overlooked. Françoise d'Eaubonne explicitly criticised orthodox Marxism when she argued in 1955 that 'changes in the socioeconomic order will not, by themselves, trigger a complete and radical change of ethic and mores.'[25] Focusing on the economy was seen as insufficient. Although they challenged dominant postwar Marxism, most intellectuals referred to classic Marxist theoreticians such as Karl Marx and Friedrich Engels to legitimise the idea that sex was a revolutionary issue. In an article titled 'Les Marxistes et l'amour' in 1961, Jean de Leyde traced the long history of Marxism and sexuality and argued that Marx and Engels were already critiquing marriage.[26] While acknowledging the limits of Marxism's sexual progressiveness—namely the USSR's failed sexual politics and traditional Marxists' hostility to psychoanalysis—he ultimately argued that Marxism had provided a space for sexual issues from the start. Defending the sexual revolution was perhaps a transgression in the postwar context, but it was ultimately justified by a faithfulness to Marx himself. More recent respected heterodox Marxists like Wilhelm Reich and Herbert Marcuse were also referred to in order to legitimise the idea of sexual revolution in France.

When students embraced the sexual revolution from 1965, they also opposed orthodox communism, embodied by the Union des Etudiants Communistes (UEC). Many of the students defending sexual claims had left or been excluded from the UEC, and moved on to the Jeunesse Communiste Révolutionnaire (JCR). However, students did not solely position themselves against traditional Marxism. Sexual claims also became a way for them to question their status in society and subvert what was expected of them as young people. Graffiti, posters and pamphlets mentioning sexuality in the most transgressive ways possible constituted a quest for subversion.[27] Many historians have swept away the political dimension of students' sexual claims on the basis that it was pure provocation with no revolutionary potential.[28] However, this transgression should be considered as fully political since it constituted a rethinking of what young people were allowed to talk about. When they wrote slogans on the walls of the Sorbonne such as 'The more I make love, the more I want to make revolution' or 'Jouissez sans entraves' ('Enjoy unfettered sex'); when they rhetorically asked in a youth newspaper of the JCR, 'Why should a seventeen-year-old teenager, who knows very well what he is entitled to, be unable to enjoy a normal sexuality [that is, to be sexually active]?,'[29] students challenged French society's expectations of a desexualised youth.[30] The peculiarly transgressive form of students' sexual politics, through graffiti, provocative slogans, suggestive drawings and so forth, should be interpreted as the invention of new ways of expressing political ideas. As Tom McDonough has argued, the 1960s saw the emergence of a new political language.[31] Students' sexual claims were also articulated with a questioning of the status of youth and the role of sexuality in young people's existences. In a demonstration against the strict rules in university accommodation in March 1968 in Paris, students held banners on which they had written 'We are adults!'[32] Students were questioning their status in society, and sexuality was one of the adult rights they claimed. The 1966 Situationist pamphlet *De la misère en milieu étudiant, considérée sous ses aspects économique, politique, psychologique, sexuel et notamment intellectuel et de quelques moyens pour y remédier* identified sexuality as one of the areas of oppression affecting students.[33] Students argued that youth sexuality was a legitimate issue to discuss collectively and publicly, just like their socioeconomic conditions.

Defending the sexual revolution therefore meant redefining politics in a context of increased dissatisfaction with an orthodox Marxism which solely focused on socioeconomic matters. This was true in the French context, but also in Germany, the UK, Italy and Spain.[34] The double-bind narrative makes manifest a disagreement within the left over where the heart of politics lies. Lasch and Hobsbawm's argument that the sexual revolution led to a double bind should be interpreted as a historical debate within the radical left where different versions of communism confronted each other, rather than as a definite attack on sexual permissiveness. Lasch and Hobsbawm came down on the side of a rather orthodox understanding of revolutionary politics, whereas those who defended the sexual revolution challenged what they described as puritanical orthodox communism. The activists who defended the sexual revolution challenged precisely the idea that personal issues were individual issues.

The activists of the 1960s were not naïvely making the personal political. They defended a revolutionary sexual revolution, holding together the structural and the intimate dimensions of the revolution, because they were aware of the tension that existed between socioeconomic structures and individual experiences. In order to address this tension, they put anti-capitalism at the core of the sexual revolution. The double-bind narrative which considers the demands for sexual liberation as only serving to reinforce the capitalist system, because of their individualist and liberal dimension, does not hold when confronted with the discourses of the 1950s and 1960s. First, the activists of the 1960s considered sex in itself as a revolutionary act because it went against market imperatives. The realm of sex was opposed to that of productivity and labour. In 1961, the philosopher Kostas Axelos defended the idea that sex constituted a model for a more authentic way of being in the world:

> Given what the world is like and what it is becoming like, can't we already consider that every time that, in a mix of ardour and distress, two beings manage to meet and to love each other—and that also means: sleep together—by experimenting with passion, with negativity and transcendence, it is a positive thing? ... Every time two beings open themselves and penetrate each other, they break the oppressive conventions of structures and superstructures, they shatter the lies we usually tell in the everyday dullness.[35]

Sex was often described as a force of resistance against the increasing mechanisation of society, against imperatives of productivity, and against anomie and social isolation. Sex and love were thought to connect human beings in a way that could not be recuperated by capitalism.

This distinction between the values of sex and those of capitalism can seem to naïvely overestimate the power of love, but it fits within a broader critique of capitalism. The question of workers was central to discussions on sexuality. The anarchist sexologist Daniel Guérin linked the sexual revolution together with the 'workers' emancipation,'[36] advocating for the reduction of 'working hours and mechanisation.'[37] The Trotskyist intellectual Boris Fraenkel also focused on work and economy in the 1966 issue of *Partisans*: 'the condition of the sexual liberation is the diminution of work, of the hours of work, the disappearance of the enslaving subordination of individuals to the capitalist organisation of work.'[38] Capitalism was thought to absorb vital energy at the expense of sexual and personal fulfilment. As the anarchist Gérard Gilles argued in an article titled 'Révolution économique, révolution érotique' in 1967, in a capitalist society, 'all human energy must serve capital.'[39] Françoise d'Eaubonne argued that capitalism also shaped sexual lives because economic necessity forced workers to settle down early, marry at a young age and, therefore, embrace the bourgeois lifestyle and its patriarchal model.[40] Daniel Guérin disagreed with d'Eaubonne's view and argued that workers were actually at the forefront of the sexual revolution: 'the sexual revolution, like its twin the social revolution, will be the workers' work.'[41] However, even if they disagreed on who would lead the revolution, all these intellectuals targeted the same enemy: bourgeois capitalism. Destroying economic alienation was therefore one of the features of the sexual revolution. These intellectuals argued it was not the only one. They opposed traditional revolutionary politics, which was solely focused on economy, for overlooking the specificity of sexual norms. However, economic analysis remained prevalent in their discourses and we cannot therefore argue that the sexual politics of the 1960s relied on a market-oriented individualism.

The sexual revolution was also conceived as anti-capitalist in the sense that it opposed the marketisation of sex in capitalist society. The intellectuals who wrote about the sexual revolution in the 1960s reacted against the capitalist uses of sex that had developed after WWII, especially in advertisement. They refused to abandon sexuality to capitalism and therefore proposed a revolutionary version of sexual liberation. Many of them were interested in Herbert Marcuse's concept of 'repressive desublimation,' which pointed to the ambiguity of a sexual liberation that accompanied the development of a market of desire.[42] Activists often denounced fake sexual liberation. In her 1964 study of advertising, the sociologist Violette Morin condemned the sexualisation of capitalism: 'eroticism became the first-class lubricant of the world economy.'[43] She was weary of a rationalised and marketised version of eroticism which neutralised the political and disruptive power of eroticism in consumer societies.[44] In 1969, the journalist Jacques Mousseau also argued that 'the possibilities for a sexual liberation are in place, but they have been deviated and exploited in favour of traditional social goals.'[45] Instead of opening the path towards a new society, eroticism had been integrated in the capitalist system already in place. The intellectuals who defended the idea of sexual revolution therefore reaffirmed the need for a revolutionary analysis of sexuality which would bring together a Marxist critique of the capitalist instrumentalisation of sex and nakedness and a defence of sexual emancipation. Denouncing a fake sexual revolution did not mean giving up on the possibility of a sexual revolution: it meant criticising a certain kind of liberation which had put revolutionary ideals aside and aiming to reconnect them with sexual matters. The Sorbonne students in the group *Nous sommes en marche*, created during May–June 1968, distinguished between the liberal cultural revolution that had already taken place, and the true sexual revolution they were fighting for:

> We used to say that if the bourgeois revolution had been about legal reform and the proletarian revolution about economy, our revolution would be social and cultural. We were wrong. Revolutionaries, let this be our self-criticism.
>
> Let's remember this: the cultural revolution already happened. Theatre, cinema, literature, fashions and dances, everything shift[ed] very quickly. Sexual revolution: NO.
>
> The sexual revolution has been nothing but a mini-skirt having sex with a sports car in the advertisement pages of a weekly-luxury-left magazine.
>
> End of the cultural revolution.
>
> Of our bodies still tied down and wounded.
>
> And the start of a sexual revolution that puts EVERYTHING in question[46]

They critiqued a sexual revolution where sexuality had been made marketable, but where people's sexualities and everyday lives would not have been emancipated. They were acutely aware of the shortcomings of the different kinds of revolutions:

1. The bourgeois revolution was legal and as it neglected economy, it got trapped in puritanism.
2. The proletarian revolution was legal and economic, and as it neglected the body, it drowned in romanticism.
3. Our revolution must be legal, economic and sexual; failing that, it will be sacrificed on the obsessional scaffold of violence and sadistic eroticism.[47]

Their defence of the sexual revolution does not seem naïve here—it was, rather, informed by a critique of traditional revolutionary politics. They carefully distinguished the sexual revolution that they defended from depoliticised individualism. In another text written in the same week, the same group again stated their revolutionary stance:

The revolutionary ideology is not 'humanist.' The revolutionary ideology is political because it refuses to separate the social from the individual, the economy from politics, work from leisure, reality from utopia, science from ideology, culture from knowledge, education from its content, the use from the object, the hard facts from abstractions, reason from emotion, love from sexuality, pleasure from eroticism, etc.[48]

The term 'humanist' here refers to a depoliticisation, to the individual dimension. The sexual revolution was not only about changing one's individual practices, but it was also tied to a revolutionary ideology and functioned in conjunction with the politico-socioeconomic revolution. Given the anticapitalist nature of these discourses, current critiques which depict the sexual revolution as flawed from the start and as necessarily leading to a double bind need to be challenged.

In the context of the Cold War, the sexual revolution went against two ideologies: communism and capitalism. Defending the idea of sexual revolution first constituted a way to challenge orthodox communism and to rethink the revolution in a more embodied way.[49] The sexual revolution was also a reaction to a depoliticised cultural revolution that was underway in capitalist liberal democracies. The current narrative of double bind overlooks the specificity of the 1950s and 1960s context, when the sexual revolution constituted an innovative rethinking of revolutionary ideals. Discourses on the sexual revolution therefore cannot simply be brushed aside as liberal and individualistic: claiming that the actors of the sexual revolution were politically naïve is ahistorical.

DISENTANGLING THE DOUBLE-BIND NARRATIVE

Returning to the historical sources allows us to challenge the narrative of the double bind. It is problematic to put the responsibility of the double bind on those who initially defended the sexual revolution. The capitalist co-optation of the sexual revolution is less a feature of the revolutionary discourses on sex than a feature of capitalist societies themselves. It was recuperated by other actors in society, who saw in these discourses an opportunity for marketability.

However, the boundary was not always perfectly clear between the revolutionary version of the sexual revolution and a more consumeristic version. A few sex shops and pornographic magazines in the late 1960s used the political rhetoric of the sexual revolution to justify their commercial activities. When the journalist Jacques Mousseau created the erotic magazine *Plexus* in 1969, he explained his vision of sexual politics in a book published in the same year where he argued that the sexual revolution was a deeply political question. He criticised mainstream pornographic magazines like *Playboy*, he quoted Reich and Marcuse, and he considered his erotic magazine a contribution to a more political sexual revolution. Interestingly, *Plexus* published articles reflecting on sexuality and politics—for instance, articles presenting the ideas of Reich—but also erotic pictures. It constitutes an interesting liminal case as it participates both in making sex a revolutionary question and in making a business out of it. The case of the journalist and sex shop creator Louis Dalmas also exemplifies this ambiguous boundary between revolutionary sexual politics and the marketisation of sex. Former member of the Résistance and Trotskyist activist after the war, he also founded one of the first Parisian sex shops in the early 1970s. He considered this business as the pursuit by other means of his political revolutionary beliefs. As Baptiste Coulmont has explained, Louis Dalmas fits into a 'commercial and political dual logic.'[50] In the UK, a similar dual logic lay at the heart of Malcolm McLaren and Vivienne Westwood's shop SEX which opened in London in 1974. Despite the commercial aspect, McLaren was influenced by situationists and the shop was instrumental in shaping the punk counter-culture.[51] These examples impart further nuance to the argument made in this chapter. Towards the end of the 1960s, the radical version of the sexual revolution led to some commercial uses of sexuality that were at odds with the anti-capitalist essence of the sexual revolution.

Nonetheless, it is important to understand that these initiatives emerged in a capitalist society where the marketisation of sex was more generally in full development. The political rationalisations for sex shops and erotic magazines were rare among the booming pool of erotic products. These innovative commercial attempts were therefore subsumed in a greater trend of Western society which saw greater commercialisation of sex products in the 1970s. However, this is probably more telling of how capitalism accommodates social transformations and incorporates critiques made against its system than of any naïvety intrinsic to the sexual revolution that would inevitably lead it into a double bind. As Luc Boltanski and Eve Chiapello explained in *The New Spirit of Capitalism* in 1999, capitalism needs critiques to justify itself, reconfigure itself and survive. Capitalist and liberal regimes accommodate critiques, even the most radical ones. This is an essential feature of the capitalist system, and we should therefore be wary of blaming activists from the 1960s for their *récuperation*. If we blur the boundary between the capitalist distortions of the sexual revolution and the initial discourses on radical sexual politics, we risk simplifying these discourses and imposing a readymade narrative on these complex discourses which always clearly stated their anti-capitalist and political dimension.

Recovering the history of the sexual revolution sheds a new light on our current times. It demonstrates the possibility for a bridge between revolutionary politics and sexual politics, today commonly associated with liberal and individualistic identity politics. Looking back at the 1950s through the 1960s demonstrates how novel it was to consider politics not as a merely serious and theoretical matter but also as an existential question. Considering issues such as sexuality and relationships as political constituted a radical innovation for revolutionary politics, and feminists generalised further this politicisation of the personal in the 1970s. Even if the question of lifestyle is more associated today with capitalist individualism than with radical politics, we should refrain from only perceiving it as a neoliberal question. Eva Illouz has been particularly critical of the politics of lifestyle, which she describes as market-oriented: 'Sexuality was the key cultural value and practice bridging between "authentic" liberation projects and the commercialization of social life. "Liberation" became a consumer niche and a consumer style.'[52] Illouz considers the question of style as purely capitalist and consumeristic, and she therefore dismisses lifestyle issues as incapable of transforming societies. We could, however, argue that lifestyle is not in essence consumeristic.[53] It is also about paying greater attention to everyday experiences than traditional radical politics usually do. We can still take seriously the idea that experiences and ways of living matter to the revolution. Sexual experimentations are not *in themselves* about marketisation and consumerism. They are relationships, and therefore they will often exceed the capitalist logics they might emerge within. Illouz's critique of dating apps seems, for instance, to overlook the nature of relationships. She argues that in a capitalist society where dating apps are popular, sex and relationships are marketised.[54] This argument is also widespread in the popular press.[55] However, I want to argue that the capitalist logics behind the apps can be exceeded by the relationships that they initiate. When people encounter other people, it opens the door to a wide variety of possibilities, which cannot be reduced to capitalism. Experiences of intimacy may create an experience of connection, of community and of freedom. Experiencing these connections with otherness does not necessarily directly reinforce capitalism and individualism. We can argue then that in sexuality lies the possibility of an agency, of a practice of freedom, which might not directly make the structures of oppression crumble, but which can provide an experience that is creative and that connects people together outside a pure market logic. And this has a revolutionary potential, all the more so because it provides experiences of agency, rather than trapping people who would believe in revolutionary ideals in an inactive hope for a brighter future. If it leads to a double bind, this is only to the extent that we live in a capitalist and patriarchal society from which we cannot entirely separate ourselves. We should not blame the double bind on sexual politics.

The perfectly legitimate critique of capitalism should avoid reducing sexual matters and questions of lifestyle to capitalist and individualist logic. The idea that the revolution will come has too often justified a resigned acceptance of patriarchal and traditional norms in the meantime. In the postwar decades, the French Communist Party (PCF), the Trotskyist Party (PCI) and traditional Marxists thought that gender relations and sexuality would automatically be transformed by the overthrowing of the capitalist infrastructure. Classic Marxism did not envision any possibility of subverting hierarchies through sexuality before the advent of a revolutionary society. That is what the newspaper of the French Trotskyist party argued against Daniel Guérin's book on *Kinsey and Sexuality* in 1955:

> No workers, exploited by their everyday work, nor women always so disadvantaged can 'free' themselves sexually without a socialist revolution happening first. Only a few privileged individuals can claim to be able to fight effectively as of now for their own sexual liberation. But they only can *claim* to do so! Because no one can, in the reality of the framework of our current society, have sexual relationships that emanate freely from their physical and affective fulfilment, without any kind of constraint and any vileness. Such relationships will only thrive in a very superior phase of the socialist society, where the human being will become for another human the main source of love and plenitude, and not a constant source of all sorts of conflicts and psychological traumas.[56]

However, the hope for a radically brighter future should not justify a social and cultural status quo. The activists who defended the sexual revolution argued that revolutionaries had neglected the immediate transformation of life for too long. Why should we believe that a structural revolution alone would transform subjectivities? How could everyday lives be suddenly radically transformed without the accompanying gradual transformation of subjectivities? According to these 1960s revolutionaries, it was already time to start experimenting with relationships. Changes in sexual practices constituted a way forward towards transforming subjectivities. Only with these transformed subjectivities would the revolutionary world be truly emancipating. Sexuality could already be used as a tool of emancipation, rather than waiting for a purely structural revolution. This position strikingly echoes that of the sex-positive scholar Carol Vance during the so-called feminist sex wars in the US in the 1980s. Contrary to what radical feminists had argued in the 1970s, Vance defended the idea that a form of empowerment through sexuality was already possible in patriarchal societies: 'Feminists are easily intimidated by the charge that their own pleasure is selfish, as in political rhetoric which suggests that no woman is entitled to talk about sexual pleasure while any woman remains in danger—that is—never.'[57] A similar logic plays out in the traditional Marxist argument that we cannot discuss sexuality before capitalism has been overthrown—because that would mean indulging in individualist considerations—and in the radical feminist idea that we cannot talk about sexual pleasure until patriarchy has been overthrown. On the contrary, both supporters of the sexual revolution and sex-positive feminists argued that sexuality in itself *could* constitute a meaningful and revolutionary subversion of power dynamics and oppressive structures.

We should therefore be critical of typically Marxist or leftist discourses that blame sexual experimentation for depoliticising issues. They convey a very specific ahistorical, teleological and fatalistic narrative of the double bind. By disentangling the sexual revolution of the 1960s and 1970s from later developments and interpretations, we can rethink the double-bind narrative. Sexual politics have the potential to be revolutionary. The historical perspective enables us to see how crucial it is to consider subjectivities and everyday matters in revolutionary politics. The ideal of sexual revolution was constructed to counterbalance the simplistic vision of revolution which focused on economy. Despite the risk of recuperation that comes with defending sexual politics within capitalist societies, this tension should not lead us to fatalism. Even in our current context, platform capitalism offers intimate opportunities that can undermine market logics themselves. Applications such as OnlyFans or dating apps demonstrate how capitalist innovations do not necessarily entail alienation or marketisation. They also have the capacity to promote sexual agency and connect atomised individuals, opening up revolutionary potentials.

NOTES

1. Michel Houellebecq, *Extension du Domaine de la Lutte* (Paris: Editions Maurice Nadeau, 1994).
2. Michel Houellebecq, *Atomised*, trans. Frank Wynne (London: Vintage, 2001), 135–36.
3. Eva Illouz, *The End of Love, A Sociology of Negative Relations* (Oxford: Oxford University Press, 2019), 101.
4. Dagmar Herzog, *Sexuality in Europe: A Twentieth-Century History* (Cambridge: Cambridge University Press, 2012), 135.
5. Illouz, *The End of Love*, 46.
6. Eva Illouz, *Cold Intimacies, The Making of Emotional Capitalism* (London: Polity Press, 2007).
7. Michel Foucault, 'The Subject and Power,' *Critical Inquiry* 8, no. 4 (Summer 1982): 777–95.
8. Michel Foucault, 'Non au sexe roi' (1977), in *Dit et Ecrits, Tome III* (Paris: Gallimard, 1994), 92–130.
9. Michel Bozon, 'Révolution sexuelle ou individualisation de la sexualité?,' *Mouvements*, no. 20 (2002) 15–22.
10. Judith Coffin, *Sex, Love, and Letters, Writing Simone de Beauvoir* (Ithaca, NY: Cornell University Press, 2020), 211.
11. Lucile Ruault, 'Libération sexuelle ou *"pression à soulager ces messieurs"*? Points de vue de femmes dans les années '68 en France,' *Ethnologie française*, no. 174 (Spring 2019): 373–89.
12. Illouz, 'Chapter 3: Confusing Sex,' in *The End of Love*, 60–97.
13. Malka Malkovitch, *L'Autre héritage de 68: La face cachée de la révolution sexuelle* (Paris: Albin Michel, 2018). Malkovitch's book has been described as a firsthand testimony from a feminist finally unveiling the true abusive nature of '68's sexual liberation.
14. Michelle Zancarini-Fournel, *Le moment 68: une histoire contestée* (Paris: Seuil, 2008); Kristin Ross, *May 68 and Its Afterlives* (Chicago: University of Chicago Press, 2001).
15. Julian Jackson, 'The Mystery of May 1968,' *French Historical Studies* 33, no. 4 (2010): 629.
16. Jackson, 'The Mystery of May 1968,' 627.
17. This was probably also a consequence of the Weinstein affair, which foregrounded gendered power dynamics.
18. Eric Hobsbawm, 'Revolution and Sex' (1969), in *Revolutionaries: Contemporary Essays* (London: Weidenfelt and Nicholson, 1973), 218.
19. Hobsbawm, 'Revolution and Sex,' 219.
20. Christopher Lasch, 'The Freudian Left and Cultural Revolution,' *New Left Review* 1, no. 129 (September–October 1981).
21. Illouz, *The End of Love*, 25.
22. Illouz, *The End of Love*, 13.
23. Illouz, *The End of Love*, 7.

24. It was circulating particularly among marginal artistic milieus such as surrealists, from neo-Malthusians fighting for access to birth control in Europe and the United States, from feminist Soviet intellectuals who thought communism should address the question of women and sexuality (especially Alexandra Kollontai and Clara Zetkin), to new groups interested in sexology and sexual politics, for instance around the League for Sexual Reform in Europe.

25. Françoise d'Eaubonne, *Le Complexe de Diane:Érotisme ou féminisme* (Paris: Julliard, 1951), 23. All translations from French to English are my own.

26. Jean de Leyde, 'Les Marxistes et l'amour,' *Arguments*, no. 21 (1961): 34–37.

27. Blanche Plaquevent, 'Penser la révolution sexuelle dans les années 1960: intellectuelles et étudiantes en quête de subversion,' *Ethnologie française* 174, no. 2 (Spring 2019).

28. Julian Jackson, *Living in Arcadia, Homosexuality, Politics, and Morality in France from the Liberation to Aids* (Chicago: University of Chicago Press, 2009), 178–79; Anne-Claire Rebreyend, *Intimités Amoureuses, France 1920–1975* (Toulouse: Presses Universitaires du Mirail, 2008), 261–69.

29. 'Lycées: ni monastère ni prison,' *Avant-garde Jeunesse*, no. 4 (February 1967).

30. Richard I. Jobs, *Riding the New Wave, Youth and the Rejuvenation of France after the Second World War* (Stanford: Stanford University Press, 2007), 220.

31. He writes for instance about graffiti and situationist *détournements*. Tom McDonough, *'The Beautiful Language of My Century': Reinventing the Language of Contestation in Postwar France, 1945–1968* (Cambridge, MA: MIT Press, 2007).

32. Report on the demonstration in front of the COPAR, 16 March 1968, Police archives of Paris, FD73.

33. The English title is *On the poverty of student life: considered in its economic, political, psychological, sexual and particularly intellectual aspects, and a modest proposal for its remedy.*

34. This has been particularly the case in the German context, although the division of the country after WWII also entailed specific dynamics. Dagmar Herzog, *Sex after Fascism: Memory and Morality in Twentieth-Century Germany* (Princeton: Princeton University Press, 2005).

35. Kostas Axelos, 'L'errance érotique. Problématique de l'amour,' *Arguments*, no. 21 (1961): 21.

36. 'Kinsey et la sexualité, de Daniel Guérin,' *Populaire Dimanche*, 6 March, 1955, in Daniel Guérin papers, La Contemporaine, Nanterre, F delta 721/12/5.

37. Daniel Guérin, *Kinsey et la sexualité* (Paris: Julliard, 1955), 48.

38. Thomas Münzer, 'Sexualité et travail,' *Partisans*, nos. 32–33 (October–November 1966): 35.

39. Gérard Gilles, 'Révolution économique, révolution érotique,' *Recherches libertaires*, no. 2 (February 1967).

40. Françoise d'Eaubonne, *Le Complexe de Diane*, 21–22.

41. Daniel Guérin, *Kinsey et la sexualité* (Paris: Julliard, 1955), 111.

42. Herbert Marcuse, *One-Dimensional Man* (Boston: Beason Press, 1964); Dagmar Herzog, *Sexuality in Europe*, 135.

43. Violette Morin and Joseph Majault, *Un mythe moderne: l'érotisme* (Paris: Casterman, 1964), 22–23.

44. Morin and Majault, *Un mythe*, 41.

45. Jacques Mousseau, *L'Amour à refaire, La révolution sexuelle à la lumière des sciences humaines* (Paris: Denoël, 1969), 12.

46. Nous sommes en marche, 'Le silence et la violence,' 6 June 1968, Marianne Guillbaud Papers, La Contemporaine, Nanterre, F delta 1061 (10), File 5: Mai 68 en lettres à Paris.

47. *Nous sommes en marche*, 'Le silence et la violence.'

48. *Nous sommes en marche*, 'Avant-projet d'une révolution culturelle et sociale,' 7 June 1968, Bibliothèque Nationale de France, Paris, Mfiche Lb61–600, no. 39.

49. This was even more so in the case of the USSR, which had abandoned its progressive sexual politics in the 1920s.

50. Baptiste Coulmont, *Sex-Shops, Une Histoire Française* (Paris: Editions Dilecta, 2007), 60.

51. Jon Savage, *England's Dreaming: Anarchy, Sex Pistols, Punk Rock and Beyond* (New York: St Martin's Press, 1992), 83.

52. Illouz, *The End of Love*, 50.

53. Many thinkers have reflected on the question of lifestyle as distinct from capitalism and consumerism. Foucault wrote about lifestyles and sexual practices in Ancient Greece in *Histoire de la sexualité, 2. L'Usage des Plaisirs* (Paris: Gallimard, 1984). Marielle Macé addresses the question of style beyond consumption in *Styles, Critique de nos formes de* vie (Paris: Gallimard, 2016). We could also mention a large body of literature on the 'formes de vie,' understood as an existential question about everyday lives, beyond the simple question of consumerism.

54. Illouz, *The End of Love*, 62.

55. Ashley Fetters and Kaitlyn Tiffany, 'The Dating Market Is Getting Worse,' *The Atlantic*, 25 February 2020, https://www.theatlantic.com/family/archive/2020/02/modern-dating-odds-economy-apps-tinder-math/606982/.

56. 'Kinsey et la sexualité de Daniel Guérin,' *IVe Internationale* 13, nos. 1–3 (March 1955).

57. Carol Vance, 'Pleasure and Danger: Toward a Politics of Sexuality,' in *Pleasure and Danger: Exploring Female Sexuality*, ed. Carol Vance (Boston: Routledge and Kegan Paul, 1984), 7.

Part III

COLLECTIVE PRACTICES AND INSTITUTIONS

Chapter Eight

Two Kinds of Critical Pragmatism

Iain MacKenzie

The double bind of neoliberalism can be summed up in a question: what do we do if we want to challenge a system that encourages us to do whatever we want? Of course, there are some clarifications to this question that should be established from the beginning. The 'we' risks invoking a collective critical subject that can be rekindled from the ashes of history. However, it is best to put such utopian hopes to one side when the mantra 'be who you want to be' sits comfortably alongside 'do whatever you want' and both are so deeply integrated into contemporary forms of life. Of course, to understand how the collective critical subject has been outflanked in this way, it is important to clarify how the double bind emerged from within the disparate series of events we often summarize with the simple date, '68; perhaps the last time a revolutionary spirit gripped Europe and 'resounded across continents.'[1] Though there are many ways of trying to grasp how neoliberalism harnessed the radicalism of these events, the emphasis below is on those accounts that resist any appeal to a nascent collective subject of resistance. As such, the problem is not just how we are bound by neoliberal gestures but how forms of resistance to neoliberalism often double down on those binds rather than shake them loose. Such historical reflection invites philosophical framing. To what extent are the forms of critical thought animating practices of resistance not merely contingently ineffective but necessarily complicit in the construction of the double bind of neoliberalism? This question can be usefully raised under the banner of correlationism, a way of conceiving of the double bind of neoliberalism as simply the latest manifestation of the limitations of critical thought.[2] But does that mean that there are no ways of answering the opening question—'what do we do?'—that will not simply lead us deeper into the traps of the double bind? Are there any forms of critical thought that can motivate critical practice that do not invoke a collective critical subject, avoid recuperation within correlationism and yet that challenge the neoliberal double bind that is its latest variant? This more refined version of the opening question invites us to leave behind most critical philosophies that merely reflect practice, to consider an approach that treats philosophy itself as a form of practice; namely, pragmatism.

There are many varieties of pragmatism, notably those that frame philosophical problems by foregrounding their contribution to the maintenance of the status quo.[3] As such, pragmatism is often sidelined or occluded altogether in the standard histories of critical thought. However, there is a kernel of radicalism within many forms of pragmatism which aim to unsettle established social formations, especially those shrouded in the cloak of common-sense representational frameworks. The pragmatic approach to philosophy in this sense is guided by critical rather than conservative concerns.[4] After sketching out the emergence of the double bind, and its philosophical formulation in the problem of correlationism, therefore, this chapter will classify, clarify, and evaluate two kinds of critical pragmatism—discursive pragmatism and machinic pragmatism—with a view to articulating which, if either, offers a practically oriented way out of the double bind of neoliberalism. In amongst the 'do whatever you like' culture of neoliberalism is it possible to *select* forms of critical practice that will not become simply recuperated within the neoliberal status quo? This issue of selection is at the heart of the problem of the double bind, the core of the distinction between discursive and machinic forms of pragmatism and it is the key to unlocking which of these will offer escape from the double bind itself. For varieties of discursive pragmatism, the selection of critically effective practice can be forged within the socially constituted 'space of reasons.' In the end, though, this practice of *rational selection* will be shown to be compromised by its continuing debt to the logic it seeks to criticise. In contrast, the process of *double selection* embedded within machinic pragmatism (based on creative conceptualisation and openness to experience) will be proposed as the more effective means to untie the double bind of neoliberalism.

A BRIEF HISTORY OF THE DOUBLE BIND OF NEOLIBERALISM

The events of '68 made it clear that traditional forms of representative politics had failed. In particular, the post-WWII consensus that guided both establishment and radical political parties into uneasy complicities and compromises began to crack. While this took different forms in different countries, the temporary sense of post-conflict stability and shared purpose was broken apart as those who bore the brunt of being disciplined into this consensus began to doubt that the promised liberties would materialise. Students, in particular, erupted onto the political scene with an unprecedented force. As is now well established and acknowledged, labour movements and worker's organisations were caught off guard. Radical political parties, such as the PCF in France, couldn't control the surge of youthful protest and found themselves uneasily positioned alongside, and in some instances aligned with, their more centrist rivals. In Italy, young people took to the streets, and some became radicalised to the point of pursuing violent strategies that subsequently resulted in the so-called years of lead. German political culture was similarly shattered by student protests, especially as it became clear to the students that former Nazis still maintained positions of authority within the apparatuses of the state and its disciplinary institutions. Universities and art colleges in England were also sites of protest. Though typically less disruptive and certainly less violent, a similar sense of unease at the post-WWII consensus motivated forms of resistance to a stifling political culture. Crucially, in America the protest movements were guided in large measure by opposition to the military operations of the US government—resistance to the draft being especially important. For all the national specificities, however, we can make sense of these disparate yet connected events.

In short, there was a moment of expressive transgression: the traditional regimes of political representation established in the wake of both world wars constituted but could not contain the youthful energies unleashed onto the streets. Ruminating on this transgressive moment, Félix Guattari explained that it was not a deep political truth that was unfurled on the banners of '68, it was simply but profoundly a response to feeling 'bored to death' by the post-WWII consensus embedded in the major social institutions, universities chief amongst them.[5] Transgressing the norms of those institutions, therefore, was not done in the name of a fully-fledged idea of freedom, rather it was a search for excitement amidst stultifying boredom; as evocatively expressed by Guattari, the events of '68 were, in the end, fueled by the desire to be 'walking on air.'[6] Given this, although there were many and varied calls for new forms of democracy, more participatory and inclusive, these were doomed to failure. There was no need for an alternative system of representative politics. In effect, the surge of transgressive energy was all the statement required to escape from the tortuous dullness of disciplinary Victorian institutions in the service of postwar calm and the stultifying 'boredom' that such institutions instilled in the youth. Although various political positions emerged and institutional changes developed, the indelible mark of the events of '68 was that of an agitated excess, unconstrained by the usual patterns of political representation and attendant forms of political organisation.

The tremendous power of this assault on traditional forms of representation is captured most succinctly by two of the intellectuals who, paradoxically perhaps, were at some remove from the actual events: Foucault and Deleuze. Even though Foucault was not present in Paris during the events of May '68, and although Deleuze was present and sympathetic he was largely concerned with finishing his doctoral thesis, by the time of their conversation in 1972 titled 'Intellectuals and Power,' Deleuze captured not just the heart of Foucault's oeuvre but the spirit of '68 in this famous phrase: 'the indignity of speaking on behalf of others.'[7] Having other people speak on one's own behalf in the name of securing the post-WWII consensus had become unbearable; it was just too 'boring' to hear the intellectuals, the party aficionados and the state hacks declare that they knew best. It was time, especially for the youth, to speak up for themselves, on their own behalf. It is true that in finding their own voice they often spoke in paradox and riddles, but there was something wildly creative and inspiring in shattering the binds of common sense. This was most famously captured in the graffito, 'Be realistic—demand the impossible!.' In amongst the moments of resistance against the apparatuses of state conformity there was acknowledgement that the demands of emergent movements should not conform to the representative structures of the state. It appeared that the time had come to find forms of expression in all domains without representatives, and to search for a way of being with each other where no one would dare to speak on behalf of anyone else.

Reflecting back, this search for a new form of non-representative politics is usually characterised as a failure because the dominant organs of the state coalesced once more to establish consensus. There is truth in this, of course. Much of the rebellious energy simply exhausted itself and what remained of the youthful spirit of change and innovation was harnessed in the service of new state organisations. It was, for example, neatly captured and contained in the forested suburbs of Paris in Vincennes. Political parties reconvened, albeit with revitalised youth wings, and in many respects the old complicities and conformities were reforged alongside the reinstitution of old forms of discipline. However, the transgressive ethos of '68 did not get wholly reabsorbed into these reinvigorated disciplinary systems. In fact, the events of '68 helped to establish something much more lasting that has come to shape our political life to this day. In the wake of '68, aspects of the creative spirit of transgression were encouraged and embraced, but only if they could be put into the service of profit. Across the developed industrial economies, the mid-1970s saw the rise of the entrepreneur, inspiring innovation within business and able to conjure up profitable opportunities within new hubs of creative capitalisation. One of the main legacies of '68, therefore, is a world of exciting new freedoms (for a few) where excess was encouraged but controlled for the sake of new opportunities in wealth creation. Disciplining subjects in the name of consensus was gradually replaced, in complex and uneven ways for sure, by the mechanisms of control which could harness entrepreneurial innovation. By the 1980s, throughout the major economies of the time, it wasn't the students who broke the conventional disciplinary rules; it was the financier, the venture capitalist and the 'Yuppies' who embodied the creative excess of '68. For this small group, everything was allowed as long as the profit margins were as excessive as the behaviour. They could indeed 'be realistic and demand the impossible,' as long as there was profit to be created.

In the wake of financialisation and its excesses, the social world was transformed. As the old regimes of representation became less and less relevant, there arose a new twist on an old idea: individualism. The old idea was that individuals made up society by way of contracts and the free exchange of labour and that these were forged with respect to ensuring the safety and prosperity of all. This modern form of individualism, that had so effectively undermined divinely sanctioned monarchies, established the complicities of labour and capital through disciplinary institutions that ensured individual desire was locked into the logics of welfare capitalism. After the events of '68, the new twist on this modern idea was that individuals should no longer work for the good of society, for anything as base as gross domestic product. Rather, the new entrepreneur would work at the limits of social acceptability purely for the sake of profit without domestic constraints. Any old institutions that got in the way, had to be transformed, worked around or torn down. For all that many of the disciplinary mechanisms are still functioning throughout advanced industrial economies they are becoming less and less important, replaced by totalising institutions of control.[8] In short, neoliberal ideology is the spirit of '68 incorporated within global capitalism and then embodied in the free-thinking, excessive entrepreneur who can serve as the aspirational model for us all. For all that liberalism has always valued the individual, in this new twist it is the excessive entrepreneurial individual that is valorised; the one that seeks profit above all else, with no regard for the disciplinary institutions that have enabled individual freedoms to flourish collectively. The anti-representationalist spirit of '68 was transformed into this neoliberal spirit of transgression. In its purest form, the entrepreneur represents no one, works for no one, and lives solely to generate profit.

From '68 to today, this new form of individualism has been diagnosed in a myriad of ways. Insight can be garnered from Christopher Lasch's *The Culture of Narcissism*, Charles Taylor's *Sources of the Self*, and more recently Luc Boltanski and Eve Chiapello's *The New Spirit of Capitalism* (and many more).[9] Whatever perspective is adopted, there is acknowledgement that the transformation towards new forms of self-expression is core to, what is now often referred to as, neoliberal ideology. These are new not just because they reinvigorate individualism against the rise of welfarism, but because they seek justification outside of any sense of consensus or the common good, other than the generation of profit. To the extent that the generation of profit is increasingly naturalised, embedded within a discourse of the real, regimes of justification tend toward the claim that my self-expression is mine alone.[10] This marks the end of the representational model of individualism, whereby the individual who engaged in the social and economic contracts of modern liberal democratic capitalism was doing so on behalf of the whole nation. What we see instead is the steady deflation of the individual who speaks on behalf of others, and the hyperinflation of the individual that will only speak on its own behalf. Deleuze's comment to Foucault, that 'you taught us the indignity of speaking on behalf of others,' was not simply acknowledgement of Foucault's tireless critique of representational modes of thinking and acting. It was, no doubt unwittingly, a prefiguring of the ideology we have come to know as neoliberalism—that we can now only speak on our own behalf. As we will explore below, however, this is not the necessary outcome of seeking an alternative to representationalism.[11]

The hyperinflation of individuals speaking on their own behalf only captures one side of the legacies of '68. The other side is that the nature of the available forms of opposition to individualism has also been transformed. If one is not winning the game of neoliberalism then it is by no means clear what one can do about it, given that the totalising institutions of control that help it to function make it increasingly impossible to speak on behalf of others. The politics of collective mobilisation has had to change, moving away from established universal categories of subject position such as class and away from particular subjectivities in need of inclusion within the liberal capitalist consensus. Instead, protests against the neoliberal regimes are increasingly organised around the mobilisation of common sense, not rebellion against it. This gesture, by appealing to shared experiences, marks the terrain of new kinds of folk politics from both left and right. While there are subtleties and nuances surrounding the emergence and nature of all protest movements, practices of resistance in and against the rise of neoliberal hyper-individualism are movements that look to express simple nativist truths about how we should get along with each other if everybody speaks (the same) common sense (on their own behalf). There is no need for tough ideological battle lines as long as everybody simply understands what we have in common—unfortunately, there is no consensus about what we have in common, and these movements are typically held together by a range of empty signifiers including, for example, 'the 99%,' 'taking back control,' 'being an American' and 'our community.' The old battle lines between and within left and right do not hold their value anymore. In the wake of '68, the dignity of speaking only on one's own behalf has become the mantra of an individualist politics that embraces and yet controls its transgressive energy and a collectivist politics that fuels folk forms of opposition characterised by leaderless movements and occupations that hark back to notions of community and country.

This captures the double bind in the legacies of '68. *Les événements* fatally undermined the politics of representation such that we can now only speak on our own behalf as individuals in the name of simply maximising what is best for us; and, if we are unable to maximise our profit then we can only speak on our behalf as members of a community that cannot be represented except by how we speak of it, on our own terms as an aggregate of individuals called the 'populous,' the 'people,' the 'community' and so on. In this respect, current forms of resistance to neoliberalism can only give sustenance to its individualist roots. Given this double bind, and as we live through the long wake of '68, we might be tempted to think that there is no way out; we may think we can choose only between options in which we will lose out either way, if by loss we mean the furtherance of neoliberal ideology. What I will explore below is the idea that the excess and energy of '68's anti-representationalist politics did not necessarily have to become the control of that transgressive behaviour in the complementary forms of neoliberal individualism and nativist folk politics. There is, at least we can suppose there to be, a space between anti-representationalism and repeated (individual and collective) self-presentation; a space that signals a route out of the double binds. For this space to be delineated, however, we must turn the brief historical sketch into a philosophical problem.

THE DOUBLE BIND AS A PHILOSOPHICAL PROBLEM

This brief historical sketch of how the anti-representationalist excess of '68 transformed into neoliberal hyper-individualism and nativist folk politics requires a firmer philosophical footing in order to establish the problem at stake. It is important, in other words, to establish what sits behind the movement from anti-representational politics to a politics of repeated (individual and collective) self-presentation. This can be done by situating it in a broader philosophical domain, which will have the additional benefit of establishing the ways in which these new forms of self-expression and folk politics simply reinstate representationalism. The philosophical nature of this problem, though not the solution as we will see, has been established by Quentin Meillassoux in his book *After Finitude*. The case for this claim is based on situating neoliberalism within the framework of, what he calls, 'fideism.' This will help us view neoliberalism as a reflex of the reflexive dynamic at the heart of modern individualism, one that has managed to incorporate the challenges to it embedded in the events of '68. We need to begin with a short reconstruction of *After Finitude*.

While *After Finitude* has rightly been celebrated (although also increasingly challenged) because of the post-critical philosophical agenda to which it points, it is primarily shaped by its withering assessment of the philosophical and political legacies of modern European critical thought. As such, it provides a compelling resource when thinking about why it should be that the events of '68 have been recuperated within new forms of individualism and control such that any protest against these new forms is based on harking back to forms of common sense that '68 was supposed to have overcome. He begins the analysis back at the high point of modern individualism, philosophically speaking. Meillassoux recognises that critical thought is aimed against all forms of ideological dogmatism (claims that simply presume the givenness of their founding axioms) but he is at his most politically astute when arguing about the ways in which the critical injunctions against dogmatism have led to a new form of fanaticism. He puts it succinctly: 'the more thought arms itself against dogmatism, the more defenceless it becomes before fanaticism.'[12] Indeed, it is not simply because critical thought is unable to challenge fanaticism that it is defenceless, it is because critical thought has brought it into existence that it cannot overcome it. As he says, 'contemporary fanaticism cannot . . . simply be attributed to the resurgence of an archaism that is violently opposed to the achievements of Western critical reason; on the contrary, it is the effect of critical rationality.'[13] As we look further into why this is the case, we can understand the sources and nature of the fanaticisms that reside within contemporary individualist and populist forms of neoliberalism.

What is the nature of critical rationality such that it has led to fanaticism? On Meillassoux's account, the great gesture of critical thought was to call into question all forms of dogmatism by insisting upon the unimpeachable correlation between thought and being. Correlationism is 'the idea according to which we only ever have access to the correlation between thinking and being, and never to either term considered apart from the other.'[14] One of the crucial consequences of this gesture is that all claims about the world, and our place in it, are claims that must be qualified as claims 'for us.' This has the effect of deflating dogmatic certainties both philosophically and, importantly, politically. However, it also set in train a way of talking about the world and our place in it that found new forms of fanatical expression precisely defined by the codicil 'for us.' According to Meillassoux, the critical tradition has opened up new forms of religiosity (religious expression and all forms of 'blind faith') that stretch across the secular and atheistic domains as well, in which the 'for us' becomes unimpeachable. This is what Meillassoux calls 'fideism.' It can be summed up as the 'belief that belief is all there is' and in the wake of the critical undermining of dogmatism it 'reinforces religious obscurantism' to the extent that critical philosophy is unable to distinguish itself from fanatically held beliefs.[15]

In the context of the events of '68, it is important to add that the fanaticism of contemporary social and political life has become split. There is the hyper-individualist fanaticism of the libertarian (of left and right) and the hyper-collectivist fanaticism of the populist (of left and right). Indeed, this means that Meillassoux's diagnosis of the present can be deepened. We can now propose that the fideist 'for us' that underpins fanaticism can be understood in two ways: it is a 'for us' that reduces to a 'for me' and it is a 'for us' that reduces to an aggregate of 'for me's.' The appeal to lived experience (shared or not) is at root an expression of the critical injunction against dogmatic claims with respect to the nature of the real. And yet, in the manner of the sceptical swing of the pendulum, lived experience becomes the only thing that counts as real. Under these conditions, the fideist principle characterises the double bind of neoliberalism rather succinctly: the only apparent challenges to fanatical expressions of individualism are those forms of fanatical collectivism, both of which rest upon the very same principle—'the belief that belief is all there is.' As such, the double bind of neoliberalism has been forged from the transgressive excess of '68 and insinuated itself into the logic of oppositional political forces that seek to challenge the neoliberal paean to 'do whatever you want to do.'

In response to this problem, Meillassoux argues that while we must retain the critical gesture against dogmatism, and thereby never return to the ideological disasters such dogmatism fosters, we must nonetheless 're-discover in thought a modicum of absoluteness' to break out of correlationism and thereby overcome the fanaticism engendered by fideism. Inventive as this gesture is, however, it risks returning thought to a form of rationalism that will give succour to dogmatism. In the rest of this discussion, a different route will be taken, one which accepts the dangers of fideism emerging within critical thought but that aims to find the resources to challenge this from within the critical tradition itself. What is required of critical thought for this to be a possible outcome? We can put it two ways. On the one hand, we would need to establish a non-correlationist form of critical thought that is still recognisably critical in intent—that is, able to delimit the domain of the known. On the other hand, we may say that this requires a thoroughly non-representationalist version of critical thought. But can critical thought be non-correlationist and non-representationalist? In short, it is these overlapping tasks that we can articulate as the core of pragmatist readings of Kant's project, albeit retrospectively. The claim is that pragmatist readings of Kant's critical injunction can open up the ways to criticise dogmatism and neoliberal versions of fideism.

Why pragmatism? As famously expressed by Richard Rorty, pragmatism does away with the idea that philosophy should be a mirror of nature[16] and, in this sense, the claim is that pragmatists are the most thorough going anti-representationalist thinkers and that this is what's required to embrace the challenge of the events of '68 without engendering new forms of representationalist fanaticism. However, what is meant by a pragmatist reading of Kant is by no means straightforward (and cannot be fully explored here). What we can say is that there are two dominant perspectives, each of which attempts to explore what we can know about the world and how we know what we know about the world without recourse to a transcendental subject and its contemporary variant, the 'for me' of neoliberalism. Or, to put it another way, we can explore two versions of pragmatism that ground both the what and the how of critical thought in what we do.

TWO KINDS OF CRITICAL PRAGMATISM

The brief sketch of the historical conditions of the double bind of neoliberalism and how this is underpinned by the critical turn in modern epistemology leaves us in a quandary. On what basis can we critically engage with the emergence of neoliberal individualism and its complementary oppositional folk politics, if they are the result of the incorporation of transgressive excess into the critical codicil, 'for us'? For all that the modern revolutionary moments that instantiated liberal regimes across the Western world (and beyond) created liberties 'for us' against arbitrary rule and tyranny, they also functioned through the construction of manifold disciplinary institutions: schools, factories, clinics, psychiatric hospitals, universities and so on. The routinisation these disciplinary apparatuses brought to bear on peoples' lives, especially in the wake of WWII, led to the boredom, the stultifying lack of potential, that induced *les événements de mai '68*. As some of the energy of '68 was absorbed back into these institutions, though not without change, it was also folded into new ways of working and living that transformed the 'for us' that was based on a liberal 'for all of us' into a 'for us' that has become a neoliberal 'for me' as an individual and a 'for me, aggregated' as a collective. Therefore, the critical tradition that instantiated the disciplinary institutions (as well as the freedoms) has also provided the basis for the mutation of those institutions (and the smooth, unfettered life they promise) into regimes of control. Oppositional political forces gather around communities of common sense that appeal to notions of shared experience that ultimately rest upon the same fideist principles as the neoliberalism they seek to criticise. So, what is to be done?

From a philosophical point of view, there are a range of contemporary responses to this question. One might hope to reach outside the correlationist circle, into a realm of being uncorrelated to the thinking subject, so as to demonstrate the limited and dangerous nature of thinking that always resolves itself in a 'for us.' This is the tactic adopted by Meillassoux. An alternate path has been sketched out whereby the correlationist circle is not pierced but suspended, held in stasis, so that we might at least consider what would happen if we do not always think about what being means 'for us.' This route has been taken, in distinctly different ways, by Giorgio Agamben and Francois Laruelle.[17] As understood here, though, these attempts to move through critique or to suspend it are inevitably bound to reinstate the problem of indifference created by the rationalist/empiricist debate that animated the critical project in the first place. In short, critique cannot be left behind or suspended. Rather, the task is to reanimate critique in the face of this new manifestation of the problems it engenders. The critique of critique must always start afresh. But how is this to be done when contemporary neoliberalism and current forms of oppositional folk politics have incorporated the transgressive critique of disciplinary apparatuses into their very fabric? What is left of critique if transgression has become a norm?

In the wake of the double bind of neoliberalism the critical task is to occupy the centre of the relationship between thought and being and embrace the dynamism of, what Meillassoux calls, the correlationist two-step without reproducing dogmatism or scepticism. This is what we might call 'the critical mix': the mixture of concept and sensation within critical pragmatism that avoids a rigid architecture of their relationship with respect both to the ends of critique and to the grounds of critique. Putting it another way, the key task is to express the transcendental conditions of '*what* we know about the world' and '*how* we know what we know about the world' in a manner that retains the contingency of both. But are there variants of contemporary thought that can express the contingency of the real and of thought while remaining within the transcendental apparatus that provides the necessary criteria for positive claims that challenge both neoliberal hyper-individualism and populist folk politics?

Two kinds of transcendentalism offer an answer to this question: we will call them transcendental naturalism and transcendental aestheticism. The transcendental naturalist claims that what we know about the world must inform our understanding of how we come to know the world but equally that how we know the world is not a mere reflection of what we know about our place in it. The first criterion disqualifies the sceptical deflation of the sciences as just one form of thought amongst others and embraces the broadly progressive quality of our understanding of nature, including our place in it. The second criterion disqualifies accounts of the subject that presume we are in some sense beings whose cognitive faculties simply reflect fundamental categories of nature. In fact, on this account, all knowledge of the world is social and discursive rather than subjective and reflective. This is the position developed by Ray Brassier; in his reading of Wilfrid Sellars, in particular.[18] Similarly, transcendental aestheticism rests upon two pillars: we can know the world by transforming it; and this process of transformation is best understood as an artistic one that engenders the learning that conditions knowledge. There are two fundamental claims animating this position: first, cognition is the result of a process called learning; secondly, the process of learning itself is not engendered by either a subject endowed with universal categories of understanding or by the unruly imposition of objects in the world upon the subject, but by encounters. The first claim establishes that learning is a critical practice that challenges what we think we know, introducing contingency at the level of what is known. The second challenges the claim that how we know what we know is the result of a discursive framework of conceptualisation, claiming instead that it is a shock to the system of conceptualisation by way of an 'encounter' with 'something in the world' that 'forces us to think.'[19] The artistry involved is that of being worthy of the encounter in order to challenge what we think we know (a claim about the contingency of thought) whilst remaining open to the possibility of new sensations in the world (a claim about the contingency of the world). This position is grounded in a post-Kantian interpretation of Deleuze and Guattari.[20]

These two kinds of transcendentalism are fundamental to our two kinds of critical pragmatism. The similar ways they treat the contingency of both thought and world establishes their respective debt to the critical project. The different emphases they place on the dynamic relationship between thought and being draw out the debates about how we come to know what we know. That said, the shared commitment to the critical project and to the dynamism of the correlationist circle mean that, in pragmatist language, we can say that these two forms of transcendentalism are seeking to avoid any lurch back to unsupportable notions of 'the given.' But how they seek to establish the critical force of philosophy without recourse to the given is different in each case. Given the reliance upon discursively constituted norms for the generation of reasonable knowledge claims, the transcendental naturalist can be called a 'discursive pragmatist.' Given the reliance upon the dynamic structures that condition learning, the transcendental aestheticist can be called a 'machinic pragmatist' (following Brassier). Which of these is better equipped to give us critical purchase on the guiding question: what do we do if we want to challenge the system that encourages us to do whatever we want?

The terms of this discussion, in many respects, have already been established by Brassier's critique of Deleuze and Guattari's machinic pragmatism in *A Thousand Plateaus*.[21] In general terms, according to Brassier, the key to understanding how this form of pragmatism operates can be summarised through the relationship between theory and practice in the book; '[p]ractice and theory realise one another: theoretical concepts are effectuated in practice; practical imperatives are formulated in theory.'[22] In a more particular manner, he rightly highlights the important role of the fifth 'approximate characteristic' of the rhizome: mapping. Mapping, in short, is one of the means by which this realisation between theory and practice is made possible. Contrasted throughout the book with the representationalist gesture of tracing our concepts off the world, mapping is a creative process of experimenting with how we might forge practical interventions in the world. In this sense, mapping should be understood as the activity of creative conceptualisation.[23] As Deleuze and Guattari also say, mapping has 'to do with performance, whereas the tracing always involves an alleged "competence".'[24] And, in these ideas of creative experiments performed without regard for whether they are performed competently or not, Brassier finds a problem at the heart of machinic pragmatism. He argues that if there is no criterion for demarcating when processes of mapping can be regarded as competently done or not, then it is impossible to contrast machinic pragmatism with 'the utilitarian compromise which is the fabric of the everyday.'[25] In other words, for all the conceptual invention of *A Thousand Plateaus* it remains a book compromised by not being able to give reasons for why we must disrupt the 'utilitarian order of fixed goals, standards and practices through which reality is reproduced.'[26] Without a criterion of competence, according to Brassier, Deleuze and Guattari can only rely upon assigning an unwarranted positive value to creative processes that bring about the destratification of social strata. Undoing the social fabric, it would seem, appears to have a normative dimension that is under-developed and under-explained in Deleuze and Guattari's otherwise rigorous critique of stratified social forces and norms. As Brassier puts it: 'everything in the book relies upon giving a positive sense to the *de* in destratification, or delimitation, but this positive sense is merely the inversion of the limitation of absolute movement that it cannot but presuppose as its starting point: stratification.'[27] As such, Brassier charges Deleuze and Guattari with being the heirs of '68, in the sense of their complicity with the positive valorisation given to expressive transgression and subsequent appeals to both hyper-individualism and ineffable notions of common sense. Deleuze and Guattari's unbridled positivity toward destratification is ill-equipped to offer a critique of our current situation because there can be no *reason* for justifying any criterion of competence with respect to the creative process of mapping.

The appeal to reason is important as it is fundamental to the discursive pragmatism animating Brassier's critique of Deleuze and Guattari. Of course, appeals to reason come in many forms and it is important to specify that what is at stake in this pragmatic version is an appeal to the practice of 'asking for and giving reasons' as social activity rather than an appeal to an individual cognitive faculty. This pragmatist approach to reason is drawn from Wilfrid Sellars's reading of Kant. As part of his deep pragmatist engagement with Kantian themes, Sellars argued that when we make claims to know, we are *doing* something; namely, placing them within a space of reasons where inferences can be drawn, such that the usefulness of these within the whole system of knowledge can be checked so as to guide our sense of success or failure. Sellars called this 'the logical space of reasons.'[28] Making claims about the world allows us to select those that sustain the system of knowledge as understood while recognising that all claims are fallible and the system itself is open-ended. This idea of the space of reasons has been given further elaboration in the work of Robert Brandom. In his work, Brandom has sought to 'make explicit' the relationship between the claim being made and the system of knowledge within which it functions.[29] In so doing, he has developed a fully fledged account of the discursive constitution of knowledge: 'it is part of the pragmatism of *Making It Explicit* to insist that in the order of understanding, discursive practice has a certain priority: one cannot understand what facts and concepts are without also understanding the practice of making claims and inferences.'[30] In summarising this practice, Brandom has come up with his own resonant phrase: 'we are always inside the game of giving and asking for reasons.'[31] It is this feature that warrants the label discursive pragmatism: the game of giving and asking for reasons is a discursive practice, one that has emerged contingently from the processes of human evolution but that is not reducible to those processes. Two key features follow. First, we cannot engage in meaningful discussion about what is reasonable to assert (and what is not) without appeal to anything but the fully fledged social nature of thought. In this respect, it would appear that the 'for me-ness' of contemporary neoliberal practice is readily susceptible to challenge on the basis of the social nature of all claims to knowledge. Secondly, we can also motivate an ethical theory, according to Brandom, that does not commit the pragmatist to the presumption that good reasons for action are really just forms of instrumental reason.[32] The right thing to do, it would appear, is embedded in the normativity of the discursive practice of giving and asking for reasons. On the face of it, then, Brassier's invocation of the pragmatism of Sellars and Brandom has provided a serious challenge to Deleuze and Guattari's machinic pragmatism and done so from within a discursive pragmatist framework capable of selecting what to do on the basis of a form of rationality that motivates ethical forms of life. Neoliberalism, it would seem, must be challenged within the space of reasons and the social interaction this rationalism implies must be made explicit against the individualism of contemporary life. It is a profound vision, but is it as powerful as it would appear?

The debate between these forms of pragmatism is emerging rather than established. That said, we can draw key threads together by looking at a couple of important responses to discursive pragmatism, how this affects the project Brassier outlines and what alternative readings of Deleuze and Guattari's practice of mapping can be given that might offer the selection of competence required without resorting to the idea of the space of reasons. With respect to the first of these, the challenge is oriented around whether the 'social' aspect of the discursive can be consistently maintained. Habermas, for example, has criticised Brandom for articulating the social basis of 'the game of asking for and giving reasons' in a contingent manner that amounts to epistemological passivity vis-à-vis our everyday world of utility.[33] A stronger 'universal pragmatics' is needed, for Habermas, if the critique of liberal modernity in all its forms is to be properly motivated. Given that Habermas appeals to an ideal universal space of discursive rationality, while we are in the domain of competing pragmatisms, we don't need to follow Habermas here. Nonetheless, it is interesting to note that Brandom faces the same critique that Brassier's Brandom-inspired position makes of Deleuze and Guattari. It alerts us, that is, to the delicate balancing act that all pragmatisms face, between complicity and critique. In addition, it is notable that in responding to Habermas, Brandom makes appeal to the spontaneity of individuals: 'although there must be a receptive element in our cognition, there is also a crucial role played by spontaneity.'[34] This is an important aspect of the pragmatist response to universal pragmatics as it keeps open the possibility of radical transformation in the game of asking for and giving reasons. However, once conceded, this lurch to spontaneity has other consequences. Is it merely that we humans are able to refine constantly our practices of reason giving, or is it that the very game itself could be transformed in radical ways, even to the point of its not being as intrinsically social as Sellars, Brandom and Brassier insist? This line of questioning has been picked up by Gibbard and David Roden, in different ways. Gibbard makes the argument that some of Brandom's key claims could be held by a non-social thinker.[35] Notably, if being sapient as Brandom would have it means that we are able to infer and inference requires some sense of keeping score on oneself, then does such score-keeping have to be discursively or socially grounded? Roden makes the same point but in a different context: imagining post-human beings, he argues that they could be beings able to keep score, in ways that do not require the measuring of their inferences against public standards—a position he takes to be fatal for the discursive pragmatist project of Brassier.[36] But aren't these both rather abstract responses to pragmatic claims about the irreducibly social nature of raising reasons for our actions?

This is not the case if we have already entered a world in which the game of asking for and giving reasons has already been radically transformed. Perhaps we do not need the thought experiments of Gibbard or Roden to see that we are already in a world in which the social nature of reason giving has been replaced by the justificatory system of beliefs about belief. Brassier charges Deleuze and Guattari with complicity in a liberal world of individualism but, after '68, we are now in a world where the liberal consensus of discipline and freedom is being increasingly supplanted by a neoliberal world of control and smoothness. I take this to be the real worth of the journey through Meillassoux's claims about correlationism. As the strong correlationist gesture manifests socially and politically, in a world of fanatical fideism 'the belief that belief is all there is' makes any appeal to reason seem outdated and ineffective. While people can have their beliefs questioned and challenged within the space of reasons, it is increasingly impossible to move the debate beyond a stalemate as the rules of the game are not in themselves agreed. For the discursive pragmatist the game must be a game of asking for and giving reasons, but for the neoliberal individual, for example, the only game of justification is that of stating one's beliefs and believing that to be the only game available. No appeal to science, to the evolutionary development of discursive practices of cognition, will circumvent the belief in the unquestionable nature of one's own beliefs.[37] In effect, Brassier (through Sellars and Brandom) has articulated a neo-rationalism that is only effective with respect to the historical problem of an emergent liberalism. In the transformation of liberalism that has come with its incorporation of the expressive transgression signalled by '68, it has become immune to the rigours of the discursive, as the regime of justification is not to be found in the reasonableness of one's beliefs but in the belief that one's beliefs are self-justificatory.

Perhaps this is an all-too-historical claim, contestable in many respects? That may be so, but we can take the engagement between discursive and machinic pragmatisms a little further. Brassier's careful rendering of the argument immediately suggests that whatever worth we might find in machinic pragmatism, it is undermined with respect to selecting the mappings that succeed as distinct from those that fail. But it is intriguing to note that Brassier's account of mapping—we recall that it is the fifth 'approximate characteristic of the rhizome'—does not address its partner characteristic, the sixth: decalcomania. Decalcomania is the practice of transferring images on to the world, in which sense it can be understood as a process of learning; that is, a process of change through experience. Just as it important to move beyond tracing social formations toward the more constructive task of mapping them, it is equally important that we use our map of the world and we do so by transferring it into everyday use. This can be a practical process of interpreting how effective our maps are, but it can also be a practice whereby our transformative maps of the world are continuously selected with respect to their transformative consequences. As such, the creative experimentalism of mapping is always to be done hand-in-hand, so to speak, with various assessments of the maps with respect to whether or not they are useful tools. In short, with more to be said, machinic pragmatism does not prioritise the disruption or the stratification; rather, it operates through a process of double selection, from the perspective of the destratified and the stratified. We can say this in general terms: Brassier presents the prioritisation of the *de* in destratification as an ontological manoeuvre with ethical consequences. In thinking about the dual aspect of mapping and transferring the map, we get an epistemological project that embraces the discursive space of reasons but that also has an account of how it is that reasonable claims come to be formed and how their use can be challenged with respect to our critical commitments. But how are these critical commitments sustained? It would be tempting to say by an idea of 'practices of emancipation'—but this would be to say too much for the machinic pragmatist, as it would import a normative regime that would be unsustainable on its own terms. But we can say, with an echo of Marx, that the usefulness is defined in terms of the changes they can bring about?[38]

One of these, indeed, is neoliberalism itself. It is crucial that critical theorists recognise the role critique has played in establishing that which most critical thinkers today want to criticise: the hyper-individualism and nativist common sense of right and left. This, once again, is the importance of Meillassoux's insight into correlationism. However, his route out is not to be followed when what is needed is for critique to reforge itself from within the fires of the neoliberalism it has created, not least through the events of '68.

CONCLUSION

Are we any closer to establishing a way out of the double bind of neoliberalism? Is there a way to figure out what is to be done in a world that entreats us to do anything we want? From within the post-representational world of pragmatic philosophy, on the grounds that the critique of representation was central to the emergence of the world that we inhabit, the discursive pragmatist offers the space of reasons and the hope that once people are coaxed into the game of asking for and giving reasons, they will see that forms of hyper-individualism and/or aggregative collectivities cannot be inferred as consistent with what we know about the world and how we know this. I have argued above that the ship of the social sailed away precisely because of the events of '68 and that trying to jump back on board is unlikely to be an effective strategy. Moreover, it is a strategy that requires a social vision of the discursive that is weak with respect to its differentiation of contingent discursive norms from the normativity of discourse. Accepting this risk, the machinic pragmatist nonetheless embraces the practice of mapping the world with a view to experimenting with how well the maps we create challenge the status quo. In effect, this was what was done in the wake of '68; what this means, though, is that it can be done again from within the logic of neoliberal fanaticism.

So, what is to be done in a world in which we are invited to do whatever we want? It is useful to begin by recalling Deleuze's summary of Foucault's oeuvre and its importance in our understanding of how '68 sowed the seeds for the double bind of neoliberalism: 'you taught us the indignity of speaking on behalf of others.'[39] This powerful sentiment no doubt set the tone for a world in which we can only speak on our own behalf, justified by the belief that our beliefs are all that matter. What the pragmatic turn is showing us, however, is that the swing of the pendulum away from speaking on behalf of others to speaking only on one's own behalf is exactly that—a swing within the same logic of a critical thought limited by correlationism. From the machinic pragmatist perspective defended here, though, this swing of the pendulum can be stopped, and an alternative logic put in place. Adopting the tone of Deleuze's remark we can now say that what we can do in the face of the neoliberal double bind is 'speak on behalf of the other in oneself (through creative conceptualization, mapping) and listen to the other that speaks to you (through an openness to experiential learning, decalcomania).' Only this process of ongoing double selection will enable us to animate critical interventions against the neoliberal claim that one can do whatever one wants.[40]

NOTES

1. Jana Ndiaye Berankova, Michael Hauser and Nick Nesbitt 'Preface: The Last European Revolutions?,' in *Revolutions for the Future: May '68 and the Prague Spring*, ed. Jana Ndiaye Berankova, Michael Hauser and Nick Nesbitt (Lyon: Suture Press, 2020), 7.

2. Quentin Meillassoux, *After Finitude: An Essay on the Necessity of Contingency* (London: Continuum, 2008).

3. For example, the defence of liberalism in Richard Rorty, *Contingency, Irony, and Solidarity* (Cambridge: Cambridge University Press, 1989).

4. For a good overview of the relationship between Kantian critical thought and pragmatism, see the essays collected in Gabriele Gava and Robert Stern, eds., *Pragmatism, Kant and Transcendental Philosophy* (London: Routledge, 2015).

5. Guattari interview with Virginie Linhart, quoted in Francois Dosse, *Gilles Deleuze and Felix Guattari: Intersecting Lives* (New York: Columbia University Press, 2010), 171.

6. Guattari interview with Linhart, quoted in Dosse, *Gilles Deleuze and Felix Guattari*.

7. Gilles Deleuze and Michel Foucault, 'Intellectuals and Power,' in *Language, Counter-Memory, Practice: Selected Essays and Interviews by Michel Foucault*, ed. Donald F. Bouchard (New York: Cornell University Press, 1977), 209. My thanks to Anna Cutler for drawing out this connection.

8. Iain MacKenzie and Robert Porter, 'Totalising Institutions, Critique and Resistance,' *Contemporary Political Theory*, no. 20 (2021): 233–49.

9. Christopher Lasch, *The Culture of Narcissism: American Life in an Age of Diminishing Expectations, Reissue Edition* (New York: W.W. Norton & Company, 2018); Charles Taylor, *Sources of the Self: The Making of the Modern Identity* (Cambridge, MA: Harvard University Press, 1992); Luc Boltanski and Eve Chiapello, *The New Spirit of Capitalism* (London: Verso, 2018).

10. Mark Fisher, *Capitalist Realism: Is There No Alternative?* (Winchester: Zero Books, 2010).

11. In this respect, the argument of this chapter is aligned with that of Mitchell Dean and Daniel Zamora, *The Last Man Takes LSD: Foucault and the End of Revolution* (London: Verso, 2021).

12. Meillassoux, *After Finitude*, 48.

13. Meillassoux, *After Finitude*, 49.

14. Meillassoux, *After Finitude*, 5.

15. Meillassoux, *After Finitude*, 49.

16. Richard Rorty, *Philosophy and the Mirror of Nature* (Princeton: Princeton University Press, 1981).

17. For discussion of these alternatives see Iain MacKenzie, 'Critique in an Age of Indifference,' *Theory and Event* (forthcoming 2022). This article also discusses why Meillassoux's route out of correlationism is not the one to take.

18. See R. Brassier's engagment with the work of Wilfrid Sellars, for example: 'Nominalism, Naturalism, and Materialism: Sellars' Critical Ontology,' in *Contemporary Philosophical Naturalism and Its Implications*, ed. B. Bashour and H. Muller (Routledge: London, 2013).

19. Gilles Deleuze, *Difference and Repetition* (New York: Columbia University Press, 1994), 139.

20. Though they don't all agree on the consequences, key texts that have established the importance of reading Deleuze alongside Kant include, but are exhausted by, the following: Alberto Toscano, *The Theatre of Production: Philosophy and Individuation between Kant and Deleuze* (Basingstoke: Palgrave Macmillan, 2006);

Christian Kerslake, *Immanence and the Vertigo of Philosophy: From Kant to Deleuze* (Edinburgh: Edinburgh University Press, 2009); Edward Willat and Matt Lee, eds., *Thinking between Deleuze and Kant: A Strange Encounter* (London: Continuum, 2009); Craig Lundy and Daniela Voss, eds., *At the Edges of Thought: Deleuze and Post-Kantian Philosophy* (Edinburgh: Edinburgh University Press, 2015).

21. Ray Brassier, 'Concrete Rules and Abstract Machines: Form and Function in *A Thousand Plateaus*,' in *A Thousand Plateaus and Philosophy*, ed. Henry Somers-Hall, Jeffrey Bell and James Williams (Edinburgh: Edinburgh University Press, 2018), 260–79.

22. Brassier, 'Concrete Rules and Abstract Machines,' 261.

23. Gilles Deleuze and Felix Guattari, *What Is Philosophy?* (New York: Columbia University Press, 1994).

24. Gilles Deleuze and Felix Guattari, *A Thousand Plateaus* (London: Athlone Press, 1992), 12–13.

25. Brassier, 'Concrete Rules and Abstract Machines,' 278.

26. Brassier, 'Concrete Rules and Abstract Machines,' 262.

27. Brassier, 'Concrete Rules and Abstract Machines,' 278.

28. Wilfrid Sellars, *Empiricism and the Philosophy of Mind with an Introduction by Richard Rorty and Study Guide by Robert Brandom* (Cambridge, MA: Harvard University Press, 1997).

29. Robert Brandom, *Making It Explicit: Reasoning, Representing and Discursive Commitment* (Cambridge, MA: Harvard University Press, 1998).

30. Brandom, 'Facts, Norms and Normative Facts: Reply to Habermas,' *European Journal of Philosophy* 8, no. 3 (2002): 356–74, 357.

31. Brandom, *Making It Explicit*, 648.

32. Brandom, 'Facts, Norms and Normative Facts.'

33. Jurgen Habermas, 'From Kant to Hegel: On Robert Brandom's Pragmatic Philosophy of Language,' *European Journal of Philosophy* 8, no. 3 (2002): 322–55.

34. Brandom, 'Facts, Norms and Normative Facts,' 358.

35. The nuances of this claim, and associated claims, are laid out in his sensitive review of Brandom's *Making It Explicit*: Allan Gibbard, 'Thought, Norms, and Discursive Practice: Commentary on Robert Brandom's Making It Explicit,' *Philosophy and Phenomenological Research* 56, no. 3 (1996): 699–717.

36. David Roden, 'On Reason and Spectral Machines: Robert Brandom and Bounded Posthumanism,' in *Philosophy After Nature*, ed. R. Braidotti and R. Dolphijn (London: Rowman & Littlefield International, 2017), 99–120.

37. As well as the texts mentioned in note 9 which give (alternative) accounts of its emergence, the hyper-individualism of neoliberal politics can be read profitably through debates about the public sphere. In this respect consider, Robert Asen, 'Neoliberalism, the Public Sphere, and a Public Good,' *Quarterly Journal of Speech* 103, no. 4 (2017): 329–49. A compelling account of the neoliberal relationship between individualism and populism can also be found in Adam Kotsko, *Neoliberalism's Demons: On the Political Theology of Late Capital* (Redwood City: Stanford University Press, 2018).

38. Karl Marx, 'Theses on Feuerbach,' in *Karl Marx: Selected Writings*, ed. D. McLellan (Oxford: Oxford University Press, 2000).

39. Deleuze and Foucault, 'Intellectuals and Power,' 209.

40. My thanks to Anna Cutler, Gaby Hernandez de la Fuente, Jonjo Brady and Charles Bowen for their insightful reading of early drafts.

Chapter Nine

May '68: An Institutional Event

Gabriela Hernández De La Fuente

INSTITUTIONS AND MAY '68

The legacies of May '68 can be examined not only through the theoretical developments often known as post-structuralism,[1] but also through their institutional expression. This is the approach taken by Benoît Dillet, Iain MacKenzie and Robert Porter, who understand post-structuralism as both an intellectual and an institutional event. This implies thinking of post-structuralism as something that happened in the form of ideas, while also thinking about how those ideas brought something new into existence, which cannot be reduced exclusively to the history of ideas.[2] The problem of institutions is also important because throughout the events of May '68 they became the target of the most radical side of the movement, which was characterised by the call for autonomy and the suspicion of structures of authority—ideas that could not be easily accommodated within existing political and social institutions.[3] Institutions of various kinds were increasingly becoming sites of challenge and contestation; not only the apparatuses of the state but any type of associative structures including art and cultural institutions, the universities, the factory and trade unions, the police, psychiatric institutions, the Communist Party (PCF), etcetera. In fact, as Kristin Ross explains, the work for a new social order was carried out 'in spite of those institutions, or outside them, or in their place.'[4] Therefore the urgent task arose of creating new institutions compatible with the radical ethos of the movement, institutions outside of the state and of traditional party politics. An example of this type of institution is the University of Vincennes, also known as Paris VIII—an experimental university that was created as a response to the events of May '68. However, this radical experiment only lasted until 1980, when the university was reincorporated back into the traditional university system through its move to Saint-Denis.

The problem of recuperation is one side of the double bind of neoliberalism. This double bind can be understood as a lose-lose situation, where we can either attempt to work within institutions even though any creative potential may be recuperated (this is the case whether you work within an already existing institution or a new one like Vincennes); or we give up resistance at the institutional level but are still subjected to newer forms of control beyond the institution. For example, Alexander Galloway identifies a new form of technological control that follows a different logic than that established in existing bureaucratic institutions: 'Protocol functions largely without relying on hierarchical, pyramidal or centralised mechanisms.'[5] This new form of control '*operates outside institutional, governmental, and corporate power*, although it has important ties to all three.'[6] Galloway is right to point out that new technologies bring about a change in the nature of control and not an emancipation from it.[7] However, this does not mean that we should give up working within institutions. As MacKenzie and Porter remind us, new technologies and new forms of control transform institutions, they do not necessarily replace them.[8] Furthermore, as Félix Guattari warns us, we cannot ignore institutions because they play a central role in the creation of subjectivity. A good example of this is the work that was carried out at La Borde, an experimental psychiatric institution established in 1953. After the examination of Vincennes and its legacy, we will detour from Vincennes to La Borde to show that abandoning the task of working within institutions would imply giving up on the task of creating new forms of subjectivity, and without new subjectivities radical movements can be easily recuperated by the system—as in the case of May '68.

VINCENNES: A UNIVERSITY UNLIKE ANY OTHER

Having established the importance of focusing on institutions, we can examine the creation of Vincennes. The University was created as a direct response to the May '68 movement. As Bernard-Henri Lévy describes it, the creation of Vincennes can be understood as an attempt 'to bring together the institutional and epistemological aspirations of May to forge a new kind of university.'[9] Furthermore, as Christelle Dormoy-Rajramanan argues: 'Given the scale of the protests against traditional university organisation, political leaders could not but react.'[10] To maintain order, the National Education Minister, Edgar Faure, had to negotiate with the students, as he acknowledged the need to democratise universities.[11] It is also important to mention the government's positive attitude towards education at the time. This was evident, for example, in the scale of job creation following May '68 (61,000 new jobs in total within the national education system); and in the number of new universities created (more than twenty-six new universities, including three experimental centres, between July 1968 and February 1969, of which Vincennes was one).[12] Faure, described as 'left-wing' by Dormoy-Rajramanan,[13] was receptive to the students' demands and gave ample freedom to the team that created Vincennes, which was composed of lecturers and professors.[14] One of the lecturers involved in the creation of Vincennes was Hélène Cixous, who recruited academics mostly from departments of philosophy, psychoanalysis and literature; and according to Jacques Rancière, she 'wanted all the Althusserians in philosophy and all the Lacanians in psychoanalysis.'[15] The intellectuals hosted by Vincennes included Gilles Deleuze, Michel Foucault, Jean-François Lyotard and Jacques Derrida.

However, the importance of Vincennes cannot be reduced to the prominent intellectuals it hosted. Some key aspects that made Vincennes different from other universities were: its openness to candidates without traditional qualifications and to mature students; its unusual opening hours in order to accommodate student workers (Monday to Saturday, from 9 a.m. to 10 p.m.); the left-wing ideology of most of the staff; and the attempt to open up the decision-making bodies of the university.[16] Although these aspects came about as a direct result of the many debates around education and institutional structures during the protests (and before), it is important to note that 'students had not won on all fronts.'[17] For example, teachers remained mostly in control of the organisation of universities and pedagogical change, as the push for greater student participation fell short.[18] Ultimately, Vincennes came into existence and reflected the complex negotiation with the government and among the teachers, who had conflicting ideas regarding the role of the university in society: 'Vincennes was the convergence of various contradictory objectives.'[19] These conflicting objectives included: the push for an open university in order to broaden the access to education; the more elitist university project of avant-garde research; and the technocrat view, which wanted to bring the university closer to the professional world and make the university more compatible with the job market.[20] Overall, while according to Julian Jackson, Vincennes can be seen as an example of how the government was 'not always successful in neutralizing the spirit of 68,'[21] it is also true that the government was able to re-establish order by giving the trouble-makers their own space, as argued by Dormoy-Rajramanan.[22] François Dosse makes a similar point to Dormoy-Rajramanan's: 'Radical politics developed freely, well removed from society, in the middle of the forest, which surrounded the campus like a quarantine fence.'[23]

Even though Vincennes played a key role in different subversive experiments in the 1970s, in areas such as education, psychiatry and ecology, ultimately 'the initial project gradually slipped out of the hands of those who first imagined it.'[24] After withstanding constant underfunding and a series of internal power struggles and divisions, the radical experiment came to an end in 1980, when the government moved the university to Saint-Denis.[25] This brings us to the question of the legacy of May '68: was the movement simply co-opted by the logic of neoliberalism? The incorporation of Vincennes back into the traditional university system seems to suggest this. As Ross notes, the claim that 'nothing happened' in May '68 is quite common (particularly in sociology and the mainstream media), and tends to be grounded either in the observation that major institutions such as the university remained unchanged, or in the claim that the rupture of system was recuperated into logic of the same.[26] As we will see in the next section, however, Deleuze and Guattari provide an alternative reading of May '68, where they argue that if May '68 did not happen, this is because it remains an incomplete event. Recuperation, therefore, is not the end of the story.

MAY '68 DID NOT HAPPEN

The problem of claiming that nothing happened in May '68 is that we miss the opportunity of learning from the events, even if the experiment did fail at the end in recuperation. In a short piece titled 'May '68 Did Not Take Place,' Deleuze and Guattari provide an alternative way of thinking about the legacy of May '68 by looking at it as an *event*. In this piece, Deleuze and Guattari define an event as that which cannot be reduced to 'any social determinism, or to causal chains' because it produces a 'breaking with causality . . . which opens up a new field of the possible.'[27] The possible, according to them, does not preexist the event, it is created by it.[28] This means that the concept of the possible is not based on what already exists in the world, or we risk merely replicating our reality without being able to grasp the conditions of the creation of the new. For Deleuze and Guattari, creation does not rely on readymade elements, nor does it mean creation ex-nihilo.[29] Creation happens, rather, between the negative conditions that determine our existence (history) and that which 'wrests itself from this history in order to create' something new.[30] According to Deleuze and Guattari, this is what happened in May '68—something new was created. However, the problem is that although new possibilities were created, the movement was eventually crushed by the state, closing off the possible.[31] In this sense, May '68 did not happen, not because it is unimportant or because it did not bring about a structural transformation, but because it remains incomplete, particularly in terms of the production of a new collective subjectivity (we will come back to this point when we look at Guattari's work at La Borde). This implies that there is more about events than might be at first apparent; there is more to Vincennes than its reincorporation into the university system in 1980. In Deleuze and Guattari's words: 'When a social mutation appears, it is not enough to draw the consequences or effects according to lines of economic or political causality.'[32] The event 'passes as much into the interior of individuals as into the depths of society.'[33] Therefore, as Dillet, MacKenzie and Porter argue, May '68 as an event is still alive in us: it cannot 'be safely tucked away in the past,' as it exists in the form of possibility and it can be revitalised in the present.[34] However, it is important to note that revitalising an event does not mean copying it. As Jose Rosales warns us, one of the lessons of '68 is that we need new forms of organisation and strategies for revolutionary practice. We cannot be content merely 'prolonging a political sequence that in reality has already come to pass' nor 'faithfully emulating the images of struggle that became associated with '68 as a whole.'[35] What we need, then, is a *dramatisation* of the event where we reenact it in a singular manner in the present, just as Vincennes was a reenactment of La Borde.

MAY '68 HAPPENED IN '53

If May '68 is an incomplete event—in terms of the creation of a new subjectivity—that can still be revitalised in the present, then it is pertinent to turn to another radical institutional event in order to explore the problem of subjectivity: the creation of La Borde in 1953. This institution is an experimental psychiatric hospital established by Dr. Jean Oury.[36] La Borde was created as an alternative to the traditional 'prison camp–like structure of psychiatric institutions,'[37] which, according to a group of nurses and psychiatrists that were involved in the project, could not be tolerated anymore in the postwar period. In Guattari's words: 'incapable of supporting concentration camp institutions, they undertook to transform services from top to bottom, knocking down fences, organizing the fight against famine, etc.'[38] Aside from examining the relationship between institutions and subjectivity, there are two more reasons for the detour from Vincennes to La Borde: first, we will discuss the connections between La Borde and May '68; and secondly, there is a philosophical justification for the detour, related to Deleuze and Guattari's understanding of May '68 as an event.

We can begin by looking at the connections between La Borde and the intellectuals of May '68. La Borde was described by Todd Meyers as 'a locus for intellectual and political activity during the 1960s and 1970s.'[39] The reason for this, according to Camille Robcis, is that the intellectuals that were shaped by the events of May '68—including Althusser, Guattari, Deleuze, Foucault and Irigaray (the last three worked / studied at Vincennes)—became deeply concerned about the problem of subjectivity after the failure of the '68 movement.[40] For example, as Foucault wrote in the preface to Deleuze and Guattari's *Anti-Oedipus: Capitalism and Schizophrenia*, which can be considered a May '68 book,[41] the major enemy of the book is our own fascism: 'the fascism in us all, in our heads and in our everyday behaviour, the fascism that causes us to love power, to desire the very thing that dominates and exploits us.'[42] Furthermore, Robcis argues that La Borde was seductive to intellectuals at the time due to its organisational structure, which was committed to avoiding stagnation and centralisation; as well as to Oury's reformulation of psychoanalysis.[43]

Just as La Borde had an impact on intellectuals who were shaped by May '68, the events of '68 also had an impact on psychiatry. Although there are 'violently contradictory positions' about the impact of May '68 on psychiatry,[44] according to Guattari's account: 'The institutional earthquakes of May [1968] in France did not spare the world of psychiatry.'[45] For Guattari, '68 was important because it showed the shared problems of psychiatry and universities as institutions, in relation to society. For example, there was the problem of the social segregation of students: 'The campus is a perfect image of the student world cut off from the rest of society, from the whole world of ordinary work.'[46] This is also a problem in psychiatry, which is presented as the false dilemma between either changing the hospital or organising community programs (for Guattari you have to do both).[47] Secondly, apart from the shared problems between the psychiatric hospital and universities, according to Guattari, at the time both the university and the hospital had not been totally incorporated by the technocratic state machine so they were both an important site for its critique.[48]

However, despite the shared problems and radical potential of both sites, in 'Students, the Mad and "Delinquents"' (which is published in *Psychoanalysis and Transversality*), Guattari lamented that the members of Institutional Psychotherapy, that was practised at La Borde, were not more active in the student movement: 'We must admit, however, that though members of this school did not stand completely aside from events, they were only marginally involved in them.'[49] It seems like there was a missed opportunity to forge a stronger and longer-lasting connection between institutional psychotherapy and the student movement: 'Other militants later came to the leadership of the student movement who were less concerned with these problems [the interconnection between individual psychopathological problems and the social, political and work context], and the institutional psychotherapy school gradually moved away from their problems [students' mental health problems, the absurdity of teaching methods, the experience of social segregation—issues that can be seen as symptoms of a larger crisis in society].'[50] Given this missed opportunity, it is important to create an encounter between both institutional revolutionary movements. This encounter is made possible by looking at Deleuze and Guattari's conception of the history, which emphasises the creative potential that events share, instead of their particular institutional and historical actualisations.

THE AMPLIFIED INSTABILITIES OF '53 AND '68

In 'May '68 Did Not Take Place,' Deleuze and Guattari oppose their understanding of the history of May '68 to traditional history: May '68 as an event is 'free of all normal, or normative causality. Its history is a "series of amplified instabilities and fluctuations."'[51] In order to understand this statement it is helpful to turn to Craig Lundy's work on Deleuze's (and Guattari's) conception of history. Lundy explains that throughout his work, Deleuze, provides different reasons for his attack on history (although according to Lundy, this is not Deleuze's final word on history).[52] For the purpose of this chapter, we can focus on the contrast between providing an extensive history of '68—which Deleuze and Guattari avoid—in favour of conceptualising the event as an intensive break.[53] Lundy explains this distinction as follows: 'histories are extensive series that spiral away on the surface from those intensive breaks that cause a change in kind.'[54] The intensive break is the event, which, as already mentioned, creates a break with causality. On the other hand, the role of extensive history is to capture the event in order to represent it and make sense of it, placing it in a timeline that follows the logic of cause and effect. In addition to extensive history, Deleuze and Guattari also avoid reading May '68 as a step towards the struggle that would culminate in a new state apparatus.[55] By refusing this kind of history (linear and teleological, following a cause-and-effect logic), Deleuze and Guattari highlight the radical potential of the event beyond its actualisation in particular institutions, and beyond its recuperation by neoliberalism.

Put differently, while it is true that the creative potential of institutional events can be easily captured and re-absorbed by the system (like in the case of Vincennes), and as we will see, institutional events can coexist with the system (like in the case of La Borde, and Vincennes throughout the 1970s), this is not the end of the story. As Lundy argues, events are not merely a two-step process where creation comes first and capture second—this would imply a radical finalism that Deleuze (and Guattari) reject(s).[56] The process of creation always remains open and the creative potential is not exhausted by a particular institutional event. This allows us to connect the 'instabilities and fluctuations' of May '68—in terms of the radical critique of institutions—to the 'instabilities and fluctuations' that happened back in '53 at La Borde. In this sense we can understand May '68 and the creation of Vincennes as a renovation and even an intensification or overflowing of the experiment at La Borde. Eugene B. Young explains this potential as the virtual side of the event, that cannot be explained by a linear conception of time and a cause-and-effect logic.[57] The temporality of the event works otherwise: 'there is the future and the past of the event considered in itself, sidestepping each present, being free of the limitations of the state of affairs.'[58] This conception of time relies on an open future that informs the sense of the past by changing its sense in the present. For example, an actor reenacting a play in a different manner in the present, even though the script is the same. As James Williams explains, the aim here is not to represent, but to enact the part in a novel way, bringing it back to life in a singular manner that works within the particular circumstances: 'how can I make it work with my body, with this audience, after these events, for these people, tonight?'[59] The question then becomes: How can we make the institutional event of '53 and '68 work today?

THE PROBLEM OF COEXISTENCE

We can begin by answering the question of how we can make the institutional event of '53 (and '68) work today with a reminder of the problems posed by neoliberalism for political practice. In addition to the interconnections between May '68 and La Borde, and Deleuze and Guattari's philosophy of the event that shifts the focus from the institutional expression of the event into its creative potential, there is a third reason for looking back to La Borde: the problem of coexistence with neoliberalism. While the experiment of Vincennes was reincorporated into the traditional university system in 1980, something different happened to La Borde. In a 1983 letter published in *Molecular Revolution in Brazil*, Guattari describes La Borde as '"a wealth of possibles" that might have led to something else' but eventually 'became one of the institutions that have not been directly coopted by the power of the state, but with which the power of the state gets on very well.'[60] Guattari also expresses disappointment that the experiment at La Borde had not led to a more general process of transformation outside of that institution. In Guattari's words: 'they went on revolving in a vacuum, as it were, working upon themselves. It's like a breakthrough in the domain of painting that just continues to revolve around itself.'[61] This highlights not only the problem of recuperation, but also the problem of the coexistence of institutions without wider transformation of the system. Overall, both Vincennes and La Borde contain radical potential in terms of their ideas about the problems posed by institutions, which resonate in the present; but they also both show us the problems faced by radical institution building in relation to the dominant social, political and economic system and the double bind of neoliberalism.

THE UNAVOIDABLE PROBLEM OF INSTITUTIONS

Now that we are aware of the risks of recuperation and coexistence, we can approach the positive lessons that we can learn from Guattari's work at La Borde. This task will be carried out despite all the negative attention institutions received in '68. This was described by Julian Bourg: 'Much of the "revolutionary" ambience rejected the reform of existing institutions, opting instead for idealistic visions of total social, cultural and political transformation.'[62] Similarly, according to Ross: 'All the usual mediations and institutions, be they student unions or the National Assembly, were no longer forms to be merely critiqued, exposed or denounced; they would be treated henceforth *as though they already no longer existed.*'[63] In opposition to this, as Rolnik Suely argues in a conversation with Guattari, 'Institutions aren't going to be changed by pretending that they don't exist.'[64] This implies two things: first, the recognition of the revolutionary potential of institutions; and secondly, the need to move beyond the false alternative of being either part of the institution or against it, which is problematic because it posits any alternative as being simply the negation of the instituted, instead of being open to the possibility of creating something new.[65] Guattari agrees with Suely, about the need to work within institutions. In his own words: 'One does not have a choice! Not to work in institutions.'[66] There are several reasons for this, the first one is that 'one could not consider psychotherapeutic treatment for the seriously ill without taking the analysis of institutions into account.'[67] This was one of the guiding principles of Institutional Psychotherapy, which was developed at La Borde (Guattari refers to La Borde as the 'first experiment in "Institutional Psychotherapy"' in a private establishment).[68] For this reason, institutions that resembled prisons or concentration camps were not acceptable anymore. Secondly, one does not have a choice not to work within institutions because the subject is produced at the intersection of different institutions. This implies that subjectivity is not only produced by individual and familial factors, but also by broader collective and institutional factors, which include the psychiatric hospital and the psychoanalyst's office, and also language, education, the economy, the media, etcetera.[69] It is also important to note that for Guattari subjectivity is plural, which means none of these factors take priority over the others in the creation of the subject.[70] Another way of explaining the multiple components of subjectivity is given by Deleuze and Guattari in *Kafka: Toward a Minor Literature*, where they argue that the familial triangle (father-mother-child)—which is of interest to psychoanalysis—is connected to the social milieu, the economy, the law, bureaucracy, language, etcetera.[71] This means we cannot look at the problems of the individual and the family in isolation. Our personal desires and relationships are shaped by forces beyond the individual. For example, in *Chaosophy* Guattari argues that the capitalist system functions through a particular model of desire that shapes our conception of childhood, parenthood and love, following the axiomatic of 'enjoyment = possession.' In other words: 'Individuals are modelled to adapt, like a cog, to the capitalist machine. At the heart of their desire and in the exercise of their pleasure, they have to find private ownership.'[72]

If we accept that institutions play a key role in the creation of subjectivity, this means not only that we have to be aware about how our current institutions shape us, but also, we can use institutions to create new subjectivities. This was precisely what the experiment at La Borde was trying to do: 'The institutional machine that we positioned didn't simply remodel the existing subjectivities, but endeavored, instead, to produce a new type of subjectivity.'[73] The psychiatric institution (or any other institution) then becomes 'the modelling plaster' that we can experiment with and transform.[74] In Guattari's words: 'Yet it seemed to me that subjectivity, at any stage of the socius worth considering, did not occur by itself, but was produced by certain conditions, and that these conditions could be modified through multiple procedures in a way that would channel it in a more creative direction.'[75] In the case of La Borde, the 'modeling plaster,' or institutional factors that were constantly modified to avoid a routine included 'the tangle of workshops and meetings, as well as daily life in the dining rooms and bedroom, in sports games, and cultural life.'[76] In *Chaosophy*, Guattari mentions that there were forty different activities available for one hundred patients and members of staff. The point was to encourage the patients and members of staff to participate in different activities, to develop skills they have not had the chance to develop before, in order to create new subjectivities. For example, a washerwoman was in charge of running the print workshop and editorial committee of the newspaper. Additionally, both the service personnel and the medical staff shared the responsibility of the medical tasks and the material tasks of the clinic (such as cleaning, cooking, etc.).[77] This helped to desegregate the clinic by bringing the medical staff and patients closer through the everyday chores. Furthermore, the new distribution of activities also helped to avoid imposing a hierarchy upon the different tasks and the personnel in the hospital. It is important to note that Guattari recognises the resistance and unforeseen difficulties arising from these changes,[78] but the response to any problem was guided by the aim to desegregate the doctor-patient relationship and the relationship between the medical staff and the service personnel.[79] Guattari wanted to get rid of rigid schemas in favour of taking individual and collective responsibility for life at the clinic, in order to avoid bureaucratic routines and passivity.[80] The problem of bureaucratic institutions, according to Guattari, is that they reinforce the different modes of alienation of the individual—for example between the patient and society, between nurses and doctors, between doctors and the administration, between the institution and society, etcetera.[81] Furthermore, as Dosse notes, the main motivation for the organisation of the everyday at La Borde was the following: 'Rejecting the traditional approach of isolating people with psychiatric disorders, La Borde took the preclinical approach of mixing patients and their pathologies with normal people—without forgetting that psychotic patients needed medical treatment.'[82] The point is to replace bureaucratic institutions with institutional creativity, going from 'empty repetition' to 'internal re-creation.'[83] This means that La Borde does not serve as an ideal model that we need to recreate in the present, as Guattari himself recognises, but we can use it as an inspiration for the present due to the problems it raises concerning institutional creativity. As Guattari argues: 'the ideal situation would be one in which no two institutions were alike and no individual institution ever cease[d] evolving in the course of time.'[84]

Guattari argues that this new institutional experimental approach is beneficial for the patients because it produces a change in their relationship with the world through the institution. The institution provides the means for a new collective life through the different activities at the clinic, combating alienation by encouraging collective responsibility.[85] The aim of the institution is not to restore the patient to the norm but to create new relations to the world and new subjectivities.[86] Similarly, the aim of institutionalisation is not to incorporate the patient into a preestablished institutional organisation, but to create personalised arrangements, changing the institution for each new person. In Guattari's words: 'A discussion of the process of institutionalisation has nothing to do with preestablished organisation charts and regulations; it has to do with the possibilities for change inherent in collective trajectories—evolutionary attitudes, self-organisation, and the assumption of responsibilities.'[87] Put in a more poetic way: 'The range of expressive possibilities is not given in advance like the colours in a painting, but for the most part is reserved for innovation and improvisation of new activities.'[88]

FROM INSTITUTIONAL PSYCHOTHERAPY TO INSTITUTIONAL ANALYSIS

The principle of institutional creativity is not limited to psychiatric institutions. Guattari's concern was always to create connections between different types of institutions (such as La Borde and Vincennes), and between institutions to the outside world. In his clinical practice, this helped to avoid the isolation of the patient. The idea taking collective responsibility for everyday life in the clinic was also connected to the aim of the social reinsertion of the patients.[89] An example of cultural reinsertion can be found in Dosse's account of La Borde in *Gilles Deleuze and Félix Guattari: Intersecting Lives*. La Borde organised different cultural events, including theatrical productions put on by the patients and involving the neighbouring towns. One of these events was a circus organised by the Thierrée-Chaplin couple, who met while working at La Borde.[90] Additionally, in terms of developing the professional life of the patients, Dosse provides multiple examples of Guattari encouraging patients to develop their own interests, for example, by allowing them to participate in the administrative tasks of the clinic.[91] Furthermore, the work carried out at La Borde was connected to wider global issues such as health, pedagogy and prison conditions, through the participation in various research groups on the theme of institutional analysis. As Guattari explains, the guiding principle of these research groups was the following: 'the analysis of formations of the unconscious did not only concern the two protagonists of classical psychoanalysis, but could encompass other, more ample social segments.'[92] In 1965, these research groups came together under the Federation of Study and Institutional Research Groups (FGERI); and included different types of professionals that depended on institutional affiliations such as psychiatrists, psychoanalysts, psychologists, nurses, academics, teachers, etcetera.[93] The groups were inspired by Jean Oury's work on institutional pedagogy and François Tosquelles's work on institutional psychotherapy. Guattari also created the Center for Institutional Study, Research and Training (CERFI), which was affiliated to the FGERI. The work of these groups was published in the journal *Recherches*, which 'gives voice to a group working in the social arena that is interested in analyzing the institutions where everyone works and is receptive to questions from other established groups in other disciplines.'[94] Guattari's dream was for all institutions to undergo a transformation in terms of creativity in a similar manner to La Borde, although each institution has to find its own way of doing it. In Guattari's words: 'One can only dream of what life could become in urban areas, in schools, hospitals, prisons, etc., if instead of conceiving them in a mode of empty repetition, one tried to redirect their purpose in the sense of permanent, internal re-creation.'[95]

CONCLUSION

The legacy of '68 cannot be limited to the history of ideas and the development of post-structuralism in France. There is also an institutional side of the event, which attempted to keep the radical ethos of the movement alive in Vincennes. Although things eventually 'went back to normal' and Vincennes was recuperated back into the traditional university system, there is another side of the event that highlights the potential of the movement beyond its actualisation and recuperation. In this regard, we can connect the experimental work of Vincennes with the work carried out at La Borde. These two examples show us the importance of working within institutions in order to create new forms of subjectivity. The question of subjectivity was already being asked at La Borde, and in its institutional inspirations such as St. Alban, but '68 made this question even more relevant when, according to Deleuze and Guattari's diagnosis, the movement was unable to bring about a new collective subjectivity;[96] and when we are confronted with the problem of people desiring their own submission, as Foucault identifies in his preface to *Anti-Oedipus*.[97] Overall, we could say that both institutional events of '68 and '53 failed, or that they were recuperated, or existed within their own bubble without being a real challenge to the system. This could mean that we are doomed to failure whether we work within institutions, or outside of them. Furthermore, the problem of working outside of institutions is even more relevant now that technological developments bring about new forms of control outside of the institution. However, Guattari shows us another alternative, which is to continue working within institutions due to their central role in the creation of subjectivity. This requires us to find out both how our already existing institutions are shaping us as subjects, and how we can invent new institutions that create new forms of subjectivity. For Guattari, events are problematics that can always be taken up again and reworked—this is how we can revive the legacy of '68 and '53. The aim of this chapter was to remind us of the importance of working within institutions, however we still need to think about our current institutions and how they have been transformed by new forms of control.

NOTES

1. For an introduction to post-structuralism see: Benoît Dillet, Iain MacKenzie and Robert Porter, *The Edinburg Companion to Poststructuralism* (Edinburgh: Edinburgh University Press, 2013). The companion focuses on the work of Cixious, Irigaray, Guattari, Deleuze, Foucault, Lyotard and Derrida. This work inspired me to under-

stand post-structuralism not only as an intellectual event, but also as an institutional event, hence my focus on the institutions of Vincennes and La Borde.

2. Dillet, MacKenzie and Porter, *Companion to Poststructuralism*, xii. In their own words: 'Thinking of poststructuralism as something that happened, a richly textured body of ideas that emerged as the result of complex forces in the milieu of French intellectual life in the mid-1960s that combined to bring something new into existence, and not simply a distanced reflection on the history of ideas.'

3. Julian Jackson, 'Rethinking May 68,' in *May 68: Rethinking France's Last Revolution*, ed. Julian Jackson, Anna-Louise Milne and James S. Williams (Basingstoke: Palgrave Macmillan, 2011), 6–7.

4. Kristin Ross, *May '68 and Its Afterlives* (Chicago: University of Chicago Press, 2002), 103.

5. Alexander R. Galloway, 'Protocol,' *Theory, Culture & Society* 22, nos. 2–3 (2006): 317.

6. Alexander R. Galloway, *Protocol: How Control Exists after Decentralization* (Cambridge and London: MIT Press, 2004), 122, emphasis in the original.

7. Galloway, 'Protocol,' 318.

8. Iain MacKenzie and Robert Porter, 'Totalizing Institutions, Critique and Resistance,' *Contemporary Political Theory* 20, no. 2 (June 2021): 1–17.

9. Bernard-Henri Lévy, 'Intellectual Fictions,' in *May 68 in French Fiction and Film: Rethinking Society, Rethinking Representation*, ed. Margaret Atack (Oxford: Oxford University Press, 1999), 67.

10. Christelle Dormoy-Rajramanan, 'From Dream to Reality: The Birth of "Vincennes,"' in *May 68: Rethinking France's Last Revolution*, ed. Julian Jackson, Anna-Louise Milne and James S. Williams (Basingstoke: Palgrave Macmillan, 2011), 248.

11. Dormoy-Rajramanan, 'The Birth of "Vincennes,"' 249.

12. Dormoy-Rajramanan, 'The Birth of "Vincennes,"' 250.

13. Dormoy-Rajramanan, 'The Birth of "Vincennes,"' 249.

14. Dormoy-Rajramanan, 'The Birth of "Vincennes,"' 252.

15. Dormoy-Rajramanan, 'The Birth of "Vincennes,"' 256.

16. Dormoy-Rajramanan, 'The Birth of "Vincennes,"' 249–55.

17. Dormoy-Rajramanan, 'The Birth of "Vincennes,"' 249. It is important to note that there was also a faction of centre-leaning students who, according to Switzer, were 'sympathetic to leftist ideas—but who advocated for reform policies that worked along existing social and political chanels.' Furthermore, student centre-right and right politics did exist at the time. Adrian Switzer, 'Les événements de Mai as Theory and Practice,' *PhaenEx* 4, no. 2 (2009): 99.

18. Dormoy-Rajramanan, 'The Birth of "Vincennes,"' 250.

19. Dormoy-Rajramanan, 'The Birth of "Vincennes,"' 259.

20. Dormoy-Rajramanan, 'The Birth of "Vincennes,"' 251, 259–60.

21. Jackson, 'Rethinking May 68,' 13.

22. Dormoy-Rajramanan, 'The Birth of "Vincennes,"' 252.

23. François Dosse, *Gilles Deleuze & Félix Guattari: Intersecting Lives* (New York: Columbia University Press, 2010), 345.

24. Dormoy-Rajramanan, 'The Birth of "Vincennes,"' 260–61.

25. For an account of the last years of Vincennes see: Dormoy-Rajramanan, 'The Birth of "Vincennes,"' 260; and Dosse, *Intersecting Lives*, 345, 385.

26. Ross, *May '68*, 19, 22.

27. Gilles Deleuze and Félix Guattari, 'May '68 Did Not Take Place,' in *Two Regimes of Madness: Texts and Interviews 1975–1995*, trans. Ames Hodges and Mike Taormina, ed. David Lapoujade (New York and Los Angeles: Semiotext(e,) 2006), 233.

28. Deleuze and Guattari, 'May '68 Did Not Take Place,' 234.

29. Gilles Deleuze and Félix Guattari, *What Is Philosophy?*, trans. Hugh Tomlinson and Graham Burchill (London and New York: Verso, 1994), 19.

30. Deleuze and Guattari, *What Is Philosophy?*, 96. For a re-examination of the relationship between history and becoming in Deleuze's philosophy (and Deleuze and Guattari's philosophy) see Craig Lundy, *History and Becoming: Deleuze's Philosophy of Creativity* (Edinburgh: Edinburgh University Press, 2012). Lundy argues that this sharp opposition between history and becoming is not Deleuze's last say on the matter.

31. Deleuze and Guattari, 'May '68 Did Not Take Place,' 334–35.

32. Deleuze and Guattari, 'May '68 Did Not Take Place,' 234.

33. Deleuze and Guattari, 'May '68 Did Not Take Place,' 233.

34. Dillet, MacKenzie and Porter, *Companion to Poststructuralism*, 3. More precisely, when Dillet, MacKenzie and Porter argue that events cannot be safely tucked away in the past they are referring to the event of post-structuralism. I used this idea as an inspiration to talk about the institutional events of Vinncenes and La Borde.

35. Jose Rosales, 'Communism Is the Riddle Posed to History,' in this volume.

36. For a detailed account of the creation of La Borde and its main inspirations see: Dosse, *Intersecting Lives*, chapter 1.

37. Guattari, *The Three Ecologies*, trans. Ian Pindar and Paul Sutton (London: The Athlone Press, 2000), ix.

38. Félix Guattari, *Psychoanalysis and Transversality: Text and Interviews 1955–1971*, trans. Ames Hodges (New York and Los Angeles: Semiotext(e), 2015), 60.

39. Todd Meyers, 'Jean Oury and Clinique de La Borde: A Conversation with Camille Robcis,' *Somatosphere*, 3 June 2014, http://somatosphere.net/2014/jean-oury-and-clinique-de-la-borde-a-conversation-with-camille-robcis.html/.

40. Meyers, 'La Borde.'

41. Even though Deleuze and Guattari's take on '68 was quite different from that of the students and workers who participated in the movement, Paul Patton argues that *Anti-Oedipus* could be considered a May '68 book because, in his own words: 'it was in a spirit of mutual ambivalence and uncertainty about May '68 that the two thinkers first came together in 1969.' Paul Patton, 'Is *Anti-Oedipus* a May '68 Book?,' in *Deleuze and History*, ed. Jeffrey A. Bell and Claire Colebrook (Edinburgh: Edinburgh University Press, 2009), 211.

42. Michel Foucault, 'Preface' to *Anti-Oedipus: Capitalism and Schizophrenia*, by Gilles Deleuze and Félix Guattari, trans. Robert Hurley, Mark Seem and Helen R. Lane (Minneapolis: University of Minnesota Press, 2003), xiii.

43. Meyers, 'La Borde.'

44. Gary Genosko, *The Guattari Reader: Pierre-Félix Guattari* (Oxford: Blackwell Publishers, 1996), 43.
45. Guattari, *Psychoanalysis and Transversality*, 305.
46. Guattari, *Psychoanalysis and Transversality*, 309.
47. Guattari, *Psychoanalysis and Transversality*, 316.
48. Guattari, *Psychoanalysis and Transversality*, 306.
49. Guattari, *Psychoanalysis and Transversality*, 305.
50. Guattari, *Psychoanalysis and Transversality*, 306.
51. Deleuze and Guattari, 'May '68 Did Not Take Place,' 233.
52. Lundy, *History and Becoming*, 3–4. As Lundy explains, Deleuze rejects a conception of history as historicism, which is 'a form of history which (1) proceeds in a linear-chronological fashion, (2) obeys a standard ontology of cause-effect, (3) concerns itself with the task of representing the world (or its essence) and (4) is teleological.' Throughout his work, Deleuze criticises history for at least some of these reasons, although not necessarily all at once. However, according to Lundy, this is not Deleuze's final word on the matter of history.
53. Lundy, *History and Becoming*, chapter 1. Lundy complicates the distinction between history and becoming by arguing that history can also be intensive by working in productive union with becoming. However, for the purpose of this paper it is helpful to retain the distinction in order to show the type of history Deleuze and Guattari are trying to avoid (extensive history).
54. Lundy, *History and Becoming*, 19.
55. Paul Patton, 'Is *Anti-Oedipus* a May '68 Book?,' 211.
56. Lundy, *History and Becoming*, 19.
57. Eugene B. Young, 'Counter-actualization,' in *The Deleuze and Guattari Dictionary*, ed. Eugene B. Young, Gary Genosko and Janell Watson (London and New York: Bloomsbury, 2013), 75.
58. Gilles Deleuze, *The Logic of Sense*, trans. Mark Lester and Charles Stivale, ed. Constantin V. Boundas (New York: Columbia University Press, 1990), 151.
59. James Williams, *Gilles Deleuze's Philosophy of Time: A Critical Introduction and Guide* (Edinburgh: Edinburgh University Press, 2011), 13. See James Williams's explanation of the concept of dramatisation.
60. Félix Guattari and Suely Rolnik, *Molecular Revolution in Brazil*, trans. Karel Clapshow and Brian Holmes (Los Angeles: Semiotext(e), 2007), 136–37.
61. Guattari and Rolnik, *Molecular Revolution*, 136.
62. Julian Bourg, 'The Moral History of 1968,' in *May 68: Rethinking France's Last Revolution*, ed. Julian Jackson, Anna-Louise Milne and James S. Williams (Basingstoke: Palgrave Macmillan, 2011), 17.
63. Ross, *May '68*, 103, emphasis in the original.
64. Guattari and Rolnik, *Molecular Revolution*, 122.
65. Guattari and Rolnik, *Molecular Revolution,* 122.
66. Guattari in Genosko, *The Guattari Reader*, 135.
67. Guattari, *Psychoanalysis and Transversality*, 61.
68. Guattari, *Chaosophy: Texts and Interviews 1972–1977*, ed. Sylvere Lotringer, trans. David L. Sweet, Jarred Becker and Taylor Adkins (Los Angeles: Semiotext(e), 2009), 176.

69. Genosko, *The Guattari Reader*, 193–94.
70. Gary Genosko, *Félix Guattari: An Aberrant Introduction* (London and New York: Continuum, 2002), 50–51.
71. Gilles Deleuze and Félix Guattari, *Kafka: Toward a Minor Literature*, trans. Dana Polan (Minneapolis: Minneapolis University Press, 1986), 17.
72. Guattari, *Chaosophy*, 237.
73. Guattari, *Chaosophy*, 180.
74. Guattari, *Chaosophy*, 181.
75. Guattari, *Chaosophy*, 182.
76. Guattari, *Chaosophy*, 181.
77. Guattari, *Chaosophy*, 178.
78. Dosse, *Intersecting lives,* chapter 2. Dosse provides a critical account of the assignment of tasks at La Borde. He argues that the assignment of tasks caused anxiety for many, and that Guattari could be quite authoritarian.
79. Guattari, *Chaosophy*, 179.
80. Guattari, *Chaosophy*, 179.
81. Guattari, *Psychoanalysis and Transversality*, 27.
82. Dosse, *Intersecting Lives*, 40.
83. Guattari, *Chaosophy*, 182.
84. Guattari, *Chaosophy*, 194.
85. Guattari, *Chaosophy*, 181.
86. Guattari and Rolnik, *Molecular Revolution*, 369.
87. Guattari and Rolnik, *Molecular Revolution*, 376.
88. Guattari, *Chaosophy*, 181.
89. Guattari and Rolnik, *Molecular Revolution*, 376.
90. Dosse, *Intersecting Lives*, 62–64.
91. Dosse, *Intersecting Lives*, chapters 2 and 3.
92. Guattari, *Chaosophy*, 183.
93. Dosse, *Intersecting Lives*, 76.
94. Dosse, *Intersecting Lives*, 78.
95. Guattari, *Chaosophy*, 182.
96. Deleuze and Guattari, 'May '68 Did Not Take Place,' 234.
97. Foucault, 'Preface,' xiii.

Chapter Ten

Communist Guilt, Public Happiness and the Feelings of Collective Attachment

aylon cohen

From the 2011 Occupy movement to the most recent global wave of uprisings in 2019 and 2020, commentators will often describe contemporary revolts as 'leaderless rebellions.'[1] Unlike the movements of earlier generations, participants are no longer guided by the leadership of political parties. Instead, protestors turn to social media to organise ongoing social revolt and build momentum on the streets. Such so-called leaderless rebellions are no longer defined by the dominant political strategies of the nineteenth and twentieth centuries, with their emphasis on recruiting new members into political parties with identifiable leaders. Instead, given the ephemeral and informal organisational structure of contemporary revolt, it would appear that the dominant strategy is one of escalation, intensifying ongoing conflict until movement demands are met or until the government has fallen. As the refrain commonly heard at the occupation and in the protest goes: *we won't leave and we won't stop until* . . .

Yet, when the moment of revolt ends, as it inevitably does, will participants simply return to their ordinary lives, only to wait until the next uprising unfolds and hope that this time things might turn out differently? In her recent work, *Crowds and Party*, Jodi Dean argues that the contemporary emphasis on maintaining ongoing rebellion and prolonging the rupture of revolt is a fickle political strategy.[2] The turn away from the slow work of party-building, she contends, has been underway since 'the shift in radical politics marked by "1968".'[3] According to Dean, the upheavals of '68 initiated a new form of anarchistic politics that rejects ideas of leadership, organisation and recruitment characteristic of the party in favour of a politics of immediacy, experimentation and novelty characteristic of the event of revolt. Yet, this 'fetishistic embrace of destabilization for its own sake' has meant that the contemporary left has been unable to meet the challenge of sustaining the upswell of collective energies beyond the moment of rebellion.[4] Consequently, Dean argues, we would do well to move past the politics of '68 and to revive the party as an organisation of political struggle.[5]

Against old tropes of the party as a container of scientific truth or bureaucratic apparatus of power, Dean proposes a novel reading and defense of the party form. Inspired by the recent turn to affect in cultural and social theory, she argues that the crowd event generates a particular kind of affective sense of unity necessary for ongoing political struggle. Rather than dismiss the crowd event in favour of party organisation, Dean claims that the Communist Party can serve as an affective infrastructure capable of regenerating the feelings of collectivity that participants experience in the event of the crowd. The party is, in other words, the organisation that can prolong the collective effervescence of struggle once the moment of revolt has passed.

In this chapter, I take up Dean's challenge to reconsider the role of the party. While I agree with the move to seriously consider the affective question of collective attachment that participants of revolt experience, I am sceptical that the vision of political organisation Dean proposes can regenerate and sustain such collective feelings. I argue that central to Dean's vision of the party as an infrastructure of feeling is what I call an affective politics of communist guilt. By institutionalising practices of critique, the party aims to generate feelings of guilt as a stand-in for the experience of crowd collectivity. Far from re-establishing the kinds of cooperative social relations that Dean believes necessary for political struggle, I contend that communist guilt is likelier to engender estrangement and isolation, and thus push members away from the party than to attach them to its vision of collectivity.

Though oriented towards the feelings of unity experienced in the crowd, the politics of communist guilt are, I argue, ultimately predicated on a misunderstanding of just the sort of affective relations that emerge in the crowd event. Communist guilt is founded on a sovereign vision of the crowd as a chaotic form, where the breakdown of order within the crowd event is isomorphic with the breakdown of individuality within the crowd participant. In opposition to the sovereign grammar of chaos, I analyse the riotous crowd from the perspective of its non-sovereign participants. Drawing on Hannah Arendt's concept of public happiness, I argue that the experience of joy in the crowd event suggests not the breakdown of individuality but rather its expansion in and through others. In contrast to communist guilt then, public happiness provides an alternative understanding of how participants feel themselves united as a collective in the event of revolt. While Dean is correct to suggest that political organisations should aim to regenerate the affective sense of collectivity felt in and through the rebellious crowd, I argue that the promise of collective attachment is ultimately better secured not through a politics of guilt but rather of happiness.

COLLECTIVITY AND THE CROWD

A recurring question of contemporary political struggle is how to produce a collectivity, a sense of a 'we,' in the face of neoliberalism's atomising forces. Ours is an era, Dean writes, 'of commanded individuality. . . . Each is told, repeatedly, that she is unique and encouraged to cultivate this uniqueness. We learn to insist on and enjoy our difference, intensifying processes of self-individuation.'[6] According to Dean, the challenge of political organising is not only to overcome capitalistic processes of individuation, but also to oppose dominant ideological configurations on the left that have been captured by these neoliberal discourses of individuality. Reflecting on her own participation in Occupy Wall Street in 2011, Dean laments that whatever collective power Occupy manifested, it soon buckled under the weight of the individualism that lurked within its politics:

> The individualism of its democratic, anarchist, and horizontalist ideological currents undermined the collective power the movement was building. . . . The movement's decline (which began well before Occupiers were evicted) exposes the impasse confronting the Left. The celebration of autonomous individuality prevents us from foregrounding our commonality and organizing ourselves politically.[7]

Dominant ideological currents on the left, then, risk recuperating capitalism's emphasis on individuality and undermining long-term political struggle. As such, the problem that Dean sets up is how to prevent the forces of individuality from undermining the collective unity necessary for political organisation. How, in other words, do we produce and maintain an attachment to a collective 'we'?

The answer, for Dean, lies in understanding what happens to participants in the event of a crowd. Drawing on the work of Elias Canetti, Dean argues that in the crowd event, participants feel 'an intense experience of substantive collectivity' arising from what Canetti calls the 'egalitarian discharge' of the crowd.[8] The experience of the crowd is one of equalisation, where the collective equality of the crowd enables its members to undergo a momentary 'de-individuation.'[9] The symbolic 'distinctions of rank, status and property . . . [that keep people] firmly apart from one another' dissolve in the physical press of the crowd, Canetti writes; with 'body presse[d] against body, each man is as near the other as he is to himself.'[10] The material density of the crowd opens up, as it were, each individual to others, forming a new egalitarian association among the crowd's participants. In and through the felt intensity of bodies amassed together in the crowd, 'the individual feels that he is transcending the limits of his own person . . . for the distances are removed which used to throw him back on himself and shut him in.'[11] Whereas neoliberal and leftist injunctions to individuality only serve to further isolate people, the force of the crowd event momentarily overcomes their atomism. Accordingly, the experience of the crowd is, as Dean puts it, 'a positive expression of the negation of individuality, separateness [and] boundaries' that characterise contemporary life.[12]

Having identified this experience of collectivity in the crowd, Dean seems to propose two lines of argumentation for the party: discursive/symbolic and affective. She begins with a basic insight, one that is too often forgotten: the revolutionary crowd in the streets is always a minority of the general population. While social scientists attempt to quantify just how large this minority needs to be in order to provoke fundamental change,[13] Dean argues that such attempts to model revolutionary thresholds misunderstand the symbolic dimensions of political action. Whether the crowd in the street is understood as a fringe mob or The People requires the work of interpretation: '*How* event and interpretation are combined matters if an event is to be the cause of [The People as the] subject [of democratic politics].'[14] Accordingly, the party seeks to make sense of and instill democratic meaning into the crowd. 'For the crowd to become the people,' Dean writes, 'representation is necessary,'[15] and so the party serves as a representative apparatus that shapes the symbolic understanding of the crowd event. Representation is, in other words, the primary function of the party working to symbolically transform, or as Dean puts it, subjectivise the crowd into The People.

This vision of the party as an interpretative apparatus risks overshadowing Dean's second and more novel argument in defense of the party. The crowd 'isn't structured like a language,' she writes, 'it isn't a discursive formation.'[16] Yet, to figure the political work of the party through the logic of representation does seem to depend on a discursive figuration of the crowd. As one reviewer puts it, the party is 'an organizational form that is somehow capable of sustaining the crowd's *claim* to universality.'[17] However, as Dean's own arguments about the egalitarian discharge indicate, the crowd is not an entity that articulates *claims* on behalf of its members. Rather, the crowd is a certain kind of affective situation that enables its participants to feel themselves anew. Affect is, in other words, not a question of representation but of intensive and experiential flows of embodied life.[18] Consequently, the party is better understood not as a discursive institution that interprets or elaborates the crowd's claims but rather as an affective infrastructure that regenerates and sustains the feelings of collectivity experienced in the crowd event.

Instead of responding to the symbolic problem of representation (is the crowd a mob or The People?), Dean's focus on the question of affect tackles the organisational concern set out at the start of this essay: How do political partisans maintain an attachment to the collective once the moment of revolt has passed? Simply put, 'Crowds amass, but they don't endure.'[19] Whether participants are arrested or return home, the event ultimately draws to a close; crowd participants thus leave the terrain of active struggle only to become individuated once again, as the experience of collectivity becomes a distant memory. 'The question that emerges from these experiences [of collectivity] is,' therefore, 'how they might endure and extend, how the momentary discharge of equality that crowds unleash might become the basis for a new process of political composition.'[20] Accordingly, the problem of affect does not directly concern the spectators of the crowd so much as the participants themselves, refocusing attention on the transformative effects brought about by the crowd's egalitarian discharge.[21]

Though refocusing attention on the experience of the crowd event, Dean does not wish to fetishise the event as such, but rather to open the question of what happens after the event passes. Indeed, those enraptured with what she calls '1968's intoxication with the politics of the beautiful moment' overlook the political problem of endurance.[22] Like Chantal Mouffe's critique of post-structuralists who advocate for a world of free-floating subject positions permanently in flux and who thus miss the political moment of decision-making,[23] Dean claims that those who align themselves with the politics of the beautiful moment 'mistake an opening, an opportunity, for an end.'[24] Captivated by the moment of rupture, in other words, they miss a simple but important point that Dean never tires of repeating: the beautiful moment 'can't last forever.'[25] As such, the political challenge is to constitute a form of organisation capable of sustaining the crowd's affective force of collectivity when the crowd itself has vanished. For Dean, this organisation is the party: 'a body that can carry the egalitarian discharge after the crowds disperse, channeling its divisive promise of justice into organized political struggle.'[26] But how exactly does the party regenerate this felt sense of a 'we' at the heart of the beautiful moment?

COMMUNIST GUILT

In a letter sent to the journal of the Communist Party of the United States in 1933, an overworked member of the Chicago chapter of the Communist Party asks for guidance and support. 'I will be criticized next Tuesday night at the organizers meeting because the unit is not larger; because I have not done more,' the member writes. 'However, no matter how much I do, I always hate to show my face because there are things I do not do that I was told to do. . . . I am getting tired. I am just as much a Communist as ever, but I am not 10 communists.'[27] According to Dean, this overworked comrade illustrates how the party keeps alive the sense of collectivity experienced in the crowd event: 'The communists appearing in the *Party Organizer* measure themselves as many. The desire that expresses itself in the urgent demands they make on themselves is collective—ten communists—even as it is felt as [an] impossible . . . command.'[28] Regardless of whether the party member could fulfill his tasks, the fact that he thinks and judges himself from the perspective of the party—that such tasks required not one but ten communists—indicates, for Dean, the collectivity that this member feels.

In so far as this letter provides evidence for a sense of collectivity, the Communist Party generates this feeling in and through the practice of criticism. The party member measures himself from the perspective of the many because he knows he will be criticised at the next organisers' meeting. Such practices of criticism are, Dean argues, vital for producing a felt sense of the 'we.' The party 'incessantly charges us for failing on all fronts, *we never do enough.*'[29] This failure, however, can never be overcome, and as such is 'always felt as a requirement or compulsion, that which must be done.'[30] Caught in the double bind between the injunction that more must always be done (despite the member's already doing too much) and the impossibility of ever doing enough—that is, within an order whose terms cannot be fulfilled— party members experience what I call communist guilt. Party members feel guilty because they feel like failures, but far from drawing them away from the party, Dean argues that these feelings of failure serve as the affective glue that binds members to the collective. To feel guilty means that party members 'feel the moral pressure of the collective. . . . Each feels the inner force of their collective strength as a command or duty.'[31] By demanding of its members more than can be done, the Communist Party uses the practice of criticism in order to produce communist guilt. This guilt not only signals but also sustains a party member's attachment to the collective, thus rekindling the experience of collectivity felt in the crowd.

Far from being simply one technique among many, the practice of criticism seems to be in Dean's view a primary method for generating collective attachment. The institutionalised forum for criticism in the Communist Party is the party trial, where members are formally charged with and critiqued for failing to uphold the principles and practices of the party. For Dean, the affective value of the party trial lies in its ability to generate an experience of collectivity 'as perhaps no other element of the Party infrastructure can.'[32] As an exemplar of the trial's affective power, Dean recounts the trial of one Chicago communist party member named Ross in the mid-1930s, as detailed in Richard Wright's *Black Boy*. Though it is unclear what infractions Ross committed—he was guilty, we read, of a 'long list of political offenses'—the truth or falsity of his charges do not matter because no comrade can be innocent: 'The impossible demands of the many,' Dean writes, 'cannot not be betrayed.'[33] Watching the trial unfold, Wright remarks that Ross underwent several hours of criticism, at the end of which his 'personality, his sense of himself, had been obliterated. . . . He was one with all the members there.'[34] As in the case of the overworked party member, subjection to criticism transformed Ross's already presumed juridical guilt into an overbearing sense of affective guilt. As Wright's comments suggest, guilt appears to cultivate an experience of and thus attachment to the collective by destroying any stable sense of oneself. Through the unrelenting barrage of criticism, it is as if Ross experiences the momentary death of his own ego, and so gives himself over, as it were, to the members assembled before him. In the destructiveness of its guilt-inducing power then, the party trial counterintuitively showcases, as Dean puts it, 'an intense experience of belonging.'[35]

Whether institutionalised in the trial or in weekly meetings, such intense practices of criticism, Dean admits, show the 'ugliness of the Party,' but they also demonstrate the party's 'capacity to make the crowd felt after its dissipation.'[36] Yet, closer inspection of these examples reveals that, far from consolidating collective attachment, the practices of criticism risk alienating party members, propelling them not towards but away from the collective 'we' of the party. Consider again the Chicago party member's plea for support in the pages of the *Party Organizer*. Though overworked, the anonymous party member writes that 'I am not kicking so much about that. Here is what I do kick about. It is criticism.' Criticism induces feelings of guilt (I have not done enough), and so, unsurprisingly, this member admits that 'I always hate to show my face' at meetings.[37] This member's conflicting relationship with the party meeting (I go, but I hate doing so) derives, I suggest, from the ambivalent nature of guilt: the affective force that is meant to strengthen his attachment to the party is, ironically, the same force that also separates him from it. The practice of criticism aims to cultivate an attachment to the collective, but in doing so through the affective force of guilt, it also breeds resentment towards this very collective.

This problem was not lost on the Communist Party members. Immediately after this letter, another party member writes in the *Party Organizer* that when a comrade 'gets nothing but criticism all the time from the higher bodies, he becomes discouraged, lets down on his activity and very often drops out of the Party.'[38] This reflection on the problem of criticism, which Dean does not cite in her discussion, reveals guilt's fraught capacity to generate attachment. While guilt may be momentarily experienced as a form of collectivity, it also risks short-circuiting the very attachments it aims to sustain. The affects associated with communist guilt produce feelings of dejection, which over time tend to alienate members from the collective. In receiving criticism, the party member becomes discouraged and does less, which only seems to lead to further criticism, further discouragement, and so on. Communist guilt thus appears to generate a cycle of growing misery, eventually leading members to withdraw from the party. While Dean believes that communist guilt (I have not done enough and I can never do enough) 'relentlessly pushes [party members] from within themselves' to continue their political work,[39] party members themselves worry that this feeling also pushes comrades away from the very organizational structures meant to sustain their activity.

Central to Dean's vision of the party as an infrastructure of feeling is what I call an affective politics of communist guilt. In and through the practices of criticism, the Communist Party aims to produce feelings of guilt in order to regenerate the feelings of collectivity felt in the crowd. Though Dean does not parse out the different varieties of affect that potentially structure discrete forms of political action, we may wonder whether the political affects operative in the party are the same as those of the crowd. Given the ambivalent feelings of attachment that guilt produces, to what extent does guilt accurately reproduce and/or mirror the experience of collectivity felt in the crowd event? And if it turns out that the negative affects associated with guilt are not the same kind of affects the crowd generates, then what image of the crowd leads us to believe they are? In order to rethink the affective problem of attachment therefore, we must rethink the crowd event and the affective force of collectivity it generates.

CROWD CHAOS

'Chaos' is a commonly deployed signifier to make sense of the crowd event. Whether in reference to the beautiful moment of May '68 or its fiftieth anniversary in 2018, media commentators often turn to the language of chaos to describe the event of a riot, counterintuitively rendering the crowd intelligible as an object of unintelligibility.[40] The *Oxford English Dictionary* defines chaos as 'the formless void believed to have existed before the creation of the universe; primordial matter.'[41] In its theological signification, chaos describes that confused, formless, order-less state prior to the emergence of God. Given the historical imbrication of the theological in modern (Western) politics, as Carl Schmitt famously argued,[42] proponents of state sovereignty often employ chaos as a trope to describe what life would look like without the state, or as Thomas Hobbes calls it, the mortal God. To destroy the law, Hobbes argues, is to 'reduce all Order, Government, and Society, to the first Chaos of violence, and Civill warre.'[43] Of course, rarely does the event of the crowd—even in its manifestation as a riot—destroy the state. Yet, the grammar of 'chaos' suggests a latent potential for disorder within the crowd. The crowd, in other words, can threaten to upend the state, and return society to a prior space of ungoverned chaos.

The political grammar of chaos, I contend, draws its meaning from the symbolic logic of sovereignty. From the sovereign's perspective, chaos signifies the opposite of Law and Order. Law is Order, and so to exit the law is to exit order. Accordingly, social scientists will often propose that a defining characteristic of a riot is a situation in which the authorities have lost control.[44] From within this sovereign logic, the effects of the crowd are then read backwards onto the crowd itself: the crowd creates disorder and therefore must itself be disordered. Insofar as the crowd event threatens sovereignty, the effects of the crowd thus become a metonym for the crowd. In other words, the chaotic effects resulting *from* the crowd come to stand for the ontological chaos *of* the crowd. To take up this sovereign logic and view that which ruptures sovereign order as itself disordered is, to speak with James Scott, to see the crowd like a state.[45]

Contrary to their own anti-statist positions, many leftists will draw on this grammar of sovereignty but normatively invert its negative meaning, such that the chaos from and of the crowd becomes politically salutary for revolutionary politics. Despite Dean's critique of those who fetishise the beautiful moment, she too tends to view the crowd event as chaotic, reading the potential effects of the crowd back into the very form of the crowd:

> The crowd's chaotic moment is indeterminate. . . . The cacophony of impressions and transports of the unknown among the unknown releases a sense of the many channeled in the everyday along set paths, igniting possibilities that will appear in retrospect to have been there all along. The political challenge is maintaining fidelity to this sense of the many—the crowd discharge—without fetishizing the cacophonous rupture.[46]

Deploying the trope of chaos in order to render the crowd intelligible, Dean portrays the crowd's 'chaotic moment' as a disordered event ('cacophony of impressions'; 'cacophonous rupture') that lacks any intelligible structure ('the unknown among the unknown'). Dean thus shares with the leftists she critiques the view of the crowd as a chaotic form. In deploying this grammar of sovereignty, Dean figures the crowd not only as creating chaos but as itself chaotic.

While communist theorists such as Dean, who view the seizure of the state as a necessary aim of radical struggle,[47] may not have any issue with employing the grammar of sovereignty to read the crowd event, I suggest that there are two problems with doing so. First, reading the crowd's effects back onto the organisational form of the crowd commits a logical error, confusing the effects of the crowd with the structure of the crowd. As a result, this error hinders political analysis by obfuscating the organisational form of the riotous crowd. Second, and more important for Dean's argument, this backwards reading of the crowd as chaotic motivates her claims for the necessity of the party in the first place. The party is, as Dean describes it, 'the organizational form that marks the difference between the chaos of revolution and the building of a new political and social order.'[48] Associated with this image of chaos is the idea of the crowd event as spontaneous. As Joshua Clover observes, the Russian word *stikhiinost*, which Lenin famously used to condemn mass revolt, 'signifies both spontaneity and the chaos of nature: that which has the least degree of organization.'[49] Consistently with this view, Dean argues that the party is 'an apparatus of intensification that ruptures the everyday by breaking with spontaneism.'[50] As a chaotic and spontaneous event, therefore, the crowd event appears to offer little insight for political organising. Indeed, the party, according to this account, emerges as a response to the absence of organisational form in the chaos of the crowd event.

Lacking any organisational value, the crowd is politically meaningful for the question of organising only insofar as it provides clues as to the kind of affective experience of collectivity the party must regenerate. Insofar as chaos describes not only a symbolic condition of disorder but also an affective condition of disarray, then reading the crowd event through the grammar of chaos is not simply to see like a state but also to feel like one: the felt experience of the crowd is believed to be a felt experience of chaos, a breaking down and deformation of the crowd participant. Drawing on psychoanalysis, Dean claims that the 'subject is [*a priori*] collective' and that ideology constitutes 'the subject as an individual.'[51] What occurs then in the chaos of the crowd is a collapse of ideological interpellation and a return of the subject to its primary condition of collectivity. As Dean puts it, the crowd 'cuts out an opening by breaking through the limits bounding [the] permitted experience [constituting the subject-as-individual].'[52] The breakdown of order in the crowd is, therefore, isomorphic with the breakdown of individuality in the subject. Indeed, Dean's belief that a subject's 'sense of individuality is obliterated' in the crowd further explains why she values Wright's description of the party trial as the process through which Ross's 'personality, his sense of himself, had been obliterated.'[53] Inside the party, criticism thus becomes a method of psychic destruction and communist guilt the affective sign of its success, recreating the crowd experience of chaos-as-deformation through the disintegration of the subject's individuality.

Drawing on the grammar of sovereignty, Dean's account of the crowd's chaos not only justifies the need for the party but also organises its affective practices. If we forego this sovereign image of the crowd event as chaotic, then how else can we understand the experience of collectivity other than as a breakdown of the individual? If the affects associated with guilt do not mirror the kinds of feelings generated in the crowd, then what affective insights might the crowd reveal for the purposes of political organising?

PUBLIC HAPPINESS

Already ten days of happiness

—May 1968 Graffiti

As a trope drawn from within the grammar of sovereignty, chaos portrays the crowd as an event of disorganised horror—the nightmare of the state of nature that the sovereign imagines would exist in its absence. From the position of those momentarily ungoverned, however, the affective condition of the crowd event is more commonly described as joyful.[54] Reflecting on his experience of May '68, Eric Hazan notes that 'one thing that was clear was that it was joyous.'[55] The 'atmosphere,' Collette Danappe similarly recalls, was 'wonderful, it was really joyful.'[56] Though this is a common descriptor of leftist crowds, the left by no means has a monopoly on joy. 'There was an intense energy about it,' writes Bill Buford of his experience in nationalist English football hooligan riots, 'it was impossible not to feel some of the thrill. Somebody near me said that he was happy. He said that he was very, very happy, that he could not remember ever being so happy.'[57] How are we to make sense of the invocation of such joyful affects to describe the experience of the crowd?

In this section, I turn to the work of Hannah Arendt to provide a political analysis of crowd affect.[58] Drawing on Arendt's reflections on totalitarianism and mass society, I argue that the pleasures of the crowd are *politically* distinct from those of the mass. Where crowd theorists commonly argue that the ecstasy of the crowd is the positive feeling of a subject's loss of individuality, Arendt's work illustrates how this idea of crowd happiness erroneously ascribes a characteristic of mass society to the minoritarian figure of the riotous crowd. Attending to Arendt's distinction between private and public happiness, I argue that, far from eradicating individuality, the crowd's public happiness makes possible the development of the crowd participant's individuality. It is only in and through the expansion of this individuality, I contend, that a crowd's collective unity can emerge.

In *Origins of Totalitarianism*, Arendt describes how totalitarian movements aim to bring into being a new collective subject known as the mass. Counterintuitively, she argues that the mass is rooted not in relations of collectivity so much as anomie and isolation. The 'masses grew out of the fragments of a highly atomized society whose competitive structure and concomitant loneliness of the individual had been held in check only through membership in a class. The chief characteristic of the mass man is . . . his isolation and the lack of normal social relationships.'[59] For Arendt, the mass is a strange kind of collectivity. Unlike the individual members of a class who share common interests as a class, the individuals that make up the mass lack social relations and 'are not held together by a consciousness of common interest.'[60] Rooted in the isolation of its members, the mass is a collectivity that seemingly lacks collective unity. It is, in other words, a grouping of atomistic individuals whose relation is constituted in and through their lack of relation.

What unites the mass then, Arendt argues, is the 'feeling of superfluousness' that accompanies relations of substitutability within the mass.[61] People, as she puts it, 'insofar as they are more than animal reaction and fulfillment of functions are entirely superfluous to totalitarian regimes. Totalitarianism strives not toward despotic rule over men, but toward a system in which men are superfluous.'[62] According to Arendt, the feeling of superfluousness that unites individuals in the mass derives not from any definite social relations among individuals but from a common animality ('animal reaction and fulfillment') shared by all humans. The feeling of superfluousness is then a sense of one's interchangeability with others, given that any *particular* individual is ultimately redundant from the perspective of the mass. Accordingly, the feeling of superfluousness marks, for Arendt, the inverse of individuality, since 'individuality, anything indeed that distinguishes one man from another, is intolerable [for totalitarianism].'[63] The mass is therefore a collective subject made up of isolated men and women marked not by too much individuality but rather by its lack. Consequently, the absence of individuality constitutes the condition for the feeling of superfluousness that ultimately unites members of the mass.

Despite its negative connotation, we need not consider the feeling of superfluousness to be a negative affect. In *The Human Condition*, Arendt explains that the basic activities that reproduce bare life—activities that all humans share with animals and that do not serve to distinguish any one person from another—often produce pleasure because 'effort and gratification follow each other as closely as producing and consuming the means of subsistence, so that happiness is a concomitant of the process itself.'[64] Despite the laborious nature of the reproductive activities Arendt calls labour, the joy we feel results from the proximity between the pleasures of consumption and the effort that makes such consumption possible. The 'mark of all laboring,' she argues, is 'that it leaves nothing behind, that the result of its effort is almost as quickly consumed as the effort is spent.'[65] The gratification of eating often follows directly from the preparation of food just as the enjoyment of a clean body immediately results from the labour of cleaning it. Indeed, Arendt goes so far as to argue that such joy enables humans to go on caring for themselves despite the endless tedium of our reproduction:

> The 'blessing or the joy' of labor is the human way to experience the sheer bliss of being alive which we share with all living creatures, and it is even the only way men, too, can remain and swing contentedly in nature's prescribed cycle, toiling and resting, laboring and consuming, with the same happy and purposeless regularity with which day and night and life and death follow each other.[66]

For Arendt, the animal pleasures of labouring are of a fundamentally solitary and thus private kind of experience. In labouring, Arendt argues, 'the human body, its activity notwithstanding, is also thrown back upon itself, concentrates upon nothing but its own being alive, and remains imprisoned in its metabolism with nature without ever transcending or freeing itself from the recurring cycle of its own functioning.'[67] Caught in the endless cycle of reproduction, labour is an activity oriented not towards a public of others but rather a care for oneself.[68] Arendt's claim that the private pleasures of reproductive labour, though shared by all animals, do not form a basis for collective life develops her earlier remarks in *Origins of Totalitarianism* on the feeling of superfluousness that unites the mass in and through their isolation. 'The "happiness of the greatest number",' Arendt writes, 'conceptualized into an "ideal" the fundamental reality of a laboring humanity. The right to the pursuit of this happiness is indeed as undeniable as the right to life; it is even identical with it.'[69] What Arendt earlier names as the feeling of superfluousness rooted in a common animality and uniting individuals in the mass, she now appears to identify as mass society's ideal of 'happiness,' that is, a 'laboring humanity['s]' private happiness of the animal body reproducing itself. Given the private nature of this reproductive happiness, its elevation to an ideal in mass society indicates, for Arendt, the disappearance of politics as a collective and other-oriented activity. Similar to Dean's critique of 'the pursuit of pleasure' under neoliberalism,[70] Arendt's association of reproductive labour with private pleasure leads her to critique the demands for (private) happiness as symptomatic of the larger isolation and anomie that characterises mass society.

Though initially sceptical, Arendt later came to revise her thoughts on the political potential of happiness. Published a few years after *The Human Condition*, Arendt's *On Revolution* articulates a distinction between labour's private and self-regarding pleasures and the kinds of public and other-dependent pleasures that arise in and through political action. In her study of the American Revolution, Arendt argues that the Americans yearned for an active and participatory 'freedom they called later, when they had come to taste it, "public happiness", and it consisted in the citizen's right of access to the public realm, in his share in public power—to be "a participator in the government of affairs".'[71] Unlike private happiness, Arendt argues that public happiness emerges from the experience of collective power—that is, from participating in public with others in such a way as to organise the affairs of our common lives. Modifying her previous critique of the pursuit of happiness by differentiating between private and public happiness, Arendt now aligns the feelings of collective joy with the experience of public freedom: '[P]ublic freedom consisted in having a share in public business,' and 'the activities connected with this business . . . gave those who discharged them in public a feeling of happiness they could acquire nowhere else.'[72] Unlike the self-oriented pleasures of labour, the pleasures of political action can only emerge from the collective condition of plurality. Absent others, there is no context of individual private life that can give rise to the feeling of joy in collective action. Public happiness is, in other words, an affective sensibility of individuals in and as a collective acting in concert.

Regardless of whether we want to take up wholesale Arendt's claims regarding what she calls labour and political action, Arendt's distinction between private and public happiness helps clarify why participants in the crowd often turn to the grammar of joy to describe their experiences. In an interview on the topic of events 'happening at places like the Sorbonne' during the riotous days of May '68, Eric Hazan was asked whether 'you [thought] it was a mess?' to which he replied, 'No it was joyous.'[73] Why might the grammar of joy, or in Arendt's terms, public happiness, be an intelligible response to the idea that the uprising or the crowd itself was, to use the grammar of sovereignty outlined above, a chaotic 'mess'? The taste of happiness that accompanies political action is dependent on the joint action of others. As a feeling that arises only in and through relationship to others, public happiness is felt only insofar as a collective exists. As Arendt puts it, 'power is never the property of an individual; it belongs to a group that remains in existence only so long as the group keeps together.'[74] In order to maintain the experience of political joy then, the collective must not break apart and become individuated. In contrast to the image of the crowd as a chaotic and disorganised form, the grammar of public happiness indicates that, insofar as joy circulates throughout the crowd, the conditions for collective action must exist. If the crowd becomes a mess, then the affective relations that tie the participants together have come undone. In other words, a joyful crowd is on some level a collectively organised crowd. The 'pleasure [of political action for Arendt] is,' Peg Birmingham writes, 'the animating bond of the "we"; it provides an animating or dynamic basis for the political bond.'[75] As the affective sensibility shared among crowd participants, the feeling of public happiness provides the very cohesion that enables the collective to maintain its form.

A joyous crowd may create disorder, but it is not itself disordered. I argued above that according to Dean's account the chaos of the crowd is isomorphic with the psychic chaos that the crowd participant experiences. As the structures of individuation break down, the subject undergoes 'de-differentiation' and returns to an originary form of collective subjectivity.[76] As such, crowd theorists argue that happiness is the feeling of the crowd participant overcoming their individuality. However, as Arendt's distinction between public and private happiness suggests, these theorists have confused the private happiness of the mass—a happiness that does indeed mark a loss of individuality—for the public happiness of the riotous crowd. In other words, if Arendt's conception of public happiness more accurately describes the experience not of the mass but of the crowd, then crowd participants do not lose that which distinguishes them in the event of their unity. As Arendt argues, political action takes place in a common world that both 'relates and separates men at the same time. The public realm, as the common world, gathers us together and yet prevents our falling over each other, so to speak.'[77] Like a table that separates and unites those sitting around it, the public realm enables its participants to form common bonds with one another without destroying their differences. Emerging in and through collective action around a shared object of public concern, the feelings of public happiness enlarge one's world, as individuals find affinity with strangers where previously there was none. As Olivia Guaraldo argues, to experience public happiness through political action is, for Arendt, '[to] expand or go beyond the limits of the self, not to blur it into an indistinct entity but to *strengthen its reality*.'[78] Discovering happiness with others in and through action in public, participants find themselves collectively relating to others without losing their own distinction.

Compare these feelings of collective joy with those of communist guilt, which build unity with others only in and through destroying that which separates them. The communist party trial resembles, to borrow from Arendt, 'a spiritualistic séance where a number of people gathered around a table might suddenly, though some magic trick, see the table vanish from their midst, so that two persons sitting opposite each other were no longer separate but also would be entirely unrelated to each other by anything tangible.'[79] In the communist trial, the magic trick that evacuates the common world that differentiates party members is the feeling of communist guilt, which reaches an intensity that can, as Wright recounts in Ross's trial, obliterate each comrade's personality. Unlike the feeling of public happiness, communist guilt generates collective attachment only by erasing the differences of each individual's relationship to the object of their common concern. If communist guilt produces feelings of pleasure, then it appears more akin to the private pleasures of self-negation at the core of the feeling of superfluousness. As Arendt puts it, 'To be uprooted means to have no place in the world . . . to be superfluous means not to belong to the world at all.'[80] While communism can serve as a common object of concern, the practices associated with communist guilt are more likely to disappear this common object and with it, the affective ties that initially drew members of the party together.

Shortly before the Ross trial, Wright left the Communist Party, explaining that the party 'had never been able to conquer their fear of the individual way in which I acted and lived.'[81] 'I wanted to be a Communist,' he writes, 'but my kind of Communist,' which the party could not accept.[82] Wright wanted to struggle for a communist world and thus find affinity with other comrades in and through their shared relation to this struggle. The party, however, was unable to appreciate Wright's unique relationship to the common object they called communism, and so, refusing the forces of guilt, he simply left. Ironically, the Communist Party pushed members away by destroying the very object that not only united them but also illuminated the very differences that the party attempted to erase. Without this common world, the very conditions of their collective freedom soon withered. 'I had only asked to be free,' reflects Wright on his departure.[83] The politics of communist guilt undermined the basis of their shared world, and so made it difficult for members to collectively act. But what if Wright had tasted public happiness with others in the Communist Party? Would he still have left?

CONCLUSION

Jodi Dean's *Crowds and Party* commendably pushes political theorists and actors to think more seriously about the problems of collective attachment by centring not the power of discourse so much as the force of affect. Attending to what Elias Canetti calls the egalitarian discharge of the crowd, Dean asks us to consider how political organisations can sustain the feelings of collectivity experienced in the crowd when the crowd itself is no longer present. According to Dean, the Communist Party can and has done just that. Closer analysis of the Communist Party as an affective infrastructure illustrates that the party aimed to generate collective attachments in and through what I have called communist guilt. The party mobilised practices of criticism in order to make party members feel that they have not and cannot ever do enough for the party. Guilt thus served not only as evidence of attachment (if members were not attached to the party, then they would not feel guilty in the first place), but more importantly, as the mechanism through which to intensify and deepen this attachment.

Communist guilt, however, displays an ambivalent relation to collective belonging, as guilt seems to install resentment and separation in its very relations of attachment. It does so, I argued, because the affective force of communist guilt seeks to generate collectivity by negating a party member's distinct and personal relationship to the common object they call communism. In this, communist guilt mirrors what Arendt names the feeling of superfluousness that unites the mass together in and through their lack of particular social relations. Either the member resists this destructive force by reasserting their individuality, which ultimately entails leaving the party, or the member gives in to guilt by destroying their unique relationship to political struggle, and with that, the personal desires that initially propelled their political activity. In either case, as the Communist Party members themselves noted, a politics of communist guilt often leads to the comrade's dejection and eventual rejection of the party.

In order to rethink the affective practices of political organisation, I argued that we must rethink the image of the crowd. The politics of communist guilt is predicated on a vision of the crowd as a chaotic form, where the disorder and deformation of the crowd mirrors the psychic disintegration and breakdown of the crowd participant, returning the subject to a primary condition of collectivity. The common invocation of joy and happiness among participants of the riotous crowd, however, suggests not an image of chaos but rather of collective action. Drawing upon Arendt's concept of public happiness (in ways that may be in tension with her own work),[84] I argued that public happiness captures the affective sensibility of a crowd acting in concert. Opposed to the sovereign figuration of the crowd as a disordered and chaotic form, public happiness indicates a level of collective organisation among crowd participants. Unlike the de-differentiating and isolating happiness an individual may experience as part of the mass, the feelings of public happiness participants enjoy in the crowd reveal not the breakdown of their world but its enlargement. Members of the crowd find affinity with others in and through each participant's unique relationship to their common object of struggle. As an affective force of cohesion therefore, public happiness provides crowd participants with a felt sense of the collective 'we.'

To foreground the political affects of public happiness is not to suggest that political organisations should totally give up their practices of self-reflection and internal critique. Rather, these practices of critique should not be the primary mechanisms through which to build collective attachment. Instead of centring communist guilt, political organisations should seek to regenerate the feelings of shared unity by nurturing practices that promote public happiness. The risk remains, however, that the pleasures of political organisation may turn out to be, rather than the collective affects of *public* happiness, the atomising pleasures of private happiness that tear political collectives apart. Indeed, it is the isolating effects of these latter affects that, as Dean rightly points out, illustrate the dangers of neoliberal discourses of pleasure and individuality. As such, the happiness of political organising may generate feelings of superfluousness and exchangeability characteristic of the totalitarian mass, and in so doing, sever ties of affinity between comrades in the long term. This risk remains inherent to political organising, and the particular practices that generate public rather than private happiness cannot be determined prior to their actual use and experimentation. Understanding the differences between the private and isolating pleasures characteristic of the mass and the public and collectivity-constituting pleasures of the riotous crowd, therefore, provides a conceptual and affective horizon that can orient the work of building collective affinity in and between cycles of revolt.[85]

NOTES

1. Preceding the global Occupy movement, occupations were also a key strategy in the Arab Spring (e.g. Tahrir Square) and the 15-M Movement in Spain. In 2019, sustained revolt occurred in Hong Kong, Lebanon, Chile, France, Colombia, Sudan, Iraq, Puerto Rico, Haiti, Iran, Algeria, Bolivia and Ecuador. In 2020, Black Lives Matter riots and protests in response to the police murder of George Floyd spread across the United States and several countries across the world. For examples of commentary deploying the grammar of 'leaderless rebellion' to describe these events, see Ross Carne, *The Leaderless Revolution: How Ordinary People Will Take Power and Change Politics in the 21st Century* (New York: Plume, 2011); Gideon Rachman, Benedict Mander, Daniel Dombey, Sue-Lin Wong and Heba Saleh, 'Leaderless Rebellion: How Social Media Enables Global Protests,' *Financial Times*, 25 October 2019, https://www.ft.com/content/19dc5dfe-f67b-11e9-a79c-bc9acae3b654 (accessed 7 October 2020); Joshua Keating, 'The George Floyd Protests Show Leaderless Movements Are the Future of Politics,' *Slate*, 9 June 2020, https://slate.com/news-and-politics/2020/06/george-floyd-global-leaderless-movements.html (accessed 3 February 2021).

2. Jodi Dean, *Crowds and Party* (London: Verso, 2016).

3. Dean, *Crowds and Party*, 102.

4. Dean, *Crowds and Party*, 90.

5. On the double bind of party politics and the extra-parliamentary left as the dominant figurations of struggle post '68, see Jose Rosales's provocative essay in this collection.

6. Dean, *Crowds and Party*, 25.

7. Dean, *Crowds and Party*, 9–10.

8. Dean, *Crowds and Party*, 10.

9. Dean, *Crowds and Party*, 78.

10. Elias Canetti, *Crowds and Power* (New York: Continuum, 1973), 17, 18. Canetti's comments on physical intimacy raises the question of the material relations of proximity that define a crowd. How 'socially distanced' can a crowd become until it no longer constitutes a crowd but a distant collection of individuals? To what extent do the feelings of the crowd depend upon a certain level of bodily proximity between crowd participants?

11. Canetti, *Crowds and Power*, 20.

12. Dean, *Crowds and Party*, 77.

13. A recent paper published in *Science* suggests that number is 25 percent of the population. Damon Centola, Joshua Becker, Devon Brackbill and Andrea Baronchelli, 'Experimental Evidence for Tipping Points in Social Convention,' *Science* 360, no. 6393 (2018): 1116–119.

14. Dean, *Crowds and Party*, 91.

15. Dean, *Crowds and Party*, 80.

16. Dean, *Crowds and Party*, 135.

17. Emil Husted, 'Time to Party?,' *Ephemera* 18, no. 2 (2018): 392, emphasis mine.

18. Nigel Thrift, *Non-Representational Theory: Space, Politics, Affect* (London: Routledge, 2007).

19. Dean, *Crowds and Party*, 21.

20. Dean, *Crowds and Party*, 20–21.

21. The distinction between spectator and participant is not as neat as this formulation suggests. Even if they are not directly involved as actors in the crowd, witnesses may nonetheless feel some of the crowd's alluring affects, as the atmosphere a crowd generates extends beyond its own participants, thus potentially drawing in or repelling its spectators. Attention to the problem of crowd affect therefore opens up the question concerning the reach of the crowd's egalitarian discharge and whether those who experience it are or are not part of the crowd. Moreover, it also raises questions concerning the relationship between the crowd's representation and its affective force. That is, do positive (or negative) representations of the crowd make individuals more (or less) likely to give themselves over to the crowd? Inversely, does 'indirect' exposure to a crowd's egalitarian discharge make individuals more or less likely to ascribe democratic meaning to the crowd form? Given that Dean's account of crowd affects only seems to involve those 'directly' engaged in crowd action, this essay employs the admittedly unstable distinction between participant and witness. For a discussion on the affective quality of symbols and representation, see Sasha Newell, 'The Affectiveness of Symbols: Materiality, Magicality, and the Limits of the Antisemiotic Turn,' *Current Anthropology* 59, no. 1 (2018): 1–22.

22. Dean, *Crowds and Party*, 158.

23. Chantal Mouffe, 'Agonistic Politics between Ethics and Politics,' *Critique and Humanism* 35 (2010): 13–22.

24. Dean, *Crowds and Party*, 80.

25. Dean, *Crowds and Party*, 90.

26. Dean, *Crowds and Party*, 10.

27. 'Give More Personal Guidance,' *Party Organizer* 6, no. 1 (1933): 21–23, cited in Dean, *Crowds and Party*, 120.

28. Dean, *Crowds and Party*, 120.

29. Dean, *Crowds and Party*, 117, emphasis in the original.

30. Dean, *Crowds and Party*, 145.

31. Dean, *Crowds and Party*, 146–47.

32. Dean, *Crowds and Party*, 152.

33. Richard Wright, *Black Boy (American Hunger): A Record of Childhood and Youth* (Harper Collins e-book, 2009), 775; Dean, *Crowds and Party*, 150.

34. Wright, *Black Boy*, 788–89.

35. Dean, *Crowds and Party*, 151.

36. Dean, *Crowds and Party*, 247.

37. 'Give More Personal Guidance,' 22.

38. 'Give More Personal Guidance,' 22.

39. Dean, *Crowds and Party*, 148.

40. For instance, consider the headline of *Los Angeles Times*, 'De Gaulle Returns to France and Worst Chaos in 10 Years,' *Los Angeles Times*, 19 May 1968, I1. Fifty years later, on the anniversary of the uprising, *The Sun* headline reads: 'Paris May Day Riots . . . Bring Chaos to the French Capital.' Holly Christodoulou, 'Paris Is Burning,' *The Sun*, 1 May 2018, https://www.thesun.co.uk/news/6187929/paris-may-day-riots-far-left-anarchists-smash-windows-loot-mcdonalds-thousands-protesters-chaos/ (accessed July 2021).

41. *Oxford English Dictionary Online*, 'Chaos,' Oxford University Press (2018), www.oed.com/view/Entry/30539 (accessed 3 January 2019).

42. Carl Schmitt, *Political Theology: Four Chapters on the Concept of Sovereignty* (Chicago: University of Chicago Press, 2005).

43. Thomas Hobbes, *Leviathan* (Cambridge, UK: Cambridge University Press, 1996), 469.

44. For example, see David Halle and Kevin Rafter, 'Riots in New York and Los Angeles: 1935–2002,' in *New York and Los Angeles: Politics, Society, and Culture—A Comparative View*, ed. D. Halle (Chicago: University of Chicago Press, 2003), 347.

45. James Scott, *Seeing Like a State: How Certain Schemes to Improve the Human Condition Have Failed* (New Haven, CT: Yale University Press, 1999).

46. Dean, *Crowds and Party*, 81.

47. 'Gaining political control of the state thus remains an important goal because the state presents a barrier to political change. . . . If we do not think that the state should remain in the hands that it is in, then we lapse into the politics of the beautiful moment when we fail to factor it into our political perspective.' Dean, *Crowds and Party*, 126–27.

48. Dean, *Crowds and Party*, 131.
49. Joshua Clover, *Riot. Strike. Riot: The New Era of Uprisings* (New York: Verso, 2016), 92.
50. Dean, *Crowds and Party*, 140.
51. Dean, *Crowds and Party*, 57.
52. Dean, *Crowds and Party*, 80.
53. Dean, *Crowds and Party*, 77, 151.
54. This is not to suggest that participants do not feel fear, but rather that the terror associated with chaos does not characterise the affective sensibility of the crowd form. Insofar as terror enters the crowd, it often results from an external intervention by the state as a strategy of crowd management. See aylon cohen, 'Sovereign Chaos and Riotious Affects, Or, How to Find Joy Behind the Barricades,' *Capacious* 2, nos. 1–2 (2020): 163–64.
55. Mitchell Abidor, *May Made Me: Additional Elements of an Oral History of the 1968 Uprising in France* (Chico, CA: AK Press e-book, 2018), 60.
56. Abidor, *May Made Me*, 91.
57. Bill Buford, *Among the Thugs* (New York: Vintage Books, 1993), 87–88. Though Buford's experiences with Manchester United fans (the Inter-City Jibbers) showcases a nationalist sentiment, hooliganism is not necessarily or always nationalistic. For a more detailed exploration of the relations between English hooligans and nationalism, see John Williams, Eric Dunning and Patrick Murphy, *Hooligans Abroad: The Behaviour and Control of English Fans in Continental Europe* (New York: Routledge, 1989). For a more complex interpretation of football fans, see Simon Critchley, *What We Think About When We Think About Football* (New York: Penguin, 2017), especially 91–105.
58. Often drawing on the more philosophically oriented work of scientists, many contemporary theories of affect risk short circuiting a political analysis of feeling. For instance, affect theorists such as Brian Massumi commonly turn to scientific studies of chaos theory to argue that chaos describes a condition of emancipatory potential. Brian Massumi, *Parables for the Virtual: Movement, Affect, Sensation* (Durham, NC: Duke University Press, 2002). See also Patricia Clough, 'Introduction,' in *The Affective Turn: Theorizing the Social*, ed. P. T. Clough (Durham, NC: Duke University Press, 2007), 1–33. In doing so, however, affect theorists overlook how the state has historically mobilised the discourse and logic of 'chaos' to suppress challenges to its hegemony, and so they remain caught in the grammar of sovereignty outlined above. Rather than employ a scientific-philosophical framework to theorise affect, this section aims to escape the grammar of sovereignty by analysing the crowd through a political register attentive to the public relations of affect. On the distinction between thinking philosophically and politically, see Hannah Arendt, 'Philosophy and Politics,' *Social Research* 57, no. 1 (1990): 73–103.
59. Hannah Arendt, *Origins of Totalitarianism* (Orlando, FL: Harcourt Brace & Company, 1973), 317.
60. Arendt, *Origins of Totalitarianism*, 311.
61. Arendt, *Origins of Totalitarianism*, 311.
62. Arendt, *Origins of Totalitarianism*, 457.

63. Arendt, *Origins of Totalitarianism*, 457.

64. Hannah Arendt, *The Human Condition* (Chicago: University of Chicago Press, 1958), 107–8.

65. Arendt, *The Human Condition*, 87.

66. Arendt, *The Human Condition*, 106.

67. Arendt, *The Human Condition*, 115.

68. As Paul Voice explains, 'Digestion is a solitary act in the same way that pain is a solitary experience—we cannot digest each other's food any more than we can feel the pain of others'; Paul Voice, 'Labour, Work, Action,' in *Hannah Arendt: Key Concepts*, ed. P. Hayden (Durham, UK: Taylor & Francis, 2014), 38. The pleasures of labour thus need not and often do not involve other people. As Voice's comment on pain suggests, Arendt at times implies that bodily sensations are, by definition, private because they cannot be experientially shared with others: 'Nothing, in fact, is less common and less communicable, and therefore more securely shielded against the visibility and audibility of the public realm, than what goes on within the confines of the body, its pleasures and its pains, its laboring and consuming.' Arendt, *The Human Condition*, 112.

69. Arendt, *The Human Condition*, 108.

70. Dean, *Crowds and Party*, 30.

71. Hannah Arendt, *On Revolution* (New York: Penguin Books, 1965), 127. Arendt is quoting here from a letter sent by Thomas Jefferson to Joseph Cabell in 1816 discussing a republican system of wards.

72. Arendt, *On Revolution*, 119.

73. Abidor, *May Made Me*, 62.

74. Hannah Arendt, *On Violence* (New York: Harcourt, Brace & Jovanovitch, 1970), 44.

75. Peg Birmingham, 'The Pleasure of Your Company: Arendt, Kristeva, and an Ethics of Public Happiness,' *Research in Phenomenology* 33 (2003): 56.

76. Dean, *Crowds and Party*, 134.

77. Arendt, *The Human Condition*, 52.

78. Olivia Guaraldo, 'Public Happiness: Revisiting an Arendtian Hypothesis,' *Philosophy Today* 62, no. 2 (2018): 399, emphasis in the original.

79. Arendt, *The Human Condition*, 53.

80. Arendt, *Origins of Totalitarianism*, 475.

81. Wright, *Black Boy*, 766–67.

82. Wright, *Black Boy*, 756.

83. Wright, *Black Boy*, 763.

84. Crowds rarely display the kind of deliberation that Arendt argues is a key part of the public sphere. Indeed, riotous crowds often feature a kind of destructive violence that Arendt thought was antithetical to politics. Nonetheless, I suggest that a riotous crowd fulfills the two central conditions of Arendtian political action: public and collective activity on the one hand and natality, or the bringing about of something new in the world, on the other. See cohen, 'Sovereign Chaos and Riotous Affects,' 161–62.

85. My thanks to Krista Bonello Rutter Giappone, Lucile Richard, Matija Vlatković and the organisers and participants of the Double Binds of '68 conference held at the University of Kent, 29–30 September 2018, for comments and criticisms on earlier drafts.

Chapter Eleven

Community, Theatre and Political Labour

Unworking the Socialist Legacy of 1968

Ben Dunn

There are eighteen people sitting in a rehearsal space in Pollokshields, Glasgow, on a sunny Monday afternoon in May 2013. They are participants in *Albert Drive*, a year-long arts and performance project delivered by theatre company Glas(s) Performance that took place in Glasgow, Scotland, between July 2012 and August 2013. Tellingly, *Albert Drive* is both the title of the project and the name of the street on which it took place. As Jess Thorpe, co-artistic director of the company, explains, the project was seen as a 'collaboration between Glas(s) Performance . . . and the community of Pollokshields,'[1] and the linguistic doubling of the project's title highlights the company's ambition to develop forms of artistic practice that reflect the lives and experiences of the people they work with. The project gave rise to multiple works including a video series, letter-writing project, shared meals and guided tours of the local allotments, but these people are meeting to make a performance, due to be shown at Tramway, an art and performance venue located at the eastern end of Albert Drive, on the 6th and 7th of July 2013. As part of my doctoral research,[2] I attended the *ALBERT DRIVE Event Weekend*, an exhibition and performance event that marked the culmination of the project, and interviewed artists, residents and participants involved in all aspects of *Albert Drive*. During our interview, Laiqa, a Pollokshields resident and participant in the performance, was particularly direct in her description of the social and political dynamics of *Albert Drive*: 'Basically, lots of people from different backgrounds, and different ages, coming together . . . to just come and be a community.'

Laiqa's statement illustrates an elision that often occurs at the threshold between theatre and social context, in which creative activity is seen as equivalent to or expressive of the performative and relational structure of community itself. In the context of theatre scholarship, this equivalence is often taken for granted and, indeed, has become central to the ways in which the affective, political, and creative potential of theatre in social contexts is imagined and discussed. Theatre scholar Nicholas Ridout thematises this idea in his description of the 'good community,'[3] noting that conceptions of community as they are embedded within academic discourse and the practice of theatre itself tend to embody a 'romantic anti-capitalism' that posits community as both opposed and exterior to the logics and progress of capital. This perspective is echoed by Dani Snyder-Young who draws critical attention to the 'good intentions'[4] of theatre-makers who associate theatre's capacity to leverage change with broadly socialist articulations of agency and progress. In these instances, community functions, not as a response to capitalism's particular, localised affects, but as a symbolic rearticulation of social and political values somehow situated 'beyond capitalism itself.'[5] It is in reference to Jean-Paul Sartre's famous description of Marxism as the 'untranscendable philosophy of our time'[6] that Ridout identifies the good community as the 'unsurpassable presupposition'[7] of socially engaged and political theatre, to suggest that an assumed correlation between social practice and social good determines our understanding of theatre as a discourse in social and political values.

This study considers this presupposition as a legacy of 1968, both as a landmark in social and political history and as a '[w]orking mythology and political background'[8] for the expansion of the alternative theatre movement in Britain over the subsequent two decades. It considers how the imperative for theatre-makers to articulate their politics through the framework of community relates back to notions of agency and oppositionalism established within this context, and explores how developments in governance and capitalist discourse in the years since have destabilised the ideological ambitions that underpin this form of political labour. Finally, through the lens of Michael Hardt and Antonio Negri's theorisation of the 'altermodern,'[9] it returns to *Albert Drive* to consider an example from this project that foregrounds the possibility of a liberatory praxis between theatre and social context, beyond the restrictive dialectic of left- and right-wing concerns.

COMMUNITY, THEATRE AND WORK—
ALTERNATIVE THEATRE AND THE LEGACIES OF 1968

In his study of experimental and political theatre in Britain over the second half of the twentieth century, scholar and practitioner Baz Kershaw draws attention to the 'Myth of '68.'[10] As he explains, this description is not intended to cast doubt on the historical realities of 1968 but, rather, to highlight the exaggerated influence of events that occurred that year and, more specifically, of practices and practitioners whose genealogy might be traced back to those events, on the ways in which theatre continues to be understood and practised.

The narrative that he addresses, and which is echoed with little variation by a number of contemporaneous and contemporary studies,[11] is that the strikes and public demonstrations occurring globally that year coincided with a sense of disquiet and dissatisfaction that had been growing within British society throughout the 1960s. Against a backdrop of widespread unemployment and social division established in the first half of the 1960s, Kershaw draws particular attention to the disillusionment of, first, the radical left, and then the general public, as Harold Wilson's Labour Party abandoned their socialist principles in a series of unsuccessful attempts to control the economy after coming to power in 1964.[12] In combination with Labour's tacit endorsement of the United States' military intervention in Vietnam, and the younger generation's fervent desire to liberate themselves from the cultural and economic strictures of a class-based society,[13] the radical actions of students, protesters and trade unions throughout Europe were framed as a viable, if not necessary, opposition to the apparent failures of privilege and power embedded in British society.

Theatre practitioner and theorist John McGrath gives particularly clear voice to the reciprocal relationship between this context and the development of British theatre, citing his experiences of the May 1968 protests in Paris, France, as the impetus behind the highly influential theatre companies 7:84 and 7:84 Scotland, which he founded in 1971 and 1973 respectively. As he notes:

> The importance of the thinking around that whole time, the excitement of that whole complex set of attitudes to life which that para-revolutionary situation threw up was incredible—the thinking about ordinary life, the freshness of the approach, the urgency and the beauty of the ideas was amazing.[14]

As Kershaw observes, in an echo of the revolutionary aspirations crystalised in the general strikes and worker-led demonstrations of that year, the decade after 1968 saw a rapid proliferation of theatre companies that sought to leverage their art to foment and facilitate social change. Though aesthetically and even ideologically diverse, what became known as the alternative theatre movement could be characterised by a consistent interest in the intersection between cultural practice and forms of agency, knowledge making and productivity that were understood to embody and articulate political values. In reference to this distinction, Sandy Craig characterises theatre in the decade after 1968 as a 'cudgel of the imagination,'[15] situating theatre as a medium through which the anger and discontent of the 1960s was made manifest in cultural forms designed, not just to identify or comment on political problems, but to attack the societal conditions that were seen as the root cause of those issues.

This ambition was expressed in new models of touring and production designed to liberate theatre's aesthetic and political potential by looking beyond the audiences and conventions of the country's main stages. As Catherine Itzin observes in the introduction to a 1976 survey of alternative theatre:

> In this handbook is a list of one hundred and thirty 'theatre' companies operating in the UK at the moment. The general theatre-going public (that notorious two per-cent), for whom theatre means plays produced in theatre buildings in London's West End or on London's fringe or in regional cities, will never have heard of most of them.[16]

Itzin characterises alternative theatre as 'often community-orientated,' identified by the use of performance spaces that allow companies to work in particularly close relationship or proximity to their audiences: car parks (Insideout), town squares (Natural Theatre Company), the street (Attic Theatre), factories (Broadside Mobile Workers' Theatre), youth and community centres (Community Theatre; Half Moon Theatre) and parks, fields and the outdoors (Lumiere & Son; Mikron Theatre Company; The Puppet Tree).[17] As Kershaw observes, though some theatre companies, such as 7:84, Red Ladder and Cartoon Archetypal Slogan Theatre (CAST), made direct reference to the politics of socialist resistance in their work, the movement as a whole might be understood in relation to 'the structure of the audience's community and the nature of the audience's culture,'[18] as the forum and context within which the political dimensions of theatre practice were examined and expressed. Designated as 'alternative,' at least in part because of a rejection of mainstream cultural values and infrastructure, audiences sought out beyond these contexts were largely aligned with working class experiences and identity, and engaging with them—as audiences, participants or co-creators—was seen as commensurate with a broader liberation of counter-hegemonic ideals.[19]

It is this characteristic that most closely aligns the legacy of 1968 and the alternative theatre movement with the construct and politics of community, and helps define the double bind that sits at the heart of this articulation of theatre's social function. As Raymond Williams observes in *Keywords*,[20] despite its prominence within the imaginaries and ambitions of the political left, the term 'community' is curiously ambivalent in its politics and meaning:

> Community can be the warmly persuasive word to describe an existing set of relationships, or the warmly persuasive word to describe an alternative set of

relationships. What is most important, perhaps, is that unlike all other terms of social organization (state, nation, society, etc.) it seems never to be used unfavourably, and never to be given any positive opposing or distinguishing term.[21]

In the absence of its own uncontested definition, what the term offers is not a specific description of context or social practice but an affirmation that is used to identify and confirm otherwise abstract themes of social and political concern. As Kershaw's comments highlight, within the framework of alternative theatre, community is valued, not for its own innate discourse of social and political expression, but as a resource through which the social dynamics of political opposition might be cultivated and advanced. As aylon cohen discusses in chapter 10 of this volume, the affective and ideological rupture of 1968 is almost immediately appended by the problem of endurance, and continued reference to community as a synonym for the aspirations of the political left could be read in these terms, as an effort to organise and sustain the radical impetus associated with that year.

Commenting on the development of alternative theatre during the 1970s, David Watt characterises the intersection between theatre and social practice as a counter-hegemonic technique designed, ultimately, to disturb social order and convention through the elevation of perspectives and experiences that are assumed to represent the working class.[22] In more recent years, as the progression of capitalist governance has attenuated the 'urgency and beauty' of socialist resistance, community has come to stand in for any number of ostensibly progressive fields of socially constituted knowledge and activity, including: the cultivation of localised or uniquely politicised experiences of identity and belonging;[23] a nexus of remembrance and meaning-making;[24] the temporary articulation of communitarian values 'in convergence with place and purpose';[25] or the performative encounter with a more socially and affectively interconnected future.[26] In these more diffuse registers of agency and affect, community might be allied with Paolo Virno's articulation of 'political action' as a circumstantial discourse in politics and potentiality that takes place 'between social relations'[27] and before the material and intellectual labours through which broader constructs of social order and political life are established. In either case, however, whether in the febrile summer of 1968 or in the long decades of economic and cultural crisis that followed,[28] community's role within a discourse of socially engaged, politically motivated theatre is broadly consistent as an articulation of progressive ambitions and an ideological commitment to the radical purpose and potential of social practice.

In a study examining the history and practice of theatre as social intervention, performance scholar Nicola Shaughnessy traces this relationship through the prism of 'work.' Associating the origins of this approach with the European avant-garde of the 1920s,[29] Shaughnessy suggests that an understanding of theatre practice as political labour '[connects] historical and contemporary artists who have a common interest in socialist politics, social activism, audiences, community engagement, marginalized groups and methodologies.'[30] In common with Ridout, Shaughnessy observes a distinction between political work, as conceptualised and facilitated by theatre-makers, and the discourse and economy of capitalist leisure. In contrast to the complementary relationship between time and work under capital and the ameliorative distraction of the leisure industry,[31] a conceptualisation of theatre as work reflects a radical attempt to disturb the various labours through which capitalism is instated and reproduced by putting the practice of theatre in their place. Jean-Luc Nancy highlights the relationship between this mode of activism and the concept and practice of community, tracing a genealogy of communist or, as he prefers, 'communitarian' opposition in the twentieth century that has seen the ideological and practical equivalence between agency and labour as central to their cause. As he writes, there is no form of communitarian opposition 'that has not been or is not still profoundly subjugated to the goal of a *human* community, that is, to the goal of achieving a community of beings producing in essence their own essence as their work, and furthermore producing precisely this essence as *community*.'[32] Despite, therefore, the imprecision with which it is described and understood within the discourses of the left, the pursuit of community is seen as central to the labour of political opposition and, subsequently, theatre's social and political affects. Where, as Hardt and Negri observe, capitalist governance is sustained by the production of 'social relations and forms of life' that rely on and perpetuate the logics and structures of capitalism,[33] theatre is understood to intervene in these processes by associating the intersection between cultural practice and social context with the work of producing community itself.

With these perspectives in mind, the imperative to 'be' a community, identified earlier by Laiqa, represents a complicated legacy. While it evokes a sense of autonomous social organisation, it remains closely tied to discourses of labour, productivity and political value that lay claim to the outcomes of that work. It is, to borrow from Snyder-Young, a 'tactic'[34] that seeks, not just to interlink social practice with the aesthetic and methodological concerns of theatre, but to articulate a resistance to capitalist interests by encouraging participants to undertake specific forms of collectivist or communitarian labour. As Shaughnessy's discussion highlights, it is the ongoing influence of these imperatives, and their tendency to supersede and contextualise the contingent circumstances and practice of theatre, that remain one of the most significant legacies of 1968. Theatre's evolution in response to landmark developments in governance and cultural policy in the years since 1968—including monetarist reform of the Arts Council under Thatcher,[35] New Labour's reframing of the cultural sector as an adjunct to social and economic policy[36] and successive cuts to public funding and the promotion of private sponsorship since 2010[37]—demonstrates the capacity of artists and cultural organisations to adapt successfully to the increasingly complex demands of publicly funded cultural practice. Nevertheless, continued reference to community—as a nexus of progressive values, practice and politics—returns understanding of theatre's social and political affects to the same principal concerns.

COMMUNITY ON THE NEOLIBERAL STAGE—CONFLICTING DRAMATURGIES

At 7:30 p.m. on 7 July 2013, the back wall of Tramway's main stage is dominated by a floor to ceiling projected image of Albert Drive. Taken from the middle of the road, the image shows the length of the street, looking from its easternmost point, where it meets Pollokshaws Road, past Tramway and into Pollokshields. Set against a familiar, grey sky, the distant spire of Pollokshields Church draws the attention of the audience up and into the Drive itself. As the lights change to illuminate the space in a soft, even wash, the cast of *ALBERT DRIVE performance* make their way onto the stage to introduce themselves (see figure 11.1). Positioned at the very front of the performance space, they pass the microphone down the long line of eighteen performers,

Figure 11.1. *ALBERT DRIVE performance*. Photograph by Alan Dimmick.

each delivering a few sentences in the third person, presenting themselves to the audience as they are seen by others: 'She's the girl who makes loads of noise when walking back from school with her friends'; 'He's the guy who works in the shop all throughout the year . . . he serves everything'; 'She's the woman who's always waving to passers-by.'[38] In so doing, the performers not only tell their own stories, but the story of the group's knowledge and acknowledgement of one another and, as the performance unfolds, we are shown an intricate mapping of interconnections, private experiences and difference, overlaid against a video backdrop of the street itself. Carefully cultivated over months of weekly rehearsals, these insights embody the 'unconstrained community of fellow-feeling'[39] that Ridout and others associate with an ideological resistance to capital. Where, as Michael Feher observes, we might understand the neoliberal subject as one who seeks to protect and appreciate their own value within the unpredictable flux of a deregulated economy,[40] community is assumed to make politics and ontology a public concern by introducing all those it implicates to a conceptually or geographically localised site of discourse and veridiction. In the context of *Albert Drive*, this interest was articulated as a move away from contexts on the Drive which, due to their usage, history or location, were considered socially or culturally 'coded,'[41] towards spaces and practices that encouraged new forms of social and spatial relation. It is the resolution of participants' individuated topographies of knowledge and experience into a shared discourse of place and identity which, on the 6th and 7th of July 2013, was re-presented as community. Performed in front of an audience of family, friends and neighbours, the performance's representation of community, too, tells a story about what Pollokshields might be like: inviting the audience to consider how they might act differently to reconfigure Pollokshields' social landscape to better reflect the communitarian principles modelled in the performance.

Following performance theorist Cathy Turner, the characteristics of agency and change embedded in *ALBERT DRIVE performance* could be described as dramaturgical. As Turner suggests, if we are to consider performance as implicated in a discourse of social and political affect, we might interpret dramaturgy, not simply as the arrangement of performers, materials and events on stage, but as any coordinated series of practices, relationships and responses directed towards the ordering of knowledge and experience.[42] Dramaturgy is not, in these terms, a static, repeatable system, but a dynamic 'constellation of events, actions, interactions, performances and contexts'[43] that gives rise to its own public form. To frame *ALBERT DRIVE performance* as a discourse in dramaturgy is to acknowledge within the rehearsal process a layered interplay of productive activities that combines the development of the performance text with the interpersonal resources required to support the performative articulation of change. Thorpe highlights this ambition in her description of the background to the project:

> As a society it seems that we spend less and less time with our neighbours. Perhaps that's because our lives are so busy. Perhaps that's because there are more computer screens and mobile phones, and things that prevent us from having actual human connections but, certainly, we realised that we didn't know that much about the people that we lived alongside.[44]

The project's interest in the figure of the neighbour positions the contributions of residents and participants as a response to these concerns, and we can consider the exercises they were asked to engage with in rehearsal, and the knowledge shared and gained about other participants, as dramaturgical prompts designed to position the group's public expression as the progressive antithesis to a perceived degradation of social connection and responsibility in society as a whole. Though the staged performance makes explicit the dramaturgical dynamics of the time the group spent together, the performative and relational foundations of a specifically politicised expression of neighbourliness and community had been experienced and established long before the audience filed in.

Despite, however, the apparent autonomy that differentiates the performative work of community from the broader social and political construct of Pollokshields itself, it is precisely this articulation of change and agency that neoliberal governance could be said to undermine. As Hardt and Negri observe, the characteristics of contemporary governance instate a discourse of politics and productivity without exterior: 'a world that, for better or worse, we all share, a world that has no "outside".'[45] As they write, where we might previously have identified a distinction between the ontology of the political subject and the various economies of politics and productivity that governed their existence, neoliberal forms of governance derive their authority from the collapse of this distinction and the direct administration of 'subjectivity itself.'[46] Whilst, as Nancy observes, leftist thought has associated community with '[a]n absolute immanence'[47] that stands opposed and exterior to the interests of capital, the various epistemological and representational strategies through which the neoliberal subject understands and expresses their relationship to the world are understood to emerge from and represent the logics and values of capital itself. Miranda Joseph draws particular attention to the implications of this shift for the construct and practice of community, suggesting that, within a discourse of capitalist governmentality, the 'rhetorical invocation of community and the social relationships that are discursively articulated as community'[48] embody performative modes of production and consumption that emphasise capital's role in associating social context with form and value. Further, and as she is careful to point out, these should not be seen as a corruption of community's relationship to values and interests that are essentially social but, rather, as an authentic articulation of social practice and politics as they are made manifest under capital. These distinctions challenge the tautology of the 'good community' to emphasise the exposure of social practice and its outcomes to the forces and interests of a capitalist economy. More specifically, where *ALBERT DRIVE performance* pursued a politics founded on a differentiation between the productive activities of the group and the broader construct of Pollokshields, the condition of the neoliberal subject could be seen to undermine the ontological basis of agency and activism articulated in these terms. As Hardt and Negri write, 'we are destined to live in *this* world, not only subject to its powers of domination but also contaminated by its corruptions,'[49] and we might assume that political subjects implicated in the practice of theatre at any level are at all times also engaged in the performative articulation of neoliberalism itself.

Theatre scholar Jen Harvie draws attention to the intersection between these concerns and the context of cultural practice. As she notes, referencing the work of American economists Joseph Pine II and James Gilmore,[50] audiences and participants operating in response to neoliberal imperatives might be identified as 'prosumers': a category of economically determined agents 'who fulfil their own needs by producing what they want to consume.'[51] Harvie illustrates her discussion with a category of cultural practice that she terms 'delegated art,'[52] with reference to examples such as Punchdrunk's immersive theatre and one-to-one performances by artists such as Adrian Howells and Oreet Ashery, in which audiences are structurally and performatively essential to the constitution of the art work. As she suggests, cultural practices that share the labour of production could also be seen to expose the work of making art to the social mechanics of neoliberal production. Positioned as prosumers, participants do not simply take part in cultural opportunities curated and controlled by the artist but use their labour to enclose the cultural product or act of cultural participation within economically determined discourses of value and productivity. Here, the social and political outcomes of cultural participation are made uncertain not because the work of artists necessarily mirrors the structural and ideological constitution of contemporary capital, but because the qualities of subjectivity that emerge in the context of a neoliberal society ensure that participation itself takes on the characteristics of capitalist labour. Theatre functions, in this sense, not to liberate the labour of participants in the service of an alternative political regime, but as an interface that facilitates the translation of otherwise immaterial qualities of affect, experience, and relation into economic commodities.

Snyder-Young offers a particularly stark critique of the impact of contemporary governance on models of change and activism embedded in the ideological and methodological construct of theatre, noting: 'the utopian promise of communion, of "pure" connection with others, is undermined by the real limits of individual ontology. Humans desire connection, but not at the expense of individual identity, individual choice, and individual agency.'[53] In these terms, the problem facing theatre practitioners is not that it is impossible to articulate community through theatre or that community as it is performed and experienced through theatre might not also embody an affective and relational allusion to qualities of safety and stability missing from neoliberal society. Rather, the challenge is that the condition of the neoliberal subject transforms social labour into an economically determined discourse of value and exchange, to associate social practice in any context with characteristics of accumulation, individualism and self-expression. Feher illustrates this dynamic in his consideration of 'human capital,' suggesting that within the deregulated marketplace of the neoliberal economy, the relative value of a person's skills, experience, connections, and background are subject to the constant and incalculable flux of appreciation and depreciation.[54] Within this context, the individual is tasked, not with the production of goods or labour, but with the production of themselves as a viable commodity within the unpredictable flow of market interests. As Feher writes: 'our main purpose is not so much to profit from our accumulated potential as to constantly value or appreciate ourselves,'[55] such that all aspects of social life and activity are seen as subsidiary to a market-led economy of the self.

Following Turner, these imperatives might be read as dramaturgical prompts that intervene even in our most intimate or seemingly incidental practices to give form to the economic priorities that constitute and motivate capitalist governance. Whilst, as Hardt and Negri's discussion makes clear, contemporary governance is characterised by discourses of power and productivity that operate at a level of ontological concern, the ways in which these interests occupy the performative space of social interaction are of central importance to those interested in theatre's social and political potential. Virno articulates this paradigm as the elision of labour and political action, to suggest that neoliberal production has subsumed into itself those public resources through which we might hope to explore and articulate alternative principles of social and political relation. As he writes: '[t]here is already too much politics in the world . . . for politics as such to continue to enjoy an autonomous dignity.'[56] Against this backdrop, while participants might work together to choreograph an apparently credible expression of immanent community, they continue to act independently as neoliberal subjects to undermine the politics it ostensibly represents. More significantly, while the legacy of 1968 would seem to posit community (and collective organisation more generally) as a viable technique of resistance and change, the pursuit of agency and politics articulated in these terms would seem to occlude contemporary realities of governance and power. Originally understood as servicing the needs and experience of the marginalised and working class, theatre's ongoing pursuit of the good community now seems to collude with modern capitalism's most insidious and exploitative dynamics.

UNWORKING COMMUNITY—BEING BEYOND LABOUR

In an extended critique of contemporary articulations of community and social context, Joseph associates the complicity between community and capitalism with a discourse of supplementarity. As she suggests, community is vulnerable to the interests of capital—not because the idea of community is essentially aligned with the principles of economic expansion, but because its performative expression is structurally dependent on institutions of practice, logic and value dominated by capitalist interests.[57] Conversely, capitalist discourse can only be seen to emerge as a principle and paradigm of social relations in structural complicity with the logics and practice of community. Whilst, as Snyder-Young's comments suggest, there is a tendency from within the field to view the apparent loss of community as evidence of the progress and preeminence of capital, we might also consider community and capital to be, in Joseph's words, 'mutually dependent structures'—each extending and giving form to the other. Though the neoliberal subject could be seen to render untenable the relationship between community and discourses of change and agency articulated by the political left, community itself remains politically significant, and a performative rearticulation of its social and political structures could still offer an important counterpoint to the neoliberal equivalence between social and economic labour. It is for these reasons that, although the conditions of contemporary capital encourage us to look for resistance beyond the ideological horizon of the good community, I remain interested in community itself as a site of progressive potential that might continue to support the ambitions of academics and theatre-makers interested in the possibility of social change.

Nancy's articulation of the 'inoperative'[58] constitution and dynamics of community provides a valuable lens through which to consider the implications of community's supplementary relationship to the ideological imperatives of both the left and the right, and consider its political function beyond these regimes. In casting community as inoperative, Nancy invites a differentiation between 'community' as an innate quality of relation, and all ideological and administrative regimes that seek to identify, structure and value social practice. As he writes, 'such a thinking . . . is in effect the closure of the political'[59] as the potentiality of human relations is resolved in economies of representation and identity that seek to commodify the productive potential of social practice. Whilst my analysis has focused on the enclosure of community within neoliberal discourses of order and productivity, Nancy is emphatic in his assertion that any effort to operationalise community as a legible, repeatable network of values and practices obscures those aspects of communitarian relation that could be considered essential to community itself.

Instead, Nancy describes community in terms of the 'clinamen': 'an inclination or an inclining from one toward the other, of one by the other, or from one to the other.'[60] As Nancy conceives of it, community exists, not as practice or social context, but as an ontological dynamic that constitutes the state and condition of being as inherently and indivisibly relational. Though we exist in singular terms—'*a* body, *a* face, *a* voice'[61]—the clinamen invests being with an essential plurality that ensures there is no such thing as the truly individual. Considered in this way, 'Being "itself" comes to be defined as relational, as nonabsoluteness, and, if you will . . . as *community*.'[62] For Nancy, it is this characteristic that defines community as inoperative—for where the *idea* of community might be implicated within overarching regimes of order, value and power, to foreground its ontological constitution is to suggest, too, that community, as an expression of itself, is neither resolved nor legible. He articulates this distinction as a differentiation between a commonality of being based on shared principles of identity, value, and politics, and the unpredictable exposure of 'being-in-common,' to suggest: 'it is the work that community does *not* do and that it *is* not that forms community.'[63]

It is this distinction that I consider here as an unworking. As Ridout writes, also in reference to Nancy's discussion, for theatre practice to examine new arrangements of social and political potential, it must also be a theatre beyond work. As he suggests, if we accept that all aspects of social life, including those visible and implicated in the practice of theatre, constitute work inasmuch as they are already associated with value and functionality within a framework of capitalist production, theatre that possesses the potential to support a liberatory politics 'will first of all be a theatre in which work is somehow in question.'[64] Expanding this discussion, I would suggest, too, that a politically significant community is, similarly, a community beyond work—one that, in the absence of supplementary obligation, is able to make public something of the 'being-in-common' that Nancy considers the essence and condition of community itself. Writing on the ontology of performance, Peggy Phelan warns of the intervention of 'the reproductive economy'[65] on the gestures, bodies and politics of performance, noting that in the moment of performance the essential intent and ontology of the performer disappears within a discourse of value and meaning-making over which they have no direct control. They are, as Ridout might observe, put to work. In positing a notion of community beyond work, I do not mean to suggest that a turn to the ontology of community is somehow isolated from these concerns. Rather, where the good community confines the politics of community to its public, legible expression, I am interested in the processual uncertainty of 'being-in-common' as a different foundation from which to think and practise the politics of performance.

EVERYBODY'S HOUSE AND THE ALTERMODERN—A COMMUNITY BEYOND WORK

Hardt and Negri offer an outline for how we might consider the politics and potential of a community beyond work in their articulation of the 'altermodern.'[66] As they write, altermodernity is not defined in opposition to the social and political order precipitated and progressed by capital, which they identify as 'modernity.' Nor should it be understood as a retreat from categories of identity, relation and production established by modernity, which they classify as 'antimodernity,' and which might be allied with Ridout's good community. Rather, altermodernity represents a form of political expression concerned with the contingent circumstances and experiences of the political agent; with the social and material resources that are available to them; and, fundamentally, with a revision of the circumstances that produce the political subject as a precondition for new forms of thought and action. As they write: '[altermodernity] is two removes from modernity since it is first grounded in the struggles of antimodernity and their resistance to the hierarchies at the core of modernity; and second it breaks with antimodernity, refusing the dialectical opposition and moving from resistance to the proposition of alternatives.'[67] Crucially, as a response to the neoliberal problematic of 'too much politics in the world,'[68] altermodernity does not seek to oppose discourses of modernity directly, but to disrupt their circulation through interrelational events that disturb and reconstitute the social, epistemological and ontological foundations of capitalism's 'normative system.'[69] Where the good community articulates an antimodern ethic as a reaction against capitalism, the 'being-in-common' of Nancy's inoperative community alludes to an alternative register of awareness and subjectivity as the dramaturgical basis for altermodern structures of politics and agency.

In the context of the *Albert Drive* project as a whole, we can consider community's altermodern potential in relation to *Everybody's House*. Designed by Glas(s) Performance in collaboration with Glasgow-based firm Edo Architecture, *Everybody's House* was a transparent house, just big enough to sit six people comfortably—three on each side, facing inward (see figure 11.2)—and also accommodate a small table with a full tea set: teapot, six cups, six saucers, milk and sugar. Set on wheels and light enough to be moved by two people, every day between January 2013 and the event weekend in July, members of Glas(s) Performance would guide the house from its storage at Tramway to a different location on Albert Drive. As Vivienne Hullin, part of the project's creative team, explained in our interview: 'it was literally a transparent place where you could sit and talk. It didn't exist before, it didn't really exist after, and it was open—there was no door, you could come straight in.' Whilst some events in the house, such as live music and karaoke, were arranged by Glas(s) Performance and encouraged a reiteration of particular, prescribed modes of cultural participation, time spent in *Everybody's*

Figure 11.2. *Everybody's House*. Photograph by Abigail Howkins; House designed by Andrew McAvoy.

House was largely unstructured. As Laiqa explains, its primary purpose was simply as a space of encounter:

> There'd be someone new in that glass house everyday.... People of different age groups met, different cultures, different backgrounds, different religions.... They all got together in this one tiny, cramped house.... [I]t was just something as simple as tea and a chat and you could talk about whatever you wanted.

The name of the project was written on a sign that travelled with the house as a title and declaration that this was, in fact, 'everybody's house,' while the visible interior—artists, seats, table, tea, conversation—became a public invitation to residents and passers-by.

As Turner writes, we can understand architecture as an 'activation' of space that frames and facilitates potential in the physical environment: 'an alternative or transgressive space in dialectical relationship to the established possibilities.'[70] As Laiqa's comment suggests, we can consider *Everybody's House* in these terms, as a dramaturgical differentiation between the space and context of the house, and the broader construct of Pollokshields itself. More specifically, while the physical context of Albert Drive is already imbricated in the material and performative expression of capitalist modernity, the function and value of the house is unknown. The flow of visitors, the unpredictable nature of their interactions and the mobility of the house itself underline the importance of irresolution to the project's social and cultural expression. Where the performers of *ALBERT DRIVE performance* articulated their community as an internally coherent mapping of personal and interpersonal values, *Everybody's House* invokes an alternative logic of practice and politics in which communitarianism is expressed and experienced in the dynamic uncertainty of relational encounter.

For Hardt and Negri, the proposition of an alternative politics is contingent on the resourcing of new subjective positions from which to think and act. While the political dynamics of *ALBERT DRIVE performance*, and the good community generally, could be seen to rely on a conception of the political subject framed by the events and ambitions of 1968, *Everybody's House* represents an environment in which subjectivity itself is in question. In contrast to the self-regulating individualism of 'self-appreciation,'[71] it provides a material and performative context indivisibly exposed to the interests and influence of others, in which the logics and values that might otherwise align community with consistent registers of meaning and identity cannot be fully resolved. While this is not the truly inoperative community identified by Nancy, it could be considered its dramaturgical expression, as a performative discourse orientated towards the practice and uncertainties of collective becoming. As Hardt and Negri suggest, altermodernity reflects an alternative discourse in politics and potentiality, not simply because it opposes the characteristics and conditions of capitalist modernity, but because it exists in adjacent relation to the entire dialectic of left- and right-wing concerns. It reflects the characteristics of political work, to the extent that it requires the performative recontextualisation of social and material resources that are otherwise implicated in the constitution of an overarching socio-political regime. Where, however, notions of work align social practice with extant discourses of productivity and value, which in turn, lay claim to their outcomes, altermodernity exists only in the moment of its expression: 'as innovation which emerges, so to speak, from the inside.'[72] It is in these terms that I associate *Everybody's House* with a community beyond work: as an emergent and uncertain rupture in social and political consistency, ontologically exterior to the productive obligations of legibility and the neoliberal regime.

CONCLUSION

The fragile differentiation between the interior of the house and the material realities of the street outside underlines the vulnerability of community understood and articulated in these terms. Dislocated from the material and social structures through which community is most frequently resourced and defined, we are left to question what of this model of agency and politics might be sustained beyond the discontinuities of space and social context precipitated by the project itself. In contrast, however, to the good community's preoccupation with legibility, it is only in the absence of representation that a community beyond work could be seen to reflect a political alternative. To paraphrase Nancy, it is the work that a community does *not* do that constitutes altermodern practice.

This model stands in contrast to the warm shelter[73] or unequivocal good[74] that could be said to characterise community as an anti-capitalist position, to encourage consideration of the affective, political and relational implications of community itself. Where *ALBERT DRIVE performance* allied the politics of community with a restaging of behaviours and relationships cultivated and refined in rehearsal, *Everybody's House* suggests that both community and its possible benefits are uncertain: 'a potential relation within the practice of theatre'[75] rather than the inevitable outcome of theatre's relationship to the history and ambitions of the political left. Crucially, where, as Craig and Kershaw suggest, the legacies of 1968 identify community as a 'weapon'[76] brandished by theatre-makers to advance partisan political aims, the community of *Everybody's House* exists only as long as and to the extent that visitors are exposed to the influence and interests of one another. Its politics are contingent, not on the practice of theatre itself, but on theatre's capacity to liberate relations between work, social practice, and context, such that those implicated as participants or collaborators might reform notions of community and interrelation, value and productivity, around themselves.

It is in this sense that the *Albert Drive* project sheds new light on the imperative for participants to 'be' a community, inviting artists and scholars to think critically about the effects of the legacy of 1968 and the political left on the ways in which we understand and practise the politics of theatre. If we accept the proposition of the neoliberal subject, as framed by authors such as Feher, it is not enough to assume that participants' collaborative activities are automatically aligned with progressive goals. Rather, as Laiqa's comment highlights, when considering dramaturgies of community and political action, it is necessary to look beyond the legible dynamics of rehearsal and social practice, to consider the demands theatre makes on being itself. As *Everybody's House* suggests, it is only through a careful choreography of being that we might associate theatre with subjectivity and agency beyond the constitutive labour of the neoliberal domain.

NOTES

1. Abigail Howkins, *Albert Drive: Introducing You to Your Neighbour* (DVD), 2013.

2. Ben Dunn, 'Troubling Community: Community Theatre, Praxis and Politics in a Neoliberal Context' PhD diss., (University of Manchester, 2019). Undertaken at the University of Manchester under supervision from James Thompson and Jenny Hughes, my doctoral research examines the practice and politics of socially engaged performance, with a focus on the politics and ontology of community. *Albert Drive* is one of three case study projects at the centre of my thesis, with others associated with the Octagon Theatre in Bolton, and the Battersea Arts Centre in London.

3. Nicholas Ridout, *Passionate Amateurs: Theatre, Communism, and Love* (Ann Arbor: University of Michigan Press, 2013), 29.

4. Dani Snyder-Young, *Theatre of Good Intentions* (Hampshire: Palgrave Macmillan, 2013), 8.

5. Ridout, *Passionate Amateurs*, 29.

6. Jean-Paul Sartre, *Critique of Dialectical Reason: Volume 1 Theory of Practical Ensembles*, trans. Alan Sheridan-Smith (London: Verso, 2004 [1960]), 822.

7. Ridout, *Passionate Amateurs*, 28.

8. Peter Ansorge, *Disrupting the Spectacle: Five Years of Experimental and Fringe Theatre in Britain* (London: Pitman, 1975), 56.

9. Michael Hardt and Antonio Negri, *Commonwealth* (Cambridge, MA: Harvard University Press, 2009).

10. Baz Kershaw, *The Politics of Performance: Radical Theatre as Cultural Intervention* (London: Routledge, 1994), 90.

11. See Ansorge, *Disrupting the Spectacle*; David Bradby and John McCormick, *People's Theatre* (Totowa: Rowman & Littlefield, 1978); John Bull, *British Theatre Companies: 1965–1979* (London: Bloomsbury, 2017); Sandy Craig, ed., *Dreams and Deconstructions—Alternative Theatre in Britain* (Ambergate: Amber Lane Press Ltd., 1980); Catherine Itzin, *Stages in the Revolution: Political Theatre in Britain Since 1968* (York: Methuen, 1980); and Alison Jeffers and Gerri Moriarty, eds., *Cultural Democracy and the Right to Make Art* (London: Bloomsbury Methuen Drama, 2017).

12. Kershaw, *The Politics of Performance*, 123.

13. Kershaw, *The Politics of Performance*, 123–24.

14. In Itzin, *Stages in the Revolution*, 120.

15. Craig, *Dreams and Deconstructions*, 9.

16. Catherine Itzin, ed., *Alternative Theatre Handbook* (London and Los Angeles: TQ Publications, 1976), 1.

17. Itzin, *Alternative Theatre Handbook*.

18. Kershaw, *The Politics of Performance*, 1.

19. David Watt, 'Theatre and Political Intervention: The 70s Project in Britain Reconsidered,' *Minnesota Review* 36 (Spring 1991): 76.

20. Raymond Williams, *Keywords: A Vocabulary of Culture and Society* (London: Fourth Estate, 2014 [1976]).

21. Williams, *Keywords*, 76.

22. Watt, 'Theatre and Political Intervention,' 74–76.

23. Helen Nicholson, *Applied Drama: The Gift of Theatre* (Hampshire: Palgrave, 2005), 93–98.

24. Jen Harvie, 'Chapter 3: Remembering the Nations. Site Specific Performance, Memory and Identities,' in *Staging the UK* (Manchester: Manchester University Press).

25. In Caoimhe McAvinchey, *Performance and Community: Commentary and Case Studies* (London: Bloomsbury, 2014), 41.

26. Jill Dolan, *Utopia in Performance: Finding Hope at the Theater* (Ann Arbor: University of Michigan Press, 2005), 6.

27. Paolo Virno, *A Grammar of the Multitude* (New York: Semiotext(e), 2004), 50.

28. Eleonora Belfiore and Oliver Bennett, *The Social Impact of the Arts* (Hampshire: Palgrave Macmillan, 2010), 4.

29. Here Shaughnessy makes particular reference to the 'social-realist' experimentations of the early Soviet era Blue Blouse Groups and the development of Epic Theatre in Berlin by practitioners such as Erwin Piscator and Bertolt Brecht, 15–20.

30. Nicola Shaughnessy, *Applying Performance—Live Art, Socially Engaged Theatre and Affective Practice* (Hampshire: Palgrave Macmillan, 2012), 15.

31. Ridout, *Passionate Amateurs*, 37.

32. Jean-Luc Nancy, *The Inoperative Community* (Minneapolis: University of Minnesota Press, 1991), 2, emphasis in the original.

33. Hardt and Negri, *Commonwealth*, 133.

34. Snyder-Young, *Theatre of Good Intentions*, 3.

35. Kershaw, *The Politics of Performance*, 171–72; Andy Lavender, 'Theatre in Crisis: Conference Report,' *New Theatre Quarterly* 5 (2009 [1989]): 210–16.

36. Caoimhe McAvinchey, *Performance and Community: Commentary and Case Studies* (London: Bloomsbury, 2014), 3.

37. Jen Harvie, *Fair Play: Art, Performance and Neoliberalism* (Hampshire: Palgrave Macmillan, 2013), 155–56.

38. Howkins, *Albert Drive*.

39. Ridout, *Passionate Amateurs*, 4.

40. Michel Feher, 'Self-Appreciation; or, The Aspirations of Human Capital,' *Public Culture* 21, no. 1 (December 2009): 27, https://doi.org/10.1215/08992363-2008-019.

41. Interview with Tashi Gore, 'Getting to Know Your Neighbours in a Space that's Everybody's House,' STV, http://news.stv.tv/west-central/226299-everybodys-house-on-albert-drive-for-glass-performance-project (accessed 22 May 2018).

42. Cathy Turner, 'Mis-Guidance and Spatial Planning: Dramaturgies of Public Space,' *Contemporary Theatre Review* 20, no. 2 (2010): 149–61, https://doi.org/10.1080/10486801003682351.

43. Turner, 'Mis-Guidance,' 151.

44. Howkins, *Albert Drive*.

45. Hardt and Negri, *Commonwealth*, vii.

46. Hardt and Negri, *Commonwealth*, 2009.

47. Nancy, *The Inoperative Community*, 2.

48. Miranda Joseph, *Against the Romance of Community* (Minneapolis: University of Minnesota Press, 2002), viii.

49. Hardt and Negri, *Commonwealth*, vii, emphasis in the original.

50. Joseph Pine II and James Gilmore, *The Experience Economy* (Boston, MA: Harvard Business School Press, 2011 [1999]).

51. Harvie, *Fair Play*, 50.

52. Harvie, *Fair Play*, 29.

53. Snyder-Young, *Theatre of Good Intentions*, 97.

54. Feher, 'Self-Appreciation,' 28.

55. Feher, 'Self-Appreciation,' 27.

56. Virno, *A Grammar*, 51.

57. Joseph, *Against the Romance*, 2.

58. Nancy, *The Inoperative Community*.

59. Nancy, *The Inoperative Community*, xxxvii.

60. Nancy, *The Inoperative Community*, 3.

61. Nancy, *The Inoperative Community*, 8.

62. Nancy, *The Inoperative Community*, 6, emphasis in the original.

63. Nancy, *The Inoperative Community*, xxxix, emphasis in the original.

64. Ridout, *Passionate Amateurs*, 11.

65. Peggy Phelan, *Unmarked* (Oxon: Routledge, 2006), 146.

66. Hardt and Negri, *Commonwealth*, 102–18.

67. Hardt and Negri, *Commonwealth*, 114.

68. Virno, *A Grammar*, 51.

69. Hardt and Negri, *Commonwealth*, 59.
70. Cathy Turner, *Dramaturgy and Architecture* (Hampshire: Palgrave Macmillan, 2015), 4.
71. Feher, 'Self-Appreciation.'
72. Hardt and Negri, *Commonwealth*, 59.
73. Zygmunt Bauman, *Community: Seeking Safety in an Insecure World* (Cambridge: Polity Press, 2006), 1.
74. Joseph, *Against the Romance*, vii.
75. Ridout, *Passionate Amateurs*, 4.
76. Craig, *Dreams and Deconstructions*, 23.

Index

Adorno, Theodor W., 81–82
Agamben, Giorgio, 105, 131, 171
Alliez, Éric and Maurizio Lazzarato, 9–10, 15, 17, 34n97, 34n100
Althusser, Louis, 185, 188
Arendt, Hannah, 27, 202, 211–217, 222n68, 222n84
Ashery, Oreet, 234
Attic Theatre, 228
Axelos, Kostas, 145, 148

Badiou, Alain, 30n34, 40–45, 47–48, 52–53, 56–59, 64n53, 123, 126
Badoglio, Pietro, 92
Banfi, Antonio, 92
Barthes, Roland, 107
Baudelaire, Charles, 17
Baudrillard, Jean, 68, 108
Benjamin, Walter, 77, 82, 104
Bentham, Jeremy, 112
Berlin, Isaiah, 112, 117
Beuys, Joseph, 108
Birmingham, Peg, 214
Black Lives Matter, 49, 218n1
Blanchot, Maurice, 42, 56–58, 60
Blizzard, 115
Bobbio, Norberto, 90–93, 95, 98,
Boltanski, Luc and Ève Chiapello, 17–19, 21, 32n63, 33n83, 152, 165

Bolsheviks, 40–41, 44
Bonomi, Ivanoe, 92
Borde, La (psychiatric institution), 26, 184, 187–195, 197n36, 199n78
Bourg, Julian, 191
Bozon, Michel, 142
Brandom, Robert, 174–176
Brassier, Ray, 172–177, 179n18
Bretton Woods Agreement, 3
Broadside Mobile Workers' Theatre, 228
Brunton, Finn, 110
Bucharin, Nikolai, 94
Buford, Bill, 211, 221n57

Caillois, Roger, 105, 106
Canetti, Elias, 203, 216, 219n10
Cartoon Archetypal Slogan Theatre (CAST), 228
Center for Institutional Study, Research and Training (CERFI), 194
Châtelet, Gilles, 123, 125
Cixous, Hélène, 185
Clark, Mark W., 92
Clover, Joshua, 53–56, 64n44, 64–65n58, 210
Coffin, Judith, 142
Communist Party, 45, 89, 92, 153, 183, 205–208, 215–217; PCF (French

Communist Party), 46–47, 59, 153, 163, 183
Community Theatre, 228
Coulmont, Baptiste, 151
Craig, Sandy, 227, 241
Croce, Benedetto, 23, 90–96, 98
Csikszentmihaly, Mihaly, 117

Dada, 104
Dalmas, Louis, 151
Danappe, Collette, 211
Dean, Jodi, 26, 201–210, 213, 215, 216, 218, 219n21, 220n47
Debord, Guy, 68, 107
Deleuze, Gilles, 8, 31n41, 34n100, 124, 127–132, 136n29, 136n30, 164, 166, 178, 179n20, 185, 188, 190, 198n52
Deleuze, Gilles and Félix Guattari, 9, 11, 13–14, 29n26, 30n40, 30n41, 68, 133, 137n40, 172–176, 186–190, 192, 194–195, 197n30, 197n40
Democrazia Cristiana (party), 92
Derrida, Jacques, 185
Dewey, John, 92
Dillet, Benoît, 183, 187, 195n1, 196n2, 197n34
Dimova-Cookson, Maria, 112
Dirty New Media movement, 104
Dormoy-Rajramanan, Christelle, 184, 185
Dosse, François, 185, 193, 194, 199n78

Eaubonne, Françoise d', 145, 146, 148
Eden, Anthony, 92
Einstein, Albert, 92
Emanuele III, Vittorio, 92
Engels, Friedrich, 47, 146
Export, Valie, 107

Faure, Edgar, 184, 185
Federation of Study and Institutional Research Groups (FGERI), 194
Federici, Silvia, 9, 29n17, 30n36
Feher, Michael, 232, 235, 242

Fisher, Mark, 104, 108
Fordism/post-Fordism, 4, 6, 16, 18, 29n29
Foster, Hal, 108
Foucault, Michel, 15, 20, 32n63, 34n100, 103, 113, 127, 130, 133, 141, 142, 157n53, 164, 166, 178, 185, 188, 195
Fraenkel, Boris, 148
Fraser, Nancy, 3
Freud, Sigmund, 113
Fromm, Erich, 112
Futurism, 104

Galloway, Alexander R., 184
Gaulle, Charles de, 7, 10, 39, 47
Gasperi, Alcide De, 92
George Floyd Rebellion, 49–50, 218n1
Geymonat, Ludovico, 92
Gilles, Gérard, 148
Gilmore, James H., 114, 234
Giulianotti, Richard, 114, 115
Giustizia e Libertà movement, 90
Glas(s) Performance, 27, 225, 239
the glitch, 104, 110
Gramsci, Antonio, 90, 92, 94, 95, 115, 116
Green, T.H., 112
Guaraldo, Olivia, 215
Guattari, Félix, 6, 9, 11–14, 26, 29n26, 29n29, 30n33, 30n40, 31n42, 31n49, 31n52, 31n55, 32n63, 40, 60n3, 68, 133, 137n40, 163, 172–176, 184, 186–195, 197n30, 197n41, 199n78
Guattari, Félix and Antonio Negri, 6
Guérin, Daniel, 145, 148, 153

Half Moon Theatre, 228
Han, Byung-Chul, 105, 111
Hardt, Michael and Antonio Negri, 16–17, 21, 31n48, 34n93, 226, 230, 233–235, 238, 240
Harvey, David, 2–3
Harvie, Jen, 234
Hazan, Eric, 211, 214

Index

Hegel, Georg Wilhelm Friedrich, 69, 76–78, 80, 93
Heidegger, Martin, 117
Herzog, Dagmar, 141
Hobbes, Thomas, 112, 208
Hobsbawm, Eric, 143, 147
Houellebecq, Michel, 139–141
Howells, Adrian, 234
Huizinga, Johan, 113, 120n65

Illouz, Eva, 140–142, 144, 152
Insideout, 228
Irigaray, Luce, 188
Itzin, Catherine, 228

Jackson, Julian, 143, 185
Jacobitism, 9
Jeunesse Communiste Révolutionnaire (JCR), 146
Joseph, Miranda, 233, 236

Kant, Immanuel, 93, 170, 172, 174, 179n4, 179n20
Kershaw, Baz, 226–229, 241
Kristeva, Julia, 107

La Boétie, Estienne de, 24, 103, 106
Lasch, Christopher, 143, 144, 147, 165
Lazzarato, Maurizio, 14, 18–19
Lenin, Vladimir Illich, 95, 210
Leninist/Leninism, 8, 9, 12, 14, 22, 23, 44, 45
Lévy, Bernard-Henri, 125, 135n15, 135n16, 184
Leyde, Jean de, 146
Liberman, Anatoly, 105
Loria, Achille, 94
Lukács, György, 68, 76, 78, 94
Lumiere & Son, 228
Lundy, Craig, 189, 197n30, 198n52, 198n53
Lyotard, Jean-François, 60–61n5, 68, 107, 185

Machiavelli, Niccolò, 94, 95, 97
MacKenzie, Iain, 183, 184, 187, 195n1, 196n2, 197n34
Malkovitch, Malka, 142, 155n13
Mann, Horace, 92
Maoism, 22, 31n55, 40
Marcuse, Herbert, 113, 142, 146, 149, 151
Marx, Karl, 5, 22–23, 26, 41, 47, 53, 61nn5–8, 64n44, 67, 69–72, 74–82, 84n21, 86n70, 94, 95, 105, 113, 125, 135n17, 146, 177
Marxist/Marxism, 5, 8, 9, 14, 17, 22, 23, 51, 60n5, 67, 69, 70, 77, 80, 81, 83n3, 86n67, 90, 93–98, 116, 141, 143, 144, 146, 147, 149, 153, 154, 226
McCarthy, Paul, 107, 109
McDonough, Tom, 147, 156n31
McGrath, John, 227
McGonigal, Jane, 114
McKenzie, Jon, 113–115
McKenzie Wark, Kenneth, 114, 117
McLaren, Malcolm, 151
Meillassoux, Quentin, 25, 168–169, 171, 177, 178n2, 179n17
Meucci, Gian Paolo, 95
Meyers, Todd, 187
Michel, Albin, 142
Mikron Theatre Company, 228
Milani, Lorenzo, 95
Mitterrand, François, 14, 39, 47
Morin, Edgar, 145
Morin, Violette, 149
Mouffe, Chantal, 205
Mousseau, Jacques, 149, 151
Mussolini, Benito, 97

Nancy, Jean-Luc, 27, 40, 60n4, 230, 233, 236–238, 240, 241
Natural Theatre Company, 228
Negri, Antonio, 21, 69, 82
Nissenbaum, Helen, 110
Nous sommes en marche, 149

Index

Obfuscation movement, 110, 111, 118
Occupy movement, 55, 201, 203, 218n1
Orlan, 107
Orwell, George, 98
Oury, Jean, 187, 188, 194

Paine, Gina, 107
Pasolini, Pierpoalo, 90–93, 95, 98
Phelan, Peggy, 237
Pine II, B. Joseph, 114, 234
Piper, Adrian, 107
Postone, Moishe, 69, 77–79
Pfaller, Robert, 3
Plekhanov, Georgi, 94
Porter, Robert, 183, 184, 187, 195n1, 196n2, 197n34
Punchdrunk, 234
The Puppet Tree, 228

Rancière, Jacques, 29n31, 30n34, 31n53, 185
Red Ladder, 228
Reich, Wilhelm, 142, 146, 151
Ridout, Nicholas, 226, 230, 232, 237, 238
Robcis, Camille, 188
Ross, Kristin, 7, 45, 143, 183, 186, 191
Rouault, Lucile, 142

Salvini, Matteo, 97
Sarkozy, Nicolas, 62n14, 135n5, 140
Sartre, Jean-Paul, 135n17, 226
Savoia, Umberto di, 92
Schiller, Friedrich, 106
Schmitt, Carl, 208
Scott, James, 209
Sellars, Wilfred, 172, 174–176, 179n18
Servin, Jacques, 109, 110
Shaughnessy, Nicola, 229, 230, 243n29
Situationist International (SI), 7, 24, 83n3, 103–107, 134n2, 135n17, 151, 156n31
Smith, Kiki, 107
Snyder-Young, Dani, 226, 230, 235, 236
Srnicek, Nick and Alex Williams, 4, 34–35n101, 84n10

Sorbonne, University (Paris I), 43, 107, 146, 149, 214
Stalinism, 11, 50–51, 61n5, 92, 125, 146
Starr, Peter, 103, 107
Suely, Rolnik, 191
Sunstein, Cass R., 117
SYRIZA, 48–49, 51

Taylorism, 18
Thaler, Richard H., 117
Thatcher, Margaret, 34n92, 104, 230
Thierrée-Chaplin, Victoria and Jean-Baptiste, 194
Thorpe, Jess, 225, 233
Togliatti, Palmiro, 90, 92–95, 98
Toscanini, Oliviero, 108
Tosquelles, François, 194
Tronti, Mario, 5, 28n10, 29n19, 69, 78
Trotskyist Party (PCI), 153
Turner, Cathy, 232, 235, 240

Union des Etudiants Communistes (UEC), 146

Vamos, Igor, 109
Vance, Carol, 154
Vaneigem, Raoul, 107
Vincennes, University of (Paris VIII), 26, 164, 183–191, 194–195, 196n1, 197n25
Virno, Paolo, 6, 229, 235

Watt, David, 229
Weber, Max, 76, 115–116
Westwood, Vivienne, 151
Williams, Raymond, 228
Wilson, Harold, 227
WochenKlausur, 108
Wright, Richard, 206, 207, 210, 215, 216

The Yes Men, 104, 109, 110
Young, Eugene B., 190

Zancarini-Fournel, Michelle, 143
Zuboff, Shoshana, 118, 121n74

About the Contributors

aylon cohen is a PhD candidate at the University of Chicago and Mellon International Dissertation Research Fellow. Specialising in political theory, aylon's research combines intellectual history, queer-feminist theory and affect studies with the history of democratic thought and practice. They are currently completing a book manuscript examining how ordinary bodily practices emerge alongside and in tension with the history of ideas, with a particular emphasis on how categories of gender and sexuality shape forms of bodily activity constitutive of democratic life. aylon's work has appeared in *Capacious: Journal for Emerging Affect Inquiry* and the volumes *Subjectivation in Political Theory and Contemporary Practices* and *Tiere—Texte—Transformationen: Kritische Perspektiven der Human-Animal Studies*.

Guillaume Collett is an honorary research fellow in the Centre for Critical Thought, at the University of Kent, and currently based in the University of Malta. He is the author of *The Psychoanalysis of Sense: Deleuze and the Lacanian School* (2016), and the editor of *Deleuze, Guattari, and the Problem of Transdisciplinarity* (2019). He has edited two special issues and previously coedited the journal *La Deleuziana*. Currently, he is working on a book on Deleuze and immanence.

Ben Dunn received his PhD in drama from the University of Manchester in 2019 and is lecturer in creative practice and performance making at the University of Leeds. Informed by a background as a performance practitioner in contemporary and applied settings, his research examines the relationship between theatre practice and social context, with a focus on collectivism, politics and ontology. Recent research includes *Meet the Neighbours*, a three-year Creative Europe-funded project examining the role of cultural practice in contexts of rapid urban change, and contributions to a national study into the impacts of Covid-19 on the UK's cultural sector, led by the Centre for Cultural Value at the University of Leeds.

Daniel Fraser is a writer from Hebden Bridge, Yorkshire. His poetry and prose have won prizes and been published widely in print and online, including: *London Magazine, LA Review of Books, Aeon, Hobart, Poetry Birmingham, Magma, Mute, Radical Philosophy* and *Review 31*. His poetry pamphlet *Lung Iron* is published by ignitionpress. A graduate of the CRMEP and a current humanities excellence scholar at University College Cork, his present research project examines trauma as a philosophical category of time in postmodernity. His primary research interests are: modernist literature, Marxism, cinema and post-Kantian European philosophy.

Krista Bonello Rutter Giappone is visiting senior lecturer in English at the University of Malta, an honorary research fellow at the University of Kent and research assistant in refugee law with the Max Planck Institute for Social Anthropology. She has degrees in the social sciences, humanities, and law, including a PhD in drama and a master's in advocacy in law. She has published in the areas of digital games, critical theory and the history of subcultures. She has previously coedited the volume *Comedy and Critical Thought* (Rowman & Littlefield International, 2018) with Fred Francis and Iain MacKenzie, and is currently coauthoring a book with Lena Wånggren on labour precarity in UK higher education.

Gabriela Hernández De La Fuente is a PhD candidate in political and social thought at the University of Kent. Her PhD project focuses on developing the concept of feminist immanent critique—inspired by Judith Butler, Johanna Oksala and Gilles Deleuze. For her master's thesis, she worked on assembling an immanent conception of critique, influenced by the work of Gilles Deleuze. She teaches courses in modern political theory.

Natasha Lushetich is professor of contemporary art and theory at the University of Dundee and 2020–2021 AHRC Research Leadership Fellow. Her research is interdisciplinary and focuses on intermedia, biopolitics and performativity, the status of sensory experience in cultural knowledge, hegemony, disorder and complexity. Her books include *Fluxus: The Practice of Non-Duality* (2014); *Interdisciplinary Performance* (2016); *The Aesthetics of Necropolitics* (2018); *Beyond Mind*, a special issue of *Symbolism* (2019) and *Big Data—A New Medium?* (2020). Her recent writing has also appeared in *AI & Society; Contemporary Aesthetics; Environment, Space, Place; Media*

Theory; *Journal of Somaesthetics*; *Performance Research*; *TDR* and *The Philosophical Salon*.

Iain MacKenzie teaches political theory at the University of Kent. His research focuses on the nature and scope of critique. Recent publications include *Resistance and the Politics of Truth* (transcript, 2018), and *Comedy and Critical Thought: Laughter as Resistance* (Rowman & Littlefield International, 2018) coedited with Fred Francis and Krista Bonello Rutter Giappone.

Franco Manni is an independent scholar based in Italy. He has written on topics in twentieth-century Italian philosophy, with a particular focus on the work of Benedetto Croce, Piero Gobetti, Antonio Gramsci and Norberto Bobbio. He has contributed to debates in political theology and theological ethics as well as written on how political history and ideas are expressed in the literary works of J. R. R. Tolkien.

Christos Marneros is lecturer in law at Kent Law School, University of Kent, and visiting lecturer in legal philosophy at Riga Graduate School of Law, Latvia. His research focuses on the areas of anarchist thought, political theory, legal theory and continental philosophy. His monograph, *Human Rights after Deleuze: Towards An-archic Jurisprudence*, will be published in 2022.

Blanche Plaquevent is currently lecturer in history at the University of Glasgow. In 2021, she defended her PhD thesis titled 'Inventing the French Sexual Revolution, 1945–1970' at the University of Bristol. Her doctoral work explores how sexuality became a revolutionary topic in postwar France, tracing the emergence of the idea that the personal is political before the advent of second wave feminism. Before coming to Bristol, her interdisciplinary trajectory took her from philosophy and social sciences to contemporary history and sociology of gender and sexuality between Sciences Po Paris, Sorbonne Paris IV and the EHESS.

Jose Rosales (they/them) is an independent researcher, a founding editor of *Hostis: A Journal for Incivility* and coeditor of *Diversity of Aesthetics*, volumes 1–3. Among their published writings, recent works include the second volume in the Diversity of Aesthetics series, *foreigners everywhere*, coauthored with Claire Fontaine and Iman Ganji (Emily Harvey Foundation: 2022); 'The Reality of Destitution Is The Destitution of Reality: A Genealogy of Destituent Power,' in *Unworking*, ed. Peer Illner, (2021); '1968–2018: plus *ça* change, plus c'est la même(?)'; and 'The Black Bloc

Which Was Not,' in *Blind Field: A Journal of Cultural Inquiry*; and an interview with former Red Army Faction member Karl-Heinz Dellwo titled 'I Cannot Tell You Why You Must Fight I Can Only Tell You How I Solve Contradictions' (*Punkto Magazine*, 2021).